DATE DUE

DEC 2 9 1999			
MAY 0 3 2003			
GAYLORD			PRINTED IN U.S.A.

D0108826

The Spellbinders

The *Spellbinders*
Charismatic Political Leadership

ANN RUTH WILLNER

YALE UNIVERSITY PRESS
NEW HAVEN AND LONDON

Designed by Sally Harris
and set in Zapf International type.
Printed in the United States of America by
BookCrafters, Inc., Ann Arbor, Michigan.

Library of Congress Cataloging in Publication Data

Willner, Ann R. (Ann Ruth)
  The spellbinders.
  Includes index.
  1.Leadership. I. Title.
HM141.W523 1983   306'.2   83-5914
ISBN 0-300-02809-1

10 9 8 7 6 5 4 3 2

*To the memory of Norbert Willner
and Bella Richman Willner*

Contents

Preface

Almost half a century has passed since a small child saw the spell-bound faces of adults who listened to a confident, reassuring voice coming from the radio in a "fireside chat." During the same period, Pathé News at the movies showed that child a single rapt expression on the many faces in crowds of people whose right arms stretched out toward a posturing figure with a small mustache and a voice that regularly rose in a raucous crescendo.

Roosevelt and Hitler were dead before I reached maturity. But those childhood memories may have served as the subconscious stimulus for the long intellectual journey I have taken in the effort to unravel, understand, and explain the spells exerted by political leaders who have succeeded in inspiring, swaying, or seducing multitudes and holding their minds and emotions in thrall. Watching the political magic performed by Sukarno in the Indonesia of the 1950s probably provided a more direct stimulus.

Some of the details, detours, and bypaths of that journey may be worth a brief recounting. This work was originally begun in 1964 as a comparative study of the leadership strategies of Sukarno, Nasser, and Nkrumah. Reluctance to add another term or concept to the already overlapping and overburdened repertoire of political science led me to select Weber's concept of political charisma as the general theme relating these three leaders.

Comments from colleagues sent me in seemingly contradictory directions. A suggestion to focus my efforts on a single case study of Sukarno produced a more extensive (and still unpublished) study of his leadership than is included in this work. Advice to enlarge my sample combined with a suggestion to discard the "weak concept" of charisma led me to try to develop the latter by examining available material on fifteen apparently charismatic political leaders. Part of the results of that effort was published somewhat prematurely in 1968 in order to protect my "pioneer rights."*

Projected publication of the whole was postponed as I faced up to one reader's comments concerning the limitations of the comparative method for conveying in "full-bodied" fashion the process of charismatic legitimation and conversion replete with the "fear and trembling" surrounding it. The subsequent delay in time-consuming perusal of old newspapers and microfilm, sometimes on a day-to-day basis, had its compensations. Even with the ex post facto knowledge of the ultimate outcome of a suspenseful crisis, I sometimes felt like a traveler in a time capsule, sharing with people of the past the sensations of having lived there and then. I hope that chapter 5 succeeds in communicating some of this.

Less time-consuming but somewhat painful was the decision to discard considerable material on leaders in the original sample and limit the number to six. The cost of having developed some fairly rigorous standards for identifying charismatic politicial leaders was having to drop those for whom my evidence could not meet these standards.

As the revised and expanded manuscript circulated widely in the last six years, other additions were made. One reader's comment that the explanation for the rise of political charisma seemed incomplete without some discussion of its consequences produced chapter 9. Events involving the Ayatollah Khomeini added to chapter 4 a contemporary case serving to verify the theory. To my editor I owe my last extension of the journey. Her skepticism concerning the nonexistence of nationally recognized women charismatic political leaders since Joan of Arc added a new section to chapter 2. The additional chapter I did not add is

---

*Ann Ruth Willner, *Charismatic Political Leadership: A Theory*, Research Monograph no. 32 (Princeton: Center of International Studies, 1968).

reserved for a work tentatively titled "Lethe and Ladies: The Cultural Historical Submersion of Women Political Leaders."

For support of the initial research I am indebted to the Center of International Studies at Princeton University and to grants from the American Council of Learned Societies, the Social Science Research Council, and the Rockefeller Foundation. To my regret, it has not been possible to keep track of all those individuals who have in some way stimulated further thought in the course of almost two decades of research and reflection. I am grateful to those, some unidentified, who provided critical comments, both positive and negative, on prior manuscripts and publications. To my editor, Marian Ash, and to Reinhard Bendix, James MacGregor Burns, Harry Eckstein, and Dankwart Rustow, I am especially obligated, not only for encouragement but also for posing challenges I initially resisted but ultimately succumbed to. To the skill and patience of Alexander Metro and his colleagues at Yale University Press during a stressful period, I wish to pay a grateful tribute.

Beyond all debts are those owed to Dorothy Willner, anthropologist and coauthor of an initial publication and a subsequent one on political charisma.[†] Having introduced me to the importance of the role of myth in leadership, from a perspective differing from that of Georges Sorel, she wisely refuses responsibility for some of what I have done with it. Her sisterly affection does not soften the rigor of her criticism, the tone of our dialogues, or the acuteness of her suggestions. Since I cannot distinguish my own ideas from those of hers I have co-opted, I consider her my closet coauthor of this work as well.

[†]Ann Ruth Willner and Dorothy Willner, "The Rise and Role of Charismatic Leaders," *Annals of the American Academy of Political and Social Science* 358 (Mar. 1965), 77–88; Ann Ruth Willner and Dorothy Willner, "Charismatic Political Leadership as Conservator and Catalyst," in *Traditional Attitudes and Modern Styles in Political Leadership: Papers Presented to the 28th International Congress of Orientalists Under the Convenorship of J. D. Legge*, ed. A. R. Davis (Sydney: Angus & Robertson, 1973), pp. 17–28.

1
Clarifying the Concept of Political Charisma

"How can we make President Suharto a charismatic leader?" I was asked by Adam Malik, Indonesia's foreign minister, several years after Suharto had supplanted Sukarno as political head of that country. Malik knew, as did some other Indonesians, that my interest in charismatic political leadership had originally been sparked by my observations of former President Sukarno. To a political scientist, a political leader who had long been able to control a country without controlling a political party, a bureaucracy, or an army was a fascinating phenomenon.

Adam Malik asked that question seriously. Sukarno was then imprisoned in the Bogor Palace. A campaign to downgrade him and his regime had been going on for months. The media were daily deriding and attacking him. Nonetheless, he was still seen as a danger to his successor. For his charisma had not completely waned.

Two years later Sukarno was dead, and within less than a decade so were nearly all the other major political leaders of the mid-twentieth century who had revived the scholarly and popular interest in charisma—Mao, Nasser, Nkrumah, Ho Chi Minh, Perón, and others. Of the actual or presumed charismatic political leaders of this period, only Castro remained. Charismatic political leaders were supplanted in the media by political terrorists. And even the meaning of the term *charisma* began to disappear as the media applied it to anyone with a touch of glamour.

But like religion, which it somewhat resembles, genuine political charisma was far from dead. This was dramatically demonstrated by two events that commanded the rapt and awed attention of millions of people around the world. One was the downfall of a powerful monarch. The other was the suicide of a small society. Each was largely the product of the will and words of one individual—a charismatic leader.

In the annals of the dethronement of kings, the gradual and suspenseful unseating of Reza Mohammed Shah Pahlevi was unusual. Here was the spectacle of a practically absolute ruler, buttressed by powerful arms and allies, rendered powerless by a small old man many miles away. The Ayatollah Khomeini had come to command the absolute loyalty of countless Iranians. The impact of his will and words upon these followers had become a potent weapon sufficient to unseat a king.

History provides precedents for part of the Jonestown phenomenon—the migration of a religious sect at the call of a leader to found a new religious and political community in a distant land. But the collective suicide and murder by several hundred people at the will of their leader, James Jones, may have been unprecedented.

The charismatic leadership of Jones and Khomeini was both religious and political. But political charisma alone has produced profound consequences in this century. Gandhi, Roosevelt, Hitler, and Castro were only four examples of political leaders whose charismatic hold over millions of followers gave them leverage to transform and transcend their times and countries.

What makes for the rare and sometimes frightening phenomenon of political charisma?[1] What causes a group of people or an entire nation to fall under the binding spell of a leader, so that his word becomes their only law and his command their almost sacred duty to obey? What must a political leader have or do to elicit such unbounded loyalty and devotion? Is political charisma largely a matter of personality, or does it stem from the uses of power? And can it be artificially created by the advanced technologies of modern media?

This book is about the making of political charisma, the elements that

---

1. The terms *political charisma* and *charismatic political leadership* are here used interchangeably.

help to generate it, and the processes by which it develops. The explanation—or explanatory theory—of the genesis of charismatic political leadership is illustrated throughout by examples from the careers of noted charismatic political leaders of this century. The explanation, however, is neither timebound nor spacebound and should help to identify emerging charismatic leaders of the present and future.

Because of considerable scholarly controversy concerning the meaning of the concept of charisma and because of the wide misuse of the term by the media, two chapters precede the beginning of the explanation. This chapter is devoted to defining political charisma and to clearing up some common confusions about it. The following chapter tells how to recognize it and provides a set of indicators to identify a truly charismatic political leader.

Core Characteristics

We owe the notion of political charisma to the fertile mind of Max Weber, the outstanding German social scientist of the early twentieth century. Weber introduced the concept of the charismatic leader in the context of his now classic classification of authority or legitimate domination into three ideal types: legal or rational, traditional, and charismatic.[2] The basis of his classification is the content of the prevailing beliefs in a society that govern its dominant pattern of command and compliance.

By what right, asked Weber, do some individuals in social systems

2. Max Weber, *Economy and Society*, ed. Guenther Roth and Claus Wittich, 3 vols. (New York: Bedminster Press, 1968), 1, pp. 212–301, and 3, pp. 941–1211. For summaries and interpretations of Weber's concept of authority, see especially: Reinhard Bendix, *Max Weber: An Intellectual Portrait* (Garden City, N.Y.: Doubleday, 1960), pp. 298–99, 301–10; Joseph Bensman and Michael Givant, "Charisma and Modernity: The Use and Abuse of a Concept," *Social Research* 69 (Winter 1975), 571–80; Julian Freund, *The Sociology of Max Weber* (New York: Pantheon, 1968), pp. 232–34; W. G. Runciman, "Charismatic Legitimacy and One-Party Rule in Ghana," *Archives Européenes de Sociologie* 4, no. 1 (1963), 148–63; Dankwart A. Rustow, *A World of Nations: Problems of Political Modernization* (Washington, D.C.: Brookings Institution, 1967), pp. 149–53. For the origins of the concept and its entry into contemporary usage, see Daniel Bell, "Sociodicy: A Guide to Modern Usage," *American Scholar* 35 (Autumn 1966), 702–05.

claim to exercise command over others and gain acceptance of their claims and obedience to their directives from those others as their right?

In the legal-rational and traditional types of authority, Weber stated, rights to the exercise of authority are recognized as legitimate because of beliefs in offices or statuses that have become institutionalized in societies over time. Thus, legal-rational authority is based upon a belief in the legality of rules and in the right of those who occupy offices by virtue of these rules to give commands. The belief in the rules of a constitution, for example, confers authority upon a duly selected prime minister or president.

Traditional authority is derived from "an established belief in the sanctity of immemorial traditions"[3] and thus in statuses traditionally recognized. The status of monarch or chieftain, for example, has been achieved in different societies in different ways, such as through lineage and inheritance or ordeal and combat. But the individual who gains that status by whatever means tradition has decreed has legitimacy by virtue of belief in that tradition.

In both these types, therefore, the claim of an individual to the exercise of authority or legitimate command is recognized largely because of his/her occupancy of an office or status.

Charismatic authority by contrast is distinctly personal. It rests on "devotion to the specific sanctity, heroism, or exemplary character of an individual person, and of the normative patterns or order revealed or ordained by him."[4] Charismatic authority, therefore, is lodged neither in office nor in status but derives from the capacity of a particular person to arouse and maintain belief in himself or herself as the source of legitimacy.[5]

This specifically personal character of charismatic authority has understandably but mistakenly led to its being treated as interchangeable with charismatic leadership. As the final section of this chapter explains, charismatic leadership is not identical to charisma as the basis for au-

---

3. Weber, *Economy*, 1, p. 213.
4. Ibid.
5. For the sake of convenience, masculine pronouns are used subsequently and are to be understood as referring to persons within the category irrespective of gender.

thority in a social system, although they may overlap.[6] Nor is charisma an aspect of leadership in general, as some scholars have asserted.[7]

Charismatic leadership is a very special subtype of leadership with unusual qualities not found in leadership in general. Leadership, in the general sense of the term in common usage,[8] denotes a relatively sustained and asymmetric exercise of influence by one individual, the leader, over others, the followers. It is a patterned relationship of influence between one member of a group and its other members. Those who receive and respond to the influence, the followers, are crucial to the relationship, for a potential or an aspirant leader's claim to mold the views or direct the actions of others is not realized until the potential followers recognize and act upon that claim.[9]

The difference between charismatic leadership and this general leadership relationship can be seen by examining four dimensions that characterize follower recognition of and response to the leader. These are: (1) the leader-image dimension, (2) the idea-acceptance dimension, (3) the compliance dimension, and (4) the emotional dimension.

The leader-image dimension refers to beliefs that followers hold about the person of their leader. Leaders frequently are believed by their followers to have skills or qualities necessary to accomplish tasks or to further goals important to them. Leaders are often perceived by their followers to possess qualities regarded as admirable in their particular

6. Bendix, in *Max Weber*, pp. 301–04, is one of the few scholars who has recognized the need to distinguish "domination as a result of charismatic leadership . . . from domination as a result of charismatic authority."

7. See, for example, Renzo Sereno, *The Rulers* (New York, Evanston, and London: Harper & Row, 1968), p. 120, and Alfred de Grazia, *Political Behavior* (New York: Free Press, 1962), p. 90. For Edward Shils, charisma extends far beyond leadership and authority to cover a host of other phenomena ("Charisma, Order and Status," *American Sociological Review* 30, 2 [Apr. 1965], 199–213).

8. For approaches to and definitions of leadership influenced by social psychology and stressing interpersonal influence and interaction within groups, see Ralph M. Stogdill, ed., *Handbook of Leadership: A Survey of Theory and Research* (New York: Free Press, 1974). For a survey of studies on political leadership, see Glenn D. Paige, *The Scientific Study of Political Leadership* (New York: Free Press, 1977), pp. 1–96.

9. See the distinction between "attempted leadership" and "successful leadership" in John K. Hemphill, "Why People Attempt to Lead," in *Leadership and Interpersonal Behavior*, ed. Luigi Petrullo and Bernard M. Bass (New York: Holt, Rinehart & Winston, 1961), pp. 201–02.

cultures, such as wisdom, foresight, firmness, benevolence, guile, strength of character, or subtlety.

In the charismatic relationship, followers believe their leader to have superhuman qualities or to possess to an extraordinary degree the qualities highly esteemed in their culture. They attribute to their leader qualities commonly associated in their culture with the realm of the divine or the supernatural, with gods, demigods, or outstanding heroes.[10]

The second dimension relates to follower receptivity to a leader's statements and ideas. This idea-acceptance dimension refers to the basis on which and the extent to which followers believe and internalize a leader's definitions and ideas. There are normally many bases upon which followers can accept what a leader tells them—because it sounds reasonable, because it conforms with knowledge obtained from other sources, because it accords with their own experience, because of the leader's status or prestige, to mention only a few.

In the charismatic relationship, however, these other bases for belief either do not exist or do not count. Followers believe statements made and ideas advanced by their leader simply because it is *he* who has made the statement or advanced the idea. It is not necessary for them to weigh or test the truth of the statement or the plausibility of the idea. For *he* knows and it is therefore enough for them that *he* has said it. If he has said it, it is unquestionably true, and it must be right.[11]

The compliance dimension refers to follower obedience to a leader's directives. There are many bases upon which followers comply with commands of leaders—because they seem reasonable or lawful, because it is to their advantage to obey, because of fear of losses or penalties if they fail to comply, because of the means of coercion the leader can use, because of the leader's persuasiveness, or because of other motives.

For followers in the charismatic relationship, however, such motives

10. It should be noted that what some religions have polarized as the divine and the demonic have been seen in others as different manifestations of the same presence, for example, Shiva as both Creator and Destroyer.

11. As succinctly stated by Marion Levy, Jr., in *Modernization and the Structure of Societies*, 2 vols. (Princeton: Princeton University Press, 1966), p. 350: "In the eyes of a true follower of a charismatic leader . . . the fact that the leader says a given thing is right makes it right."

are minor or irrelevant. They comply because for them it is sufficient that their leader has given the command. If *he* has ordered, it is their duty to obey.

Noncharismatic leadership generally includes an intervening phase, however brief, between the communication of a leader's message or directive to his followers and their acceptance of or obedience to it. This phase involves followers in processes of calculation and evaluation. For even highly respected leaders cannot count on their followers to surrender to them regularly and without question the mandate to choose and judge.

This surrender, however, is typical of the charismatic leadership relationship. The followers abdicate choice and judgment to the leader. Belief and obedience are almost automatic. Followers accept and believe that the past was as the leader portrays it, that the present is as he depicts it, and that the future will be as he predicts it. And they follow without hesitation his prescriptions for action.

The emotional dimension relates to the type and intensity of the emotional commitment of followers to a leader. Leadership often involves an emotional response on the part of the followers toward a leader and, at times, a fairly strong emotional attachment. Highly popular leaders can elicit such emotions as affection, admiration, trust, and even love.

In the charismatic relationship, however, the emotions aroused are not only more intense in degree, but they are also of a somewhat different order. Followers respond to their leader with devotion, awe, reverence, and blind faith, in short, with emotions close to religious worship.[12]

It is worth noting that charismatic leaders have rarely provoked indifference, neutrality, or mild reactions. Treated as godlike by their followers, they have often been regarded as diabolic by many of those not susceptible to their appeal. Whatever underlay the kinds and intensity of emotion they have generated, even their opponents have recognized and feared them as far beyond the ordinary and even beyond the unusual in human experience.

---

12. "In its pure form," according to Bendix, *Max Weber*, p. 300, "charismatic leadership involves a degree of commitment on the part of the disciples that has no parallel in other types of domination."

Charismatic leadership can therefore be defined briefly as a relationship between a leader and a group of followers that has the following properties:

1. The leader is perceived by the followers as somehow superhuman.
2. The followers blindly believe the leader's statements.
3. The followers unconditionally comply with the leader's directives for action.
4. The followers give the leader unqualified emotional commitment.

Charismatic political leadership denotes a relationship between a political leader and a segment of his following that has these properties.

Dispelling Some Common Confusions

If popular usage has distorted the meaning and significance of charisma, it cannot be said that the scholarly community has cohesively cast a clear and unambiguous light on the subject. For years scholars have debated the precise meaning and scope of the concept, have interpreted and misinterpreted Weber's intent, and have challenged and defended the usefulness of charisma as a category for contemporary political analysis.[13] Although this controversy has provided some illumination, it has also reflected and contributed to some unfortunate misconceptions.

The appendix to this book contains some detailed analyses of the conceptual confusions and misconceptions that have marked some of the scholarship on charisma and some discussion of the logical fallacies underlying them, together with some clarification of the most controversial points. In this chapter several of the more salient issues of general concern are summarized as succinctly as possible.

The first issue concerns what properly belongs in the definition of the concept of charisma. The definition given above was not arrived at lightly. After I gave my first lecture on Sukarno as a charismatic political

13. For criticisms of the concept of charisma and its contemporary usages, see especially: Carl J. Friedrich, "Political Leadership and the Problem of Charismatic Power," *Journal of Politics* 23 (Feb. 1961), 3–24; Karl Loewenstein, *Max Weber's Political Ideas in the Perspective of Our Time* (Amherst: University of Massachusetts Press, 1966), pp. 74–88; K. J. Ratnam, "Charisma and Political Leadership," *Political Studies* 12 (Oct. 1964), 341–54; and Bensman and Givant, "Charisma and Modernity," pp. 599–614.

leader, I was subjected to a series of questions by a noted scholar well versed in the works of Max Weber. Among them were the following:

"Did Sukarno have a mission?"

"Yes."

"Did he perform some sort of miracle in his rise?"

"No."

"Did he lead an austere life removed from family comforts?"

"Certainly not."

"Then he can't have been charismatic, at least not according to Weber."

Having directly observed Sukarno's clearly charismatic hold on his followers, I was taken aback. My questioner proceeded to read a list of all the major attributes he had culled from Weber's work on charisma and assured me that if Sukarno did not have all these, he could not justifiably be called charismatic.

It took some time and thought to realize that this scholar and others were committing a not uncommon error. They failed to separate out the essential ideas that define charisma from those ideas that provide further or auxiliary information about it.

It is not surprising that this sort of confusion has occurred. Weber advanced a number of ideas about the charismatic phenomenon in his voluminous writings. Some were not organized systematically and some were phrased elliptically or ambiguously. Furthermore, some have been modified in translation.[14]

Weber's major and most detailed analyses of charisma dealt with its transformation into other types of authority. But he did discuss briefly elements in what he saw as the typical trajectory of charismatic authority, such as a condition for its emergence, a requirement for its maintenance, a probable consequence, and some of the modes by which a charismatic leader exercises authority.[15]

Unfortunately, some or most of these elements seem to have been mistakenly incorporated by some scholars into the definition of charis-

14. See appendix for a discussion of problems of interpretation arising from translations.

15. See appendix for an elaboration of Weber's theory and its elements.

matic leadership itself. Such overloading of the definition and concept is unfortunate for several reasons. These are not defining properties that specify the meaning of charisma. They are rather properties that may or may not occur in some relation to it. To include probable or possible elements in the definition of a category can lead to excluding from that category some empirical or real-world cases that do belong in it, as the example about Sukarno illustrates.

Moreover, statements that do not primarily tell what charismatic authority or leadership is but instead assert other things about it should stand apart. For, unless proved, they are theoretical propositions still subject to verification. Weber's statements expressed what he in his time believed to be central tendencies or probabilities. Weber would have been the first to acknowledge that the course of history and the accumulation of further evidence might disprove as well as confirm some of them. To lock these propositions immutably into the definition is to deprive us of the chance to test their validity.

One such statement that has commonly been assimilated into the definition is that the charismatic leader is inspired by a calling or mission and inspires others by virtue of it. As I note in a later chapter, the proclamation of a goal or mission may well play a part in generating a charismatic relationship. Insofar as it does, however, this element forms part of the explanation for the origin of charisma and not part of its definition. The same holds true of situations or times of distress, mentioned by Weber in connection with the rise of a charismatic leader. Since the element of distress is prior to and a possible cause of the appearance of charisma, it belongs in the explanation, not in the definition.

Another notion too often attached to the definition but not properly part of it is that of charisma as a revolutionary phenomenon. It is clear that a relationship that allows a leader extraordinary control over the beliefs and behavior of his followers also permits him to change them in a revolutionary manner. If these followers constitute a considerable proportion of the members of a political unit he leads, he can similarly change the latter. Should revolutionary changes take place, however, they constitute consequences of charisma; they do not define charisma itself.

Moreover, Weber's assertions about the revolutionary impact of charisma referred to the typical case, not to the universe of all possible cases. This means that not all charismatic leaders must be revolutionary in the conventional senses of the term, that is, espousing revolutionary goals, gaining office by revolutionary means, or radically restructuring a society. There can be—and have been—atypical cases of charismatic political leaders who seek to preserve a prevailing social order from falling apart or who seek to revive one from the past. Franklin Delano Roosevelt was an example of a charismatic leader who preserved the basic framework of an order that was being undermined. The Mahdi of the Sudan and Prince Diponegoro of Java were nineteenth-century examples of charismatic leaders of nativistic movements aimed at the restoration of a prior order.

Political Charisma—Virtuous or Wicked?

Some of the scholars who appear to take issue with the concept of political charisma are in reality concerned with the consequences of political charisma in action and with the morality or immorality of these consequences. As the case of Adolf Hitler has amply demonstrated in this century, the use of political charisma can result in appalling as well as awesome consequences.

Outraged or revolted by what has been wrought by some charismatic leaders and their regimes, these scholars are apparently uncomfortable with the use of the concept itself. For *charisma* is a word of Greek origin and in the vocabulary of early Christianity meant "gift of grace." From this source Weber derived the term and extended it to contexts other than the religious one. Carl Friedrich later argued that a concept originally identified with religious inspiration should not be extended to include leaders who are seized with and communicate a darkly secular fervor. How, he asked, can one class together the works of Hitler and Jesus, Mussolini and Moses? How can one apply the same notion to the leadership of Luther and of Hitler?[16]

If Freidrich wished to keep the notion of charisma pure, there are those who have considered it hopelessly contaminated. Arthur

16. Friedrich, "Political Leadership," pp. 14–16, 19.

Schlesinger, Jr., for example, has argued that we ought not to apply the notion of charisma to leaders in a democracy.[17]

Such attempts to revise or restrict the definition of charismatic leadership are neither logically nor scientifically tenable. They illustrate a kind of reasoning backward: the consequences of a phenomenon are confused with and substituted for the actual phenomenon itself and further projected on the definition of that phenomenon. The charismatic phenomenon is not the same thing as its many possible consequences and cannot be logically defined on the basis of any of them.

It is true that we can distinguish and evaluate the works of various charismatic leaders in accordance with moral, ethical, religious, social, and even esthetic criteria. We can also distinguish among the various ends served by the process of converting nuclear energy. Nuclear energy can be used to treat cancer or destroy a city, but it is the same basic process that leads to either of these results. Similarly, charismatic leadership is a relationship, an interactional process, inherently neither moral nor immoral, neither virtuous nor wicked. Such questions arise only when we wish to evaluate whether a particular charismatic leader has used the relationship in the service of good or evil.

Contemporary Charisma—Real or Counterfeit?

Another set of critics takes issue with the usefulness of the concept, because they believe that genuine charisma is dead and what passes for it today is spurious or contrived. They argue that real charisma can arise only in a certain kind of environment, one that has almost disappeared from the contemporary world, and that Weber's genuinely charismatic leader has been supplanted by pseudocharismatics, manipulators of modern mass communications.[18]

---

17. Arthur M. Schlesinger, Jr., "On Heroic Leadership," *Encounter* 15 (Dec. 1960), 7. In contrast to those who wish to dispense with the concept on moral grounds is James C. Davies, who applies a moral standard by categorizing charismatic leaders as "responsible" or "irresponsible" in *Human Nature and Politics* (New York: John Wiley & Sons, 1963), pp. 298–308.

18. Jeremiah F. Wolpert, "Toward a Sociology of Authority," in *Studies in Leadership*, ed. Alvin W. Gouldner (New York: Harper, 1950), pp. 679–701; Loewenstein, *Weber's Political Ideas*, pp. 74–88; Bensman and Givant, "Charisma and Modernity," pp. 601–14.

On the surface, this notion does seem plausible, but it does not hold up under careful analysis of the arguments advanced to support it. One argument is that charisma existed historically in societies "free of bureaucracy" and moving "on the level of myth." The political milieu natural to charisma is held to be one "conditioned exclusively, or at least to a large extent, by magical, ritualistic, or mystically religious elements." Karl Loewenstein has argued that political charisma is a phenomenon of the "pre-Cartesian world." That world and its elements have been supplanted by a highly rationalized, industrialized, bureaucratized modern world. In such a different world, he asserted, charisma cannot arise except perhaps in parts of Africa and Asia that still have a "magico-religious ambiance."[19]

Because something existed at one time in one environment, it does not therefore follow that it cannot exist at another time in another environment. And if it can be found in another environment, the argument that the first one is its only natural habitat is disproved. Ironically, Loewenstein himself undermined his argument by conceding the charisma of Napoleon, who lived in a post-Cartesian world.[20]

There is a further weakness in this argument—its linkage of myth and ritual exclusively to the domain of religion. It is true that in the past the realms of politics and religion were closely intertwined. But one need not necessarily conclude that a divorce of politics from religion automatically confers upon religion complete custody of myth, ritual, and emotion. It seems more reasonable to assume that, with the decline of religious influence in a modern secular world, political myth and ritual can command the zeal once evoked by religion.

The second part of this thesis—that modern technology and mass communications can create a counterfeit charisma or pseudo-charisma—is also dubious. Up until now, at least, mass communications have been unable to create political charisma where there has been little or no other basis for its existence. All the expenditure of money and media expertise that went toward building the image of the pre-Watergate Richard Nixon could not make him a charismatic leader. Modern

19. Wolpert, "Toward a Sociology," pp. 680, 692; Loewenstein, *Weber's Political Ideas*, pp. 79, 86.
20. Loewenstein, *Weber's Political Ideas*, pp. 80–81.

media technology may promote political charisma more broadly than in past periods, but it cannot generate it.

Yet even if the charismatic phenomenon could be artificially created through media technology, would that necessarily make it counterfeit? A statement to that effect seems to confuse the existence of charisma with the means by which it comes about. The rain that falls from artificially seeded clouds is rain nonetheless. The artificially inseminated test-tube baby is just as human as the one conceived naturally. Therefore, if the properties listed above as defining and characterizing a charismatic relationship are found to exist in a leader–follower relationship, it is a genuinely charismatic relationship, whether it came into existence fortuitously or through contrivance and calculation.

Charisma—Personality or Perceptions?

A most common misconception about charisma links it directly to the personality of the individual who is credited with it. There is a popular notion that charisma is located in a quality or combination of qualities of a person and that some leaders naturally possess a "charismatic personality" while most do not. This notion may have been derived from Weber's statement about charisma as "a certain quality of an individual personality by which he is set apart and treated as endowed with supernatural, superhuman, or . . . exceptional powers or qualities."[21]

However, a search for a set of identical or similar qualities—whether of personality, character, temperament, or style—common to all or most political leaders who have been seen as superhuman by blindly devoted followers is not likely to yield decisive results. For, apart from similarities, the variations in the individual personalities seem so great that the probability of teasing out a composite "charismatic personality type" seems small. It is difficult to consider Gandhi and Hitler as cast in the same personality mold.

Moreover, such a search would not really locate the direct source of charisma. As we have seen, charisma is defined in terms of people's perceptions of and responses to a leader. It is not what the leader is but what people see the leader as that counts in generating the charismatic

21. Weber, *Economy*, 1, p. 241.

relationship. In the quotation from Weber given above, the operative phrase is "treated as endowed." This emphasis is supported by his later statement: "What alone is important is how the individual is actually regarded by those subject to charismatic authority."[22]

Charisma, then, can be found not so much in the personality of the leader as in the perceptions of the people he leads. To locate its direct source, we must look for the factors that call forth from followers those perceptions and responses that characterize and define the charismatic relationship. And since societies and groups may differ in their dominant cultural definitions of preferred and extraordinary qualities, the content of the leadership images projected and perceived may differ.

Yet if personality cannot provide the direct explanation for charisma, it may nonetheless provide an explanation removed from but related to the direct explanation. For aspects of a leader's personality may partly determine his ability to project those images of himself that give rise to charismatic perceptions. A process of mapping personal qualities and predispositions of a sample of demonstrably charismatic political leaders might conceivably yield an intersecting set or "charismatic cluster" of commonly held attributes. This could form the basis for a personality-oriented theory underlying the direct determinants of political charisma.

Charisma as Leadership and/or Authority

One other common confusion remains to be cleared up—the confusion between charisma as leadership and charisma as the dominant basis for authority in a society. Weber (or his translators) frequently appears to have treated these as interchangeable, and other scholars have followed suit. Some who studied newly independent countries observed that their political heads had numerous charismatically oriented followers. They therefore implied or concluded, as did David Apter in the case of Nkrumah and Ghana, that charisma was the sole or dominant basis for authority in these political systems. And they credited charisma with special functions in these states.[23] Other scholars observed strong op-

---

22. Ibid., p. 242.
23. See, for example, David Apter, *Ghana in Transition* (New York: Atheneum, 1963).

position to these leaders in their own states. They therefore questioned their charisma, took issue with the claims made for charismatic authority, and further questioned the value of the concept itself.[24]

It is understandable that these disputes should have arisen, because it is not always easy to recognize the distinction between charisma as leadership and charisma as the basis for political authority. Both are derived from belief in an individual. Moreover, although traditional and legal-rational authority systems are bolstered by already existing beliefs, it is charismatic leadership and its exercise that create the belief that legitimizes and sustains charismatic authority.

The distinction between charismatic political leadership and charismatic political authority rests on the extent of the radius of charismatic support. Charismatic leadership can arise and maintain itself within a predominantly traditional authority system or within a predominantly legal-rational authority system. If and when a charismatic political leader converts the majority of members of a system into his charismatic constituency, his charisma also becomes the basis for authority in that system.

There can be mixed authority systems in states or other political units, with one or another type dominant, depending upon the mix of prevalent beliefs. Especially within contemporary new states, it has been possible for all three of these types to coexist. Cambodia under Sihanouk may have been an example. Having originally been ruler of a traditional monarchy, Sihanouk was apparently still viewed as authoritative by some people primarily for that reason, even after the system of government changed. Others recognized his authority primarily by virtue of his election to office under the constitutional system. Still others were charismatically oriented to him.

Whether or not a particular instance of charismatic political leadership is also one of charismatic authority for the social unit in which it appears depends upon the distribution of charismatically oriented beliefs within that unit.[25] Charisma as a leadership phenomenon can be

24. See, for example, Claude Ake, "Charismatic Legitimation and Political Integration," *Comparative Studies in Society and History* 9 (Oct. 1966), 1–11, and Ratnam, "Political Leadership," pp. 350–54.

25. This point is well made by Aristide R. Zolberg in *Creating Political Order* (Chicago: Rand McNally, 1966), p. 138.

said to exist wherever or whenever the relationship, as I have defined it, is established between a leader and a group of followers. For charisma to be the dominant basis for authority in a society, such a relationship must exist between a charismatic leader and most, or at least the majority, of the members of that society.

2
Identifying Charismatic Political Leaders

Confusion and controversy over the meaning of the concept have not been the only impediments to understanding the phenomenon of charismatic political leadership. Another obstacle has been the lack of clear-cut criteria for designating the category *charismatic leader* and for identifying leaders that properly fit or do not fit within it.[1] In the absence of such criteria, it is not surprising that nearly every political leader with marked popular appeal is indiscriminately tagged as charismatic by some scholar or journalist infatuated with the term.[2]

This chapter is therefore directed to making the concept operational. It specifies indicators by which the existence of a charismatic relationship between a political leader and his followers can be discerned. It provides examples of the kinds of evidence that can serve to identify genuinely charismatic political leaders and to distinguish them from others who have been mistakenly credited with charisma. Finally, it offers some guidelines for the use and interpretation of evidence.

According to the definition provided in the preceding chapter, we must look to the responses of the followers, not to the leader, in order to know whether a charismatic relationship has been established. As

---

1. Ratnam, "Charisma and Political Leadership," p. 346.
2. For example, Willard Hanna included in *Eight Nation Makers: Southeast Asia's Charismatic Statesmen* (New York: St. Martin's Press, 1964) such far from charismatic leaders as Macapagal and Ne Win.

Weber emphasized, "It is recognition on the part of those subject to authority which is decisive for the validity of charisma."[3]

From the definition of the concept we can derive three analytically distinct categories of indicators of charismatically oriented recognition. The first, referring to what I have called the "leader-image" dimension, consists of beliefs that identify the leader with realms beyond the human. It can be divided into two subcategories: (1) beliefs assimilating the leader to the divine or semidivine, and (2) beliefs that the leader possesses otherwise superhuman, supernatural, or exceptional powers or capacities.

The second category of indicator denotes unconditional acceptance of the personal authority of the leader. It can also be divided into two subcategories, one in the domain of belief and the other in the domain of action. The first relates to the "idea-acceptance" dimension and consists of convictions of the truth of the leader's statements. The second subcategory refers to the "compliance" dimension and comprises unconditional obedience to the leader's directives.

The third category includes all those indicators denoting complete emotional commitment to the leader and, by extension, to his vision or to the order he has created. Although this is an independent category of indicators of follower response, there can be some overlap between this and the other categories. Statements of emotional intensity may include substantive content pertinent to the other categories, and, conversely, expressions of ideas about the leader may be conveyed in terms that also indicate strong emotional commitment.

Another type of indicator was originally included in an earlier version of this study, that of follower beliefs in the indispensability of the leader.[4] Upon further consideration, I decided to delete it as nonessential and subject to ambiguities of interpretation. The convictions of a following that the very existence or continuity of the social order they value is directly dependent upon the life or continued presence of the leader is a logical corollary of the definition and thus implicit in the other indicators. To include the notion of indispensability as an independent indicator permits the possible inclusion of beliefs in the leader as indispensable

3. Weber, *Economy*, 1, p. 242.

4. Ann Ruth Willner, *Charismatic Political Leadership: A Theory*, Research Monograph no. 32 (Princeton: Center of International Studies, 1968), pp. 26–27.

to the performance of a certain task or as indispensable in the absence of any other acceptable alternative. These are distinctly not charismatically oriented perceptions.

The Leader as God or Savior

Among the clearest indicators of charismatic perceptions of a political leader are direct and preferably unsolicited identifications of him with the sphere of the divine or semidivine. These typically can take one of the following forms: (1) equating the leader with God or a specific deity; (2) seeing the leader as a savior; (3) linking the leader with specific founders of religions or sacred figures of a specific culture.

Examples of evidence for the first indicator in this group are the following extracts from letters written to President Franklin Delano Roosevelt:

> I have never had the urge to write to any President before, but with you it is different. . . . To me you're a god in disguise.[5]

> People are looking to you almost as they look to God.[6]

Another example is the following exchange concerning Mussolini that was overheard by Barzini.

> He is like a god. . . .
> Like a god? No, No! He is a god.[7]

An illustration of the kind of evidence appropriate to the second indicator is the following sentence from an autobiographical life history of a member of the National Socialist Party in Germany:

> My belief is that our Leader, Adolf Hitler, was given by fate to the German nation as our savior, bringing light into darkness.[8]

This sentence in a letter to Roosevelt, shortly after his first inauguration, exemplifies the linkage with a founder of a religion:

  5. Leila A. Sussman, *Dear FDR: A Study of Political Letter-Writing* (Totowa, N.J.: Bedminster Press, 1963), p. 110.
  6. Arthur Schlesinger, *The Age of Roosevelt*, vol. 2, *The Coming of the New Deal* (Boston: Houghton Mifflin, 1958), p. 1.
  7. Luigi Barzini, *The Italians* (New York: Bantam, 1964), p. 153.
  8. Theodore Abel, *Why Hitler Came to Power* (New York: Prentice-Hall, 1938), p. 244.

Yours is the first opportunity to carve a name in the halls of the immortals beside Jesus.[9]

A similar example can be found in the autobiography of another German describing his initial response to Hitler:

His appeal to German manhood was like a call to arms, the gospel he preached a sacred truth. He seemed another Luther. I forgot everything but the man.[10]

The Leader as Seer or Magician

In the same category of indicators as those specified above and also derived directly from Weber's definition is the belief of followers that a leader possesses superhuman, supernatural, or notably exceptional qualities. Precisely what beliefs about which particular qualities can be taken to constitute indicators and evidence for charismatic qualification in all or most cases would be difficult to enumerate. An enumeration such as that of Davies, specifying beliefs in the leader "as being *all*-powerful, *all*-wise and morally *perfect*" is highly abstract; moreover, the attribution of moral perfection may be specific only to some cultures.[11]

Enumeration of specific qualities with universal or near-universal applicability is hazardous because of cultural variation. Attributes that may be considered truly exceptional in one culture may be seen as no more than relatively rare in another. Similarly, different cultures may have different measures for how much of any quality so far surpasses the normal human range as to transcend human potential.

What also makes specification difficult is the nature of the accounts of followers that might serve as the basis for such a listing. Such accounts tend to refer vaguely to the "emanation of power" or the "magnetic force" that these followers sense the leaders to have. But they are rarely more specific in trying to pinpoint the "something" they sense as beyond their experience. What is emphasized are the extra effects produced in these followers by exposure to the leaders, the sense of revelation or

9. Schlesinger, *Age of Roosevelt*, p. 1.

10. Hadley Cantril, *The Psychology of Social Movements* (New York: John Wiley & Sons, 1941), p. 236.

11. James C. Davies, "Charisma in the 1952 Campaign," *American Political Science Review* 48 (Dec. 1954), 1063.

awakening, and the emotional transports they have felt. It is as if they can communicate their sense of the exceptional in these leaders only by dwelling on the extraordinary feelings aroused in themselves.[12]

Nonetheless, several attributes or clusters of attributes can be singled out as having been traditionally and widely considered to be superhuman, supernatural, or magical. Belief in a leader's possession of one or some of these qualities can serve as a valid indicator of charismatically oriented perceptions of him. One such quality is prescience, the ability to foretell or prophesy the future. Another is the closely related capacity to read the minds and intentions of others. A third is the ability to heal or harm in unorthodox ways, by will alone, by sheer presence, inadvertently, or at a distance. Ability to influence or control the elements also belongs in this category. Finally, a cluster of attributes such as immunity from harm, "magical" protection, a capacity to overcome powerful enemies or circumvent great danger may be summed up as invulnerability.

In Indonesia I encountered beliefs that Sukarno could foretell future events. Most of those who expressed such convictions could not, when challenged, give a basis for them. Some, however, offered as proof the fact that as early as 1928 he had predicted a war in the Pacific among England, Japan, and America.[13] The following statement, made to me about Sukarno by one of his supporters, illustrates the belief in a leader's capacity to read the minds of others.

> I had not seen him for months, but we had barely begun to talk before he interrupted me and told me what I was thinking and what I wanted to ask him. It was as if all my thoughts were written in my face.[14]

Sukarno was also credited by some Indonesians with a kind of hypnotic power in an interpersonal encounter, and the following recollection of one of his opponents is an example of evidence for the existence of such a belief:

> I went in to tell him how angry I was with what he had done. The moment I sat in front of him and looked into his eyes, something

---

12. The autobiographical extracts in Abel, *Hitler*, illustrate this.
13. Those who offered this testimony were from the educated elite.
14. Personal communication from a high military officer.

happened and what I wanted to say just disappeared. My anger also disappeared. It was well over an hour after I left his presence that I could recall what I had wanted to say to him.[15]

The following passage provides an example of belief in a leader's curative powers:

At Dacca, in Bengal, a man of seventy was brought before Gandhi. He was wearing Gandhi's photograph around his neck and weeping profusely. As he approached the Mahatma, he fell on his face and thanked Gandhi for having cured him of chronic paralysis. "When all remedies failed," the poor man said, "I took to uttering Gandhi's name, and one day I found myself utterly cured."[16]

An illustration of followers' beliefs in the invulnerability of a leader is given by another biographer of Gandhi, who notes that to many Indians Gandhi's first imprisonment in India came as a shock, for they "had taken it for granted that their Mahatma had superhuman powers, and that if the English tried to lock him up, he would in all likelihood fly out the window."[17]

A passage from a book about Castro by a disillusioned but formerly close follower not only provides another example of a belief in magical protection or invulnerability but also suggests how such a belief can spread and how it can persist:

Those who fought beside him in the sierra have told me how, going from one place to another in the middle of the forest, he would suddenly stop and say, "No—not there." They would change direction and go by a round-about route and learn afterwards that near those very places where Fidel had stopped—"as if struck by lightning," his comrades said—there had been enemy troops lying in ambush. This happened not once but several times. Be it intuition, magic . . . or whatever, there is a quality in the man that warns him of danger. . . .[18]

The preceding examples come largely from countries in which many

---

15. Personal communication from a former political leader.
16. Louis Fischer, *The Life of Mahatma Gandhi* (New York: Collier Books, 1962), p. 234.
17. Geoffrey Ashe, *Gandhi: A Study in Revolution* (London: Heineman, 1968), p. 234.
18. Teresa Casuso, *Cuba and Castro* (New York: Random House, 1961), pp. 137–38.

people still freely admit to beliefs in magic and the supernatural. This does not mean, however, that beliefs about the supernatural gifts of some leaders are confined to such countries. Equivalent convictions or at least close approximations of them are also held in the more industrially and scientifically developed countries. However, these are more generally expressed in different terms, such as attributing to a leader the possession of a "sixth sense," of "extraordinary luck," or of "singularly good fortune."

There seems to be little difference between the substance of what was told to me about Sukarno's ability to divine the thoughts of others and the substance of the following passage written about Mussolini by Herman Finer, a political scientist:

> Men are to Mussolini like clocks whose works are cased in glass in order that they can be seen. His penetration is extremely subtle. . . . Some people are saturated with the knowledge of mankind; they seem to have a perceptive ability in addition to the usual senses. It is an absolutely infallible and subtle prescience that formulates itself immediately a person is confronted, as though all the secrets emerged and steadily developed themselves on a highly sensitized plate. All those who are acquainted with Mussolini agree that he has this power.[19]

One would not expect a twentieth-century German to declare explicitly that nature itself surrounds his hero with signs and portents. Such a message, however, can be implicitly conveyed, as in a Nazi's description of a meeting that emphasized that the sun shone all the time Hitler was present in "proverbial Hitler weather," although it poured before his arrival and after his departure.[20]

Similarly, one would not expect a contemporary American to declaim in archaic Shakespearean style: "The heavens themselves proclaim his presence and power!" Probably most Americans could not overtly admit to the possibility of holding such beliefs. When they are expressed, they tend to be framed obliquely, preceded by such phrases as "it seems as if," or they are attributed to others. The following examples of such oblique

19. Herman Finer, *Mussolini's Italy* (London: V. Gollancz, 1935), p. 288.
20. Abel, *Hitler*, p. 152.

expressions of this type of belief come from scholarly books about Roosevelt. They refer to his trip to the midwest drought area in the summer of 1936, when rain fell for the first time in seven months:

> Most extraordinary of all was the fact that the President, by his very presence, seemed to bring the rain. . . .[21]

> Roosevelt himself seemed to take on magical qualities as his trips through the parched country time and again brought rain.[22]

> It was impossible for the most skeptical oppositionist not to conclude that Franklin was blessed with luck. His followers were inclined to rate his good fortune even higher. It seemed to many of them that a providential arranger was at work.[23]

He Says Unto Us

One of the defining characteristics of the charismatic relationship, as elaborated in the preceding chapter, and therefore one of its indicators is the unconditional acceptance by followers of the personal authority of the leader. A valid indicator that such acceptance exists, either on the level of belief or on the level of behavior, requires more than that the followers' beliefs accord with the statements of the leader or that their behavior conforms with his directives. It should demonstrate that the leader's statements constitute a sufficient source for their beliefs and his commands a sufficient motive for their obedience.

Adequate evidence should show that a following believes that something has been so, is so, or will be so or believes that something is right *because of* the leader's statements to this effect. For example, a young Indonesian worker believed that the Indonesian language was the most widely used language in the world after English. Both the high school principal in his community and I tried to convince him otherwise, with no success. Probing disclosed that the basis for his belief was someone's

21. Schlesinger, *Roosevelt*, vol. 3, *The Politics of Upheaval* (Boston: Houghton Mifflin, 1960), p. 609.

22. James MacGregor Burns, *Roosevelt: The Lion and the Fox* (New York: Harcourt, Brace and World, 1956), p. 277.

23. Rexford G. Tugwell, *The Democratic Roosevelt* (Garden City, N.Y.: Doubleday, 1957), p. 425.

assurance that Sukarno had said this in one of his speeches. If Sukarno had said it, he stubbornly repeated, it must be true. It became clear that the only way we could have shaken his conviction would have been to persuade him that Sukarno had not made such a statement.

Beliefs held that are contrary to fact and beliefs that are persisted in despite available authoritative contradictory information constitute particularly telling evidence for a charismatic orientation on the part of followers. An instance of the former is provided by Speer's account of conversations with German farmers in the Ruhr in March 1945, when that area had already been overrun by Allied forces:

> Hitler could never lose the war, they declared. "The Fuehrer is still holding something in reserve that he'll play at the last moment. Then the turning point will come. It's only a trap, his letting the enemy come so far into our country."[24]

An interesting example of persistence of belief in spite of contrary information from sources they normally regarded as authoritative is that of some Italian immigrants whom I knew. Their views of European history preceding World War II were still, twenty years later, those provided by Mussolini. Discussions with them made it clear that they were convinced that events had happened a certain way *because* that was how Mussolini had described them during their youth in Italy. On contemporary affairs, they sought and accepted what they thought to be the more authoritative opinions of their more educated neighbors, their children's teachers, and television commentators; but none of these could shake their beliefs in past history as Mussolini had portrayed it or as they recalled he had. They were, indeed, disturbed by their children's accounts of what the latter were taught at school and wondered why American schools taught "lies" about Mussolini.

For obedience to a leader's commands to serve as a valid indicator of charismatic orientations to him, it is not necessary that the command be received directly from him. Compliance to orders issued by intermediaries or by others in the name of the leader is also acceptable as an indicator, provided that it is clear that compliance is given by followers only because they believe that these originated with the leader or are in conformity with his wishes.

---

24. Albert H. Speer, *Inside the Third Reich* (New York: Macmillan, 1970), p. 446.

An example of evidence that can be derived at a distance was the settlement of a labor dispute I observed in Indonesia. The dispute was between two ethnically different groups of workers in a textile factory and the manager had tried to settle it by persuasion, threats, and bribery, all to no avail. As a last resort in the attempt to prevent a strike, he called both groups of workers together and reminded them that President Sukarno had often said that they were one nation now and if he were present he would order them to make up their differences and work together. "In the name of Bung Karno," concluded the manager, "I ask you to do what he would tell you if he were with us here today." This worked.

Strongly indicative of a charismatic orientation toward a leader are actions performed by his followers at his order despite their awareness of hardships and sacrifices that such obedience entails. An interesting example of willingness for sacrifice if the leader so requires, one that also indicates belief in the leader's omniscience, is this statement made by one of Gandhi's followers during the campaign Gandhi organized in 1908 against the ordinances imposed on Asiatics in the Transvaal: "Mr. Gandhi, he know. If he say go to prison, we go." Indeed, at one point, more than 2,500 of the 13,000 Indian residents of the Transvaal were imprisoned for obeying Gandhi's call for resistance to these ordinances.[25]

Gandhi's career provided many illustrations of such actions performed at his bidding by followers at painful cost to themselves. During the campaign against British rule in India in 1930, Gujarati peasants refused to pay the land tax, despite seizure of their land, declaring: "We won't pay until he tells us."[26]

Indicators of Emotional Commitment

The last category of indicators is concerned with the emotional dimension of follower response. It is somewhat more difficult to specify precise indicators in this category than in the preceding ones, since this one deals with intensity of expression rather than with subject matter. Thus, what-

25. Ashe, *Gandhi*, p. 116.
26. Ibid., p. 295.

ever suggests the kind of emotion normally given to or associated with gods and saviors, such as adoration and reverence, can fit this category.

The best evidence for the existence of such emotions directed toward the leader is from testimonials volunteered by followers themselves. An example of such evidence, in which the follower specifies the emotion felt, is this account by Albert Speer of his feelings toward Hitler at the end of World War II:

> Now at the end of his rule . . . although I was opposing him and had had to face up to the fact of defeat, I still revered him.[27]

It is rare that the emotion indicated is specifically mentioned in this way in statements of follower response. More often, it has to be inferred. For example, one can infer blind faith in Roosevelt from the following sentence in a letter written to him:

> I voice millions when I say we wish you could be our leader always.[28]

Pledges of lifetime loyalty whose tone approximates that of religious dedication also reflect strong emotional commitment. For example, a survey conducted in Cuba elicited the following response from a truck driver:

> I will support Fidel and the Revolutionary Government with all the efforts of my life.[29]

An Argentinian's recollection of his first meeting with Perón with its mention of willingness to sacrifice self is also illustrative of such commitment:

> From that instant I committed myself to a higher ideal and to loyalty without reservation . . . loyalty which I profess and will continue to profess, observing it at the cost of greatest personal sacrifice.[30]

27. Speer, *Third Reich*, p. 437.
28. Sussman, *Dear FDR*, p. 110.
29. Lloyd A. Free, *Attitudes of the Cuban People Toward the Castro Regime* (Princeton: Institute of International Social Research, 1960), p. 7.
30. Joseph R. Barager, ed., *Why Perón Came to Power: The Background to Peronism in Argentina* (New York: Knopf, 1968), p. 179.

The promise of absolute obedience is another indicator within this group. Two examples are given here, the first from a letter to Roosevelt written by an Iowa congressman and the second from a statement by an Italian journalist:

I will do anything you ask. You are my leader.

We want to do more and better to make Mussolini understand that we want to obey him to the death.[31]

Certain kinds of actions on the part of followers may also serve as evidence of their emotional commitment to a leader. Among such actions might be: frenzied attempts to see, reach, or touch the person of a leader; according him gestures of worship commonly offered representations of divinity; treating objects he has touched or used as sacred relics. An example of an action that suggests veneration is that of a woman in Ohio who knelt down and "reverently patted the dust where he had left a footprint."[32] Another illustration is afforded by followers of Gandhi.

When travelling by rail he was besieged wherever he halted. At one obscure station the local people swore that if the train did not stop, they would lie down on the track and let it run over them. About midnight, amid uproar, the train was sighted. It did stop. Gandhi was asleep but he staggered up and showed himself. The din died away and the crowd knelt on the platform, weeping.[33]

I use the conditional, above, in referring to indicators of action, for the validity of many of these, as is discussed below, depends upon cultural context and the affect that can legitimately be ascribed to them.

Evidence and Interpretation

If open-ended survey research on political leaders were regularly conducted on a broad scale, problems of assessing evidence to determine whether leaders are charismatic might be limited to those involved in

31. Burns, *Roosevelt*, p. 168; Finer, *Mussolini*, p. 301.
32. Burns, *Roosevelt*, p. 362.
33. Ashe, *Gandhi*, p. 219.

coding responses.[34] Not only are such surveys often prohibitively expensive but in some countries they are prohibited. Moreover, survey research cannot be conducted retroactively for leaders who have passed into history. Therefore, evidence must often be gleaned from archival material, biographies, memoirs, and accounts of journalists and other observers. Evidence appearing to contain charismatically oriented content needs to be weighed carefully and interpreted in accordance with cultural and situational contexts.

Evidence that can be given greatest weight consists of statements freely tendered by followers concerning their beliefs in and emotional attitudes toward a leader, especially when given in their own words. Examples of these are the letters to Roosevelt quoted above and the extracts from the autobiographical accounts of followers of Hitler. Next in order of usefulness are fairly concrete and detailed accounts of statements or actions of followers from which their possession of charismatically oriented beliefs and emotions can be relatively unambiguously inferred. The earlier quoted description of the man who believed himself to have been cured of illness by the repetition of Gandhi's name is a prime example of this type of evidence.

Statements representing the conclusions or evaluations of an observer or a recorder do not in and of themselves constitute valid evidence. For one does not know whether they are based on acute and multiple observations of followers or interviews with them or whether they were formed highly impressionistically or from hearsay. The difference between direct evidence and unsupported conclusion may be illustrated by two extracts from William Shirer's *Berlin Diary*, each dealing with unconditional faith in Hitler's word. The first gives the following exchange between Shirer and an elderly German he encountered in a Berlin restaurant who assured him that Germany would win the war:

> "Each side thinks it will win," I said. "In all the wars."
> He looked at me with pity in his old eyes. "Germany will win," he said. "It is certain. The Fuhrer has said so."

The second is Shirer's own assertion:

---

34. See Davies, "Charisma," for an example of such a survey.

To many Germans . . . Hitler has become infallible. They say, as many peoples throughout history have said of their respective gods: "He is always right."[35]

This assertion may well have been a distillation of many statements heard by Shirer similar to the one quoted above. Generally, however, such statements can be problematical.

Without knowledge of the data or observational bases for summary statements that, for example, Filipinos gave Magsaysay "love, adoration, worship," or that Lenin's followers in Geneva in 1905 surrounded him with "an atmosphere of worship," one hesitates to accept these as adequate evidence. Personal bias in favor of a dramatic figure often tempts journalists and even scholars into employing overstatement and hyperbole, as illustrated by the statement that Mao "by millions of Chinese is quite genuinely regarded as a teacher, a strategist, statesman, philosopher, poet laureate, national hero, head of family and the greatest liberator in history. He is to them Confucius, plus Lao-Tzu plus Marx plus Buddha."[36]

This does not mean that summary statements should be discarded out of hand. Careful scrutiny of an account in which such a statement appears may convey some impression of the author's methods of observation and analysis, degree of precision, and objectivity. Sometimes, knowledge of an author's particular bias can be helpful in assessing the weight to be given to a statement. For example, knowing that Arnaldo Cortesi, the *New York Times* correspondent in Argentina, was unfavorably disposed to Péron lends credence for me to the following statement from one of his dispatches:

There is no denying . . . that many of Señor Perón's followers believe in him implicitly and with an almost mystic faith. . . . Nobody who has watched any pro-Perón meeting doubts that some of the persons who participate in them regard him as a demigod.[37]

35. William Shirer, *Berlin Diary* (New York: Knopf, 1941), pp. 283, 587.

36. Agnes Newton Keith, *Bare Feet in the Palace* (Boston: Little, Brown, 1955), p. 245; Nikolay Valentinov, *Encounters With Lenin* (London: Oxford University Press, 1968), p. 40; quotation from Edgar Snow in Jerome Ch'en, ed., *Mao* (Englewood Cliffs, N.J.: Prentice-Hall, 1969), pp. 130–31.

37. *New York Times*, Dec. 22, 1945.

Apparent evidence of charismatically oriented responses should be considered also in terms of the cultural and situational contexts in which it appears. This is especially important in assessing audience and crowd reactions to appearances and speeches of a leader. Statements that an audience greeted a leader's appearance or speech with "thunderous applause" or "wild enthusiasm" can suggest but do not necessarily provide adequate evidence for charismatically oriented perceptions.

In some societies enthusiastic acclamation of a religious or political leader is a traditional response tendered to nearly all members of that category. In India, for example, the notion of *darshan*, the personal dispensing of a spiritual blessing by the presence of a person perceived as especially endowed, extends to almost any outstanding figure. Thus, not all *darshan*-seekers are charismatically oriented followers, although uninitiated outsiders may receive that impression from observing them. Similarly, urban Arab crowds have tended to be highly volatile, easily aroused to frenzies of enthusiasm or hostility toward political leaders. Therefore, analysis of crowd responses in Arabic cultural contexts might require distinctions between sporadic situationally determined reactions and more enduring ones.

In assessing whether audience responses can be taken as indicative of charismatic content, it is also important to attempt to distinguish between enthusiastic reactions to a leader's statements on an issue and reactions to the person of the leader. In examining accounts of audience responses, one is especially dependent upon the acuteness, eye for detail, and discriminatory powers of the observers and recorders. Sometimes, information offered within an account might provide a decisive clue, even though parenthetical to the main thrust of the account. For example, an otherwise persuasive argument concerning the apparent charisma of labor leaders in Africa who were treated with deference and could bring out thousands of people for mass meetings is vitiated, in my opinion, by the casually mentioned statement that they could not collect dues from their union members.[38]

Whether or not specific modes of behavior constitute valid evidence may depend upon the cultural meanings of such behavior. One would,

38. See William H. Friedland, "For a Sociological Concept of Charisma," *Social Forces* 43 (Oct. 1964), 21–22.

for example, discount the association of a leader's name with a divinity if such an association is conventional for most leaders in a particular culture. A leader's picture hung on the wall of a home beside pictures of religious figures could indicate charismatically oriented perceptions. Such a possibility, however, would be discounted in some locales or among some classes or groups in a society where it is customary to hang a picture of a current or past head of state beside those of religious figures.

There are special problems in isolating possible charismatic content from sentiments of grief and loss in the responses to the death of a highly popular or longtime head of state. For example, statements credited to the Cairo populace at Nasser's funeral, such as "There is no God but God and Nasser is his love" and "We dedicate our lives, our souls, our blood to carry on the mission of Gamal Abdul Nasser," strongly suggest charismatic affect.[39] They also can be interpreted, however, as more reflective of a sense of abandonment on the part of people for whom their system was their leader and had been so for over fifteen years. There can be a very sudden sense of abandonment, especially when the death of a sitting head of government or state has been occasioned by assassination. This, together with the complex emotions generated in many societies by violent death or deliberate murder, can lead to laudatory statements about the deceased and his indispensability. But perceptions of loss or of indispensability are not equivalent to charismatically oriented perceptions.

Charismatics and Probable Charismatics

Six cases of charismatic political leaders have been chosen to illustrate this explanation for the charismatic political phenomenon: Castro, Gandhi, Hitler, Mussolini, Roosevelt, and Sukarno. The seventh and most recent case is that of Khomeini, an instance of both religious and political charisma. These leaders were selected in part because they cut across a range of different cultures. Mainly, however, their selection was determined by the fact that they represent unambiguous cases. There is plentiful evidence, in accordance with the criteria and caveats stipulated

---

39. Reported on NBC television news, Oct. 1, 1970.

above, for charismatically oriented perceptions of them among various strata of their societies. In the case of Sukarno, I had the benefit of considerable opportunity for personal observations of follower responses.

Another concern in my selection was that of examining the uses of office and formal power in the generation and development of political charisma, especially on a national level. For that reason, my sample has been restricted, with the exception of Gandhi, to those charismatic leaders who have held the highest political office in their countries or, stated somewhat differently, to those in highest office who gained widespread charismatic validation at some stage in their careers. The inclusion of Khomeini was also motivated by the opportunity to illustrate competition between personal and institutionalized or royal charisma.

In a preliminary version of this study I drew on a larger sample of national leaders.[40] It also included: Ataturk, Lenin, Mao, Magsaysay, Nasser, Nkrumah, Perón, Touré, and U Nu. The evidence I could find for charismatically oriented perceptions of them in the sources available to me was either quantitatively or qualitatively insufficient for me to put them on a par with the seven cases noted above. On the basis of available evidence, however, and on the basis of judgments of specialists on their countries I have consulted, it seems safe to consider them probable charismatics, at least for some stage of their career trajectories.

Consort Charisma and the Passionate Charismatic

"Where," I was asked by someone to whom I mentioned my sample of twentieth-century charismatic political leaders, "are the women charismatic political leaders?"

Media attention in this century has often been the first clue to the emergence of a coming star in a national political firmament. In the mid-twentieth century the women who gained media attention approaching that of Castro, Mao, Nasser, or Sukarno were likely to be named Marilyn Monroe or Elizabeth Taylor if they were not members of the British royal family. The only exceptions that easily come to mind are Eleanor Roosevelt and Evita Perón, whose political prominence, at least

40. Ann Ruth Willner, *Charismatic Political Leadership*, p. 33.

in part, was initially derived from the fact that they were consorts to prominent male political leaders.

It might well be argued that for most of this century talented women were able to gain the recognition accorded their male peers mainly in the fields of popular entertainment and literature. In politics perhaps to an even greater extent than in other traditionally "male" occupations, women gained an opportunity to develop and demonstrate latent talent only accidentally or indirectly.

In most societies, rulership or even aspiring to it has generally been a male prerogative. Even though history has familiarized us with the reigns of some notable women monarchs, the few women who came to rule countries did so generally in the absence of a legitimate male heir in the direct line of succession, as regent during the minority of the male heir, and/or through specific designation by their predecessors. In sixteenth-century England, Mary Tudor and Elizabeth Tudor ruled as the result of the early death of their younger half-brother and the express will of their late father, Henry VIII. In France, during the same period, Catherine de Medici ruled as Queen Regent for her second son. Many more women, such as the late Manchu Dynasty Empress Dowager Tz'u-hsi, Theodora of Byzantium, and Madame de Pompadour, informally ruled the formal rulers as mother, consort, or concubine.

Monarchical rule succumbed to presidential and prime ministerial rule under parliamentary and electoral systems and to caesarist rule without any significant increase in the visibility of women in high political posts. Women's roles in the upper echelons of politics continued to be dependent upon and subordinate to the men to whom they were attached. These roles were not conducive to the development of an autonomous following, much less a charismatically oriented one.

If the possibility of widespread charismatically oriented responses developing in the direction of a political woman has been slight, the likelihood of discovering such a phenomenon has been slimmer. Non-consort politically active women in the last two centuries have been generally neglected by scholars, biographers, and journalists writing in English, whether because of their gender or because of their counter-establishment orientations and activities is difficult to ascertain. Not until the 1960s did there appear in English a biography of Rosa Luxemburg, Marxist theoretical economist, revolutionary activist, and, in the opinion of some, an intellectually broader and more cogent critic of Leninist Marxism than Trotsky and his disciples.[41] Emma Goldman, possibly the most publicized anarchist in America at the beginning of this century and a spellbinding orator who filled halls with more than left-wing sympathizers, faded into historical obscurity until the recent revival of the women's movement and the development of women's studies.[42]

Thus, it would require considerably more research efforts than were needed for my sample of men to ascertain whether and to what extent women leaders of suffragette, radical, and reformist movements gained charismatic recognition. My search so far has yielded only one who seems to have done so autonomously in this century on a national basis—Dolores Gómez Ibarruri, more familiarly known as La Pasionaria (The Passionate Flower). Daughter of a Basque miner, she became one of the founders of the Spanish Communist Party and in 1936 a deputy in the parliament of the Republican government, where she was renowned as an orator.

She became a heroine of the Loyalists throughout the Spanish Civil War. Her cry "No pasarán!" ("They shall not pass!") became theirs. At the onset of the Franco rebellion she spoke to the country over Madrid radio and her final words, "It is better to die on your feet than live on your knees!" rallied resistance and became the slogan of the Spanish Republic. Reports of American war correspondents at the time and their memoirs later testify to La Pasionaria's immense influence among the Spanish masses beyond the small membership of her party. From an oral history of the Spanish Civil War we learn that battalions of young and unlettered workers and peasants becoming literate as well as learning military skills wrote their first letter to their wives and the second one to her. When the bells of Madrid's churches were melted down to make armored cars, the first one was named after her.[43]

41. J. P. Nettl, *Rosa Luxemburg* (London: Oxford University Press, 1966), pp. 7, 11–13.

42. See, for example, Margaret S. Marsh, *Anarchist Women* (Philadelphia: Temple University Press, 1981).

43. Vincent Sheean, *Not Peace But a Sword* (New York: Doubleday, Doran, 1939), p. 183; Herbert L. Matthews, *Half of Spain Died: A Reappraisal of the Spanish Civil War* (New York: Charles Scribner and Sons, 1973), p. 67; Hugh Thomas, *The Spanish Civil War* (New York: Harper & Brothers, 1961), p. 140; Ronald Fraser, *Blood of Spain: An Oral History of the Spanish Civil War* (New York: Pantheon Books, 1979), p. 232; *New York Times*, Aug. 2, 1936, Sept. 2, 1936.

Most suggestive of charismatic appeal, however, is Vincent Sheean's recollection of a meeting of the Central Committee of the Spanish Communist Party on May 23, 1938. The government of moderate Socialist López Negrín had issued a declaration of war aims that included encouragement of capitalist enterprise and respect for regional liberties. La Pasionaria spoke in support of the program in a speech lasting several hours that was critical of the "revolutionary infantilism" of those who thought industry could be run without middle classes and wage differentials. To Sheean "it seemed as if she was asking these people to stop being Communists altogether, at least until the war was won."[44] The audience, dismayed and shocked at first, responded with enthusiastic cheers when she concluded.

That same decade saw an American president's wife who might have gained personal political charisma had her efforts not been so closely linked with her husband's career that they contributed to his charisma. According to an Associated Press reporter, Eleanor Roosevelt was better known to New York State politicians in 1928 than was her husband, Franklin, the candidate for governor.[45]

In a sense the Roosevelts come close to approximating a case of dual political charisma in that Eleanor's extraordinary activities, unparalleled in the history of American First Ladies, and her unflagging advocacy of the rights and causes of hitherto submerged sectors of the American people redounded to the credit and contributed to the charisma of Franklin. That popular perceptions of her did not appear to cross the border between extreme admiration (as well as considerable hostility in some quarters) and charismatic orientation may have had something to do with how she perceived and enacted her role. Clearly independent minded, she nonetheless publicly depoliticized and minimized her political successes.

The Peróns seem to have been a clear case of dual political charisma. While Evita (as Eva Duarte de Perón was popularly known) also contributed to Juan Domingo's charisma, she did appear to have gained a charismatically oriented following of her own as well as one overlapping with his. Hers consisted primarily of women among the poor. Indeed, she exemplifies the phenomenon of a woman whose uses of power

---

44. Sheean, pp. 182–89.
45. Lorena A. Hickok, *Reluctant First Lady* (New York: Dodd, Mead, 1962), p. 17.

helped to crystallize charismatically oriented perceptions. Her power and control of communications were considerable and were partly directed toward satisfying her apparently great need for adulation. This makes it somewhat difficult, although not impossible, to distinguish between what might have been commandeered ritual tributes to her saintliness and genuinely charismatic ones.[46]

Within the last decade, three women have exercised power as the chief political executives in their respective countries. Neither Indira Gandhi nor Golda Meier nor Margaret Thatcher appears to have catalyzed any significant charismatically oriented following, however much they may have been admired by some segments of their societies.

Marginals and Misnomers

Lastly might be mentioned those cases of political leaders who do not meet the criteria for the possession of charisma but for whom its attribution or appearance has some justification. They are marginal cases who might be termed *quasi-charismatics*. One type within this general category is that of the leader with derived or designated charisma. He is the heir of the residue of charisma inherited from close association with or linkage to a clearly charismatic leader. In my opinion, Nehru exemplifies this type. Some segments of the Indian public may well have responded to Nehru in ways that weighed more toward charisma than *darshan*. Yet one cannot help suspecting that this must have been a secondary charisma, that those responses were tendered to Nehru as designate of Gandhi and inheritor of Gandhi's mantle or as a tribute to Gandhi through the person of Nehru.

Some of the leaders listed above as probables might be more fittingly classified as quasi-charismatic because of the problem of establishing the genuineness of their apparently charismatic acclaim. This problem

46. Considering her prominence, it is surprising that as of this writing there has not appeared in English a solid scholarly biography of Eva Perón. A semifictionalized biography is John Barnes, *Evita, First Lady: A Biography of Eva Perón* (New York: Grove Press, 1978). I found most useful an anthropological study, J. M. Taylor, *Eva Perón: The Myths of a Woman* (Chicago: University of Chicago Press, 1979), and am especially grateful to George and Deborah Blanksten for their recollections of their personal observations while engaged in research for George I. Blanksten, *Perón's Argentina* (Chicago: University of Chicago Press, 1953).

arises in cases of closed systems in which the cult of leadership is officially cultivated and propagated. It is minimized in the cases of leaders like Hitler and Mussolini whose charisma was visible before they instituted closed systems. The case of Mao, however, seems not too clear. Sympathetic visitors during the Yunan period, such as Edgar Snow, did not observe or at least did not write about any charismatically oriented follower perceptions. These seem to have emerged and flowered after the institution of the cult of Mao and the onset of a repressive regime.

A similar difficulty arises in the case of Lenin. The posthumous myth of Lenin's charisma is so firmly established that there is a tendency to overlook the fact that in 1917–18 he had his way over the objections of his closest followers not because of their absolute belief in his judgment but through the force of his will and his logic and by his threats to withdraw. Similarly often forgotten is that during this period his support from the Petrograd populace waxed and waned.[47]

Perhaps the most unusual kind of marginal case is postmortem charisma or, more precisely, postmortem retroactive attribution of charisma. In his lifetime, John F. Kennedy did not generate a charismatically oriented following, although he was a striking and glamorous figure. The manner of his death and the staging of his funeral invoked some classic and close to universal myths, as Dorothy Willner has demonstrated, and associated him and his family with their protagonists. Not only was Kennedy assimilated to the Lincoln legend but also to the myths of King Arthur and Camelot, Oedipus of Greece, and Christ and others martyred in their youth.[48]

Possibly a marginal type but more likely a misnomer when credited with charisma is the case of the political leader popularly considered indispensable in a crisis. DeGaulle, frequently referred to as charismatic by scholars as well as journalists, is a case in point. In having a mission, he undoubtedly fitted one part of Weber's description of the charismatic leader. He was seized by an inner vision and believed it the duty of the French people to follow him. Moreover, as Mauriac first noted and as the Hoffmans later described in detail, he carefully and artistically fash-

---

47. Adam Ulam, *The Bolsheviks* (New York: Macmillan, 1965), pp. 330–32; David Shub, *Lenin* (Garden City, N.Y.: Doubleday, 1948), pp. 188–96, 237–38, 253.

48. Dorothy Willner, "Ritual, Myth and the Murdered President," in *The Realm of the Extra Human*, ed. A. Bharati (The Hague: Mouton, 1976), pp. 401–20.

ioned himself in advance to act out in classic style the role of the transcendant hero.[49]

Yet evidence that DeGaulle was so perceived by many of the French people seems difficult to obtain. The only source I was able to find is problematical, consisting of campaign statements made by Gaullist deputies seeking votes in an election and obviously wishing to ride on DeGaulle's coattails. Other sources suggest that DeGaulle was followed not so much because he inspired others by his vision or his person but because in a crisis he seemed "le seul possible," "le seul qui essaie de sauver France." Because DeGaulle was seen as the sole alternative in 1958, his subsequent performance gained him substantial popularity and deep respect from his countrypeople. But apparently, as Werth states, he "was not 'adored' the way Hitler or Mussolini had been."[50]

On the issue of the borderline between perceptions suggesting charisma and those indicating indispensability, the case of Nasser after Egypt's defeat by Israel in the 1967 war provides an interesting example of varied interpretations of the same phenomenon. The phenomenon was an outpouring of the Cairo populace hysterically refusing to accept Nasser's genuine or feigned attempt to resign. While some commentators have taken this as clear proof of Nasser's continued charisma, others have argued that it merely testified to the inability of Egyptians to imagine any other leader of the system that Nasser had instituted and ruled for well over a decade. Unfortunately, none of the sources consulted provided detailed or direct evidence of Egyptian participants' individual perceptions.[51]

49. David Schoenbrun, *The Three Lives of Charles de Gaulle* (New York: Atheneum, 1968), p. 11 and passim; Henry Ehrmann, *Politics in France* (Boston: Little, Brown, 1968), p. 161; François Mauriac, *DeGaulle* (Garden City, N.Y.: Doubleday, 1966), p. 42; Stanley Hoffman and Inge Hoffman, "The Will to Grandeur: DeGaulle as Political Artist," in *Philosophers and Kings*, ed. Dankwart A. Rustow (New York: George Braziller, 1970), pp. 248–316.

50. Mattei Dogan, "Le Personnel Politique et la Personnalité Charismatique," *Revue Française de Sociologie* 6 (1965), 305–24; Philip E. Converse and George Dupeux, "DeGaulle and Eisenhower: The Public Image of the Victorious General," in *Elections and the Political Order*, ed. Angus Campbell, Philip E. Converse, Warren Miller, and Donald E. Stokes (New York: John Wiley & Sons, 1966), p. 297; Alexander Werth, *De Gaulle: A Political Biography* (New York: Simon and Schuster, 1965), p. 219.

51. Those taking this episode to illustrate Nasser's charisma include: R. Hrair Dekmejian, *Egypt Under Nasir: A Study in Political Dynamics* (Albany: State University of New

Similarly borderline are the apparent but ephemeral quasi-charismatic reactions to individuals that are at root responses to situations in which a particular stance is symbolized by an individual. Senators Eugene McCarthy and George McGovern seemed to generate, respectively, in 1968 and 1972 something akin to charismatic responses from younger people. But even at those times and certainly in retrospect it could be seen that these were not so much responses to the persons as they were to the person-as-symbol of the situational and ideological concerns of the Vietnam generation.

In my initial version of this study I referred to Churchill as a possible situational charismatic. It was tempting to envision him as one of a long line of legendary and historic heroes, starting with St. George, who came to the rescue of England in her time of desperation. Unable, however, to find evidence of charismatically oriented perceptions of Churchill by his countrypeople, I also suggested that the British may not be susceptible to charismatic affect, that they can admire and esteem but not adore. This suggestion has since been confirmed by Dennis Kavanagh in his study of Churchill's leadership.[52]

York Press, 1971), pp. 46, 302, 307; John P. Entelis, "Nasser's Egypt: The Failure of Charismatic Leadership," *Orbis* 18 (1974), pp. 457–59; and Jean Lacouture, *Nasser* (New York: Knopf, 1973), pp. 311–13. Anthony Nutting, *Nasser* (London: Constable, 1972), pp. 17, 425, is an example of those who favor the indispensability argument, that is, "Nasser was the only rock to which they could cling" (p. 425).

52. Ann Ruth Willner, *Charismatic Political Leadership*, pp. 75, 86; Dennis Kavanagh, "Crisis, Charisma and British Political Leadership: Winston Churchill," paper delivered at Ninth World Congress of Political Science, Montreal, Aug. 1973.

3
Political Charisma: Contexts and Catalysts

The preceding chapters have provided a definition of political charisma and operational indices for identifying it. This chapter offers the beginning of an explanation for the emergence of charismatic political leadership. I start with a summary of the elements commonly held to account for political charisma and proceed to a critical analysis of them. Because I have found prior attempts, including my own, to explain political charisma somewhat simplistic, I then briefly outline a revised explanation. Those elements that I have found, upon further thought, to be most salient in the emergence and development of political charisma are described in greater depth and detail in the succeeding chapters.

Three sources seem to have provided the primary bases for current and conventional views concerning the preconditions and causes of charismatic political leadership. The first is Weber's work, in which charisma is associated with times of "distress" and "extraordinary" situations.[1] The second consists of theories concerning collective and especially revolutionary movements, a source considered useful on the assumption that overlapping categories such as charismatic leadership and revolutionary leadership can be similarly explained.[2] The third

---

1. Weber, *Economy*, 3, pp. 1111, 1117.
2. Hadley Cantril, *The Psychology of Social Movements* (New York: Wiley, 1941), and Neil Smelser, *Theory of Collective Behavior* (New York: Free Press, 1962) have been among the most influential sources. For an excellent synthesis and development of theories on revolution, see Ted Gurr, *Why Men Rebel* (Princeton: Princeton University Press, 1970).

source is comprised of early studies of Hitler's rise to power, the assumption behind their use presumably being that factors explaining the appeal of one charismatic political leader have relevance for the class of such leaders.[3]

The formula for the generation of political charisma conventionally begins with a situation of extreme social stress or crisis, often one producing major deprivations. Such a situation evokes in people psychic anxiety and distress. If political authorities seem unwilling or unable to cope with or alleviate the crisis, people become alienated from the political system and susceptible to the political appeal of a strong leader who can be seen as the symbol and the means of rescue from distress. Should a leader and movement appear with a doctrine that holds out hope, they react to him with a charismatically oriented response.[4]

Whether through emulation or autonomous thought, there seems to be relative consensus concerning the elements combining to produce political charisma and concerning their order or sequence, that is: (1) a crisis situation, (2) potential followers in distress, and (3) an aspirant leader with (4) a doctrine promising deliverance. There is controversy, however, concerning which element tends to constitute the primary cause or chief precipitant of political charisma. Some analysts place major emphasis upon the social situation or context of crisis.[5] Others see the chief source of charisma in the psychic states of the followers.[6] Still others stress the primacy of the mission, doctrine, or issues that the aspirant leader exploits.[7]

Before analyzing these elements and demonstrating how this formula falls short as a satisfactory explanation of the genesis of political charisma, I might note the lack of emphasis given to the leader. In aspects

3. Abel, *Why Hitler Came to Power*; Hans Gerth, "The Nazi Party: Its Leadership and Composition," *American Journal of Sociology* 45 (Jan. 1940), 517–41.

4. This version or variants of it can be found in William H. Friedland, "For a Sociological Concept of Charisma," *Social Forces* 43 (Oct. 1964), 18–26; Smelser, *Theory*, pp. 313–81; and Ann Ruth Willner, *Charismatic Political Leadership*, pp. 34–48.

5. For example, Friedland, "Sociological Concept."

6. George Devereux, "Charismatic Leadership and Crisis," in *Psychoanalysis and the Social Sciences*, ed. Warner Muensterberger and Sidney Axelrod (New York: International Universities Press, 1955); James V. Downton, Jr., *Rebel Leadership: Commitment and Charisma in the Revolutionary Process* (New York: Free Press, 1973); and Alexander Mitscherlich, "Changing Patterns of Authority: A Psychiatric Interpretation," in *Political Leadership in Industrialized Societies*, ed. Lewis J. Edinger (New York: Wiley, 1967).

7. See, for example, Ratnam, "Charisma and Political Leadership."

other than that of chief expounder of the doctrine or chief rhetorician, the leader has generally been seen as the least, if not the last, of the factors explaining political charisma. This is not so strange as it may seem, for contemporary students of leadership and other social scientists have long since forced Carlyle's hero off center stage and supplanted him as a maker of history with a host of collectivities. The single individual who seems to transcend social forces tends to be seen as no more than the product of collective needs, collective values, collective crises, or collective actions.

This view of leadership as a latent force, to be called or summoned into being by a collective impulse, is not confined to social scientists. "The call for leadership," a renowned philosopher has asserted, "only appears when a collective desire has reached an overwhelming strength and when, on the other hand, all hopes of fulfilling this desire in an ordinary way have failed. At these times, the desire is not only keenly felt but also personified. It stands before the eyes of man in a concrete, plastic, and individual shape. The intensity of the collective wish is embodied in the leader."[8]

In a similar vein, a prominent psychoanalyst has written: "There are periods in history which are identity-vacua, when a sudden sense of alienation is widespread. . . . It is in such periods that the leaders' deep conflicts and special gifts have found their 'activities on a large scale,' and they have been found and chosen by contemporaries possessed of analogous conflicts and corresponding needs."[9]

It may be this perspective on leadership that indirectly accounts for what I find to be one of the major limitations of the conventional formula for political charisma: the neglect or minimization of the role of the leader as active initiator or catalyst of charismatically oriented perceptions of himself. As I seek to show below, the actions of the leader himself have generally been a major factor and sometimes the major factor in the generation of political charisma. Moreover, the leader can also play a prominent part in activating the other elements.

This suggests not only the necessity for including some additional elements in an expanded and revised explanation of the genesis of politi-

8. Ernst Cassirer, *The Myth of the State* (Garden City, N.Y.: Doubleday, 1955), p. 352.
9. Erik H. Erikson, *Insight and Responsibility* (New York: Norton, 1964), p. 204.

cal charisma. It also suggests a revision of the sequence of elements or even the possibility of several different sequences producing political charisma with different elements in the primary place. Before looking to the role of the leader and to the possibility of alternative sequences, I examine the other elements in the conventional formulation in part to ascertain whether they are necessary or merely conducive to the generation of political charisma.

Social Crisis and Psychic Distress

It seems intuitively plausible that severe social stress or crisis can lead to psychic distress and political disillusionment and that these in turn can result in susceptibility to an individual leader. One's intuitions are aided or perhaps catalyzed by recalling the war, inflation, and depression that preceded Hitler's rise to power in Germany, the war and internal violence that preceded Mussolini's in Italy, and the depression that preceded Roosevelt's presidency in the United States.

War and its aftermath generally constitute a dramatic and pervasive collective social and psychological crisis for a society, involving as they usually do loss of life, separations of families, economic hardships, and social dislocations. If the consequences of war include defeat and occupation, the economic hardships and social dislocations for many people can be magnified. At the same time, the psychological props of patriotism and propaganda that may have justified or rationalized deprivations for them earlier are removed. Apathy, anxiety, alienation, and resentment are some of the emotions that can result and the two latter can be directed toward governmental authorities whom people might hold responsible for their plight or for not doing something about it.

Even a victorious war can result in a social crisis engendered by the problems of restoring a peacetime economy and providing employment to demobilized veterans. Those exhausted by wartime efforts and deprivations may be impatient and resentful at the slim yields and slow pace of restoration. Some may feel an even sharper sense of relative deprivation if they are members of groups that have been led by wartime promises to expect postwar social transformations and increased opportunities in their favor.

Severe economic crises such as extreme inflation or depression can be in some respects as psychologically traumatic as war, if not more so. To most people, unversed in economics, these are causeless and purposeless. This can produce not only anxiety about economic survival and social status but even disorientation and panic about what the future might hold.

A similar element of unpredictability characterizes crises of internal violence. Apart from the fact that internal violence and terrorism can hinder normal life and livelihood, even violence and terror directed at specific targets tend to take their toll of others, heightening anxiety and resentment.

Social crisis and psychic distress may seem quite logical as linked proximate causes for the generation of political charisma. To establish whether they have indeed been major causes, however, requires some empirical investigation. One would have to state with confidence that known cases of charismatic political leadership have invariably or generally been preceded by severe social crises and psychic stress.

It is true that the rise of many charismatic leaders to political power has been preceded or accompanied by crises. However, it is important to make a distinction, one that is often forgotten, between power and charisma. Some charismatic political leaders have gained charismatic recognition before the achievement of formal political power and others only after it and mainly by virtue of how they have used that power. Crisis and distress may contribute to gaining widespread political support and national office without necessarily generating charismatic affect. Without attention to this essential distinction, a spurious relationship can be, and has been, made between crisis and charisma.

An examination of the six cases of political charisma dealt with in this study suggests that only two, those of Hitler and Roosevelt, seem to conform sufficiently closely to the preconditions of crisis and psychic distress specified in the conventional formula. In the other cases the relationship seems relatively remote or nonexistent.

The case of Hitler certainly seems to strengthen the association between crisis and the generation of charisma. Before Hitler's entry into German politics, Germany had successively undergone the crises of war and defeat, quasi-revolution, and partial occupation. Germans of all groups resented the terms of the Versailles Treaty and especially the occupation of the Rhineland. In the autobiographies of a sample of

National Socialists obtained by Theodore Abel, the themes of nationalist bitterness, sense of betrayal, and desire for revenge are pervasive.[10]

In 1923 came the occupation of the Ruhr by France and Belgium, which occasioned a great sense of outrage in many Germans, and the runaway inflation. For those on salaries and wages, the latter was a crisis but for the middle classes whose investments and savings were swept away, it was practically catastrophic. The suddenly impoverished, fearful of loss of status as well as anxious about economic survival, lost confidence in a governmental system that could permit this. Bewilderment and anxiety were combined with resentment at the sight of industrialists and speculators who seemed enriched by the inflation.[11] According to Abel, one-fourth of his sample of Nazi respondents wrote of the inflation as having been a major crisis in their personal lives.[12]

After a brief period of economic recovery, there came another and far more prolonged economic crisis: the depression that began in 1929 and whose effects in Germany have been termed "devastating."[13] Unemployment doubled from 3 million in September 1930 to more than 6 million in January 1932. In the latter year, when the government cut unemployment compensation, about 15 to 20 million people were on the dole. The psychological trauma brought on many suicides, not only of bankrupt businessmen and bankers but also of members of the middle classes fearful of facing the social stigma they attached to poverty.[14]

On the surface, the economic depression and its psychological effects appear to have been the major precipitant for the widespread growth of general, if not necessarily charismatic, support for Hitler and his party. For the ranks of the latter swelled dramatically after the onset of the depression, more than doubling between 1929 and 1930 and doubling again the following year; and the proportion of votes received by the National Socialists rose from 2.6 percent in 1928 to 18.3 percent in 1930.

However, there are grounds to question the primacy of the depression

10. Abel, *Hitler*, pp. 36–37, 42, 46, 48, 100.

11. Cantril, *Psychology*, p. 222; Joachim C. Fest, *Hitler* (New York: Vintage Books, 1975), p. 148.

12. Abel, *Hitler*, pp. 121–22.

13. Fest, *Hitler*, p. 268.

14. Alan Bullock, *Hitler: A Study in Tyranny* (New York: Harper, 1960), pp. 152–53; Cantril, *Psychology*, p. 223; Fest, *Hitler*, pp. 268–69.

crisis and of economic hardship generally as the chief inducement to conversion to the Nazi cause. The figures given by Abel for his sample of National Socialists reveal that about four-fifths of them had never changed occupation or been unemployed and could be judged economically secure at the time of joining the party.[15] Moreover, Peter Merkl, who has reanalyzed the Abel protocols in much detail and with considerable analytic and statistical sophistication, has found in them no support for the thesis of the depression as a major motivating factor, although the role of economic motives generally is not excluded but was relatively less than generally assumed.[16] It is conceivable that for many a more important factor was the cumulative effect of the successive crises that progressively undermined their confidence in the existing system and, with the final crisis, impelled them into the Nazi camp.

Merkl's analysis strongly suggests that the different crises had differential impacts on different groups, with respect to their politicization and to their conversion to the cause of National Socialism. Generation, class background, and rural or urban provenience provided some of the denominators of difference.[17]

The reasons for conversion to a cause, however, may not be quite the same as conversion to a charismatic attachment to its leader. Although Hitler's charisma for large masses of Germans appears to have been generated after his accession to power, there is evidence that some of his followers perceived him in charismatic terms during the early years of his political career.[18] Merkl's analysis of the Abel sample indicates that 18.1 percent of the respondents were "Hitler cultists" or charismatically oriented followers as of 1934.[19]

The autobiographies of this group show that they had initially become politicized mainly by the shock of defeat and of the foreign occupation and also by economic problems and antagonism to the "Marxist revolution."[20] Many of the postwar generation reported themselves as having

15. Abel, *Hitler*, pp. 313, 315.
16. Peter Merkl, *Political Violence Under the Swastika* (Princeton: Princeton University Press, 1975), pp. 366, 562.
17. Ibid., pp. 668–78.
18. Abel, *Hitler*, pp. 152–53; Fest, *Hitler*, p. 154.
19. Merkl, *Political Violence*, p. 453.
20. Ibid., p. 463.

become politicized as a result of conflict over the occupation of the Ruhr.[21] Specific motives reported for joining the National Socialist Party included the comradeship of stormtroopers, economic problems, and especially friction with the occupation.[22] It appears, at least from these data, that the psychic shocks engendered by wartime defeat and by its consequences may have been more significant than those produced by economic deprivation as a basis for charismatic conversion to Hitler.[23]

In the case of Roosevelt the economic depression was the single overriding crisis. The shock of the collapse of the stock market in 1929 and of the steadily worsening conditions thereafter may have been greater for Americans than the impact of the depression was for Germans or for nationals of other countries. For in the United States, the economic crisis broke upon a period of considerable prosperity marked by expectations of greater prosperity to come. Details of that crisis and its effects are spelled out in chapter 5 in relation to the genesis of Roosevelt's political charisma soon after he assumed office. Here it need only be noted that this was the clearest case of a direct relationship between crisis and despair on the one hand and charisma on the other.

Certain parallels between the rise to power of Mussolini and of Hitler have caused these cases to be treated as similar instances of charismatic leaders of revolutionary movements who came to power in part because of crises, some of their own making, and because of the weaknesses of the preceding regimes. Nevertheless, despite the similarities there were differences, especially with respect to the relationship between crisis and charisma.

It is true that Mussolini's rise to political prominence and power was also preceded and accompanied by crises, although none perhaps of the magnitude of some that afflicted Germany. It might even be said that Italy was in a state of recurrent crisis from shortly after the end of World War I to 1922, when Mussolini took office. In part these crises were the result of frustrated expectations, for extravagant wartime promises had led various groups to anticipate a new social and economic order. When

21. Ibid., p. 670.
22. Ibid., p. 463.
23. Merkl assigns this factor greater weight for the entire group of Nazi converts (ibid., p. 711).

expected gains failed to materialize, these groups attempted direct change through protests and violence.

The year 1919 brought not only a sharp inflation but a wave of strikes by leftist labor unions and the beginning of peasant takeovers of land in the countryside. The same year there was outrage at the treatment accorded Italy's claims at the Versailles Peace Conference, particularly the claim to Fiume, leading to belief in the "mutilated victory." Inflation, strikes, and land seizures continued in 1920, as did shortages of coal and other vital commodities. The rise in the price of bread by decree of Prime Minister Nitti may well have been felt as a personal crisis by many families. The most dramatic crisis of that year, however, was the occupation of many factories by workers.

Such activities produced in the minds of the members of the upper and middle classes the fear of an imminent full-scale socialist or communist revolution. Industrialists and landowners, indignant at government inability to curb the radical unions and leagues of farm workers, financed Fascist paramilitary groups that moved against them. The year 1921 was marked not only by growing unemployment and a bank crisis. It was the year of escalation of violence almost to the point of civil war, as rightists fought leftists in fields and factories for veritable control of entire municipalities and regions.[24]

Mussolini and his Fascist movement undoubtedly gained from the fear of left-wing revolution felt even by small shopkeepers, peasant proprietors, and petty civil servants. The disillusionment with a series of inept governments, the desire for an end to violence, and the wish for a "strong hand" at the helm of government may have more than reconciled many Italians to Mussolini's March on Rome in 1922. Crises, including those he helped to create, undoubtedly aided Mussolini's attainment of power.

However, it cannot easily be demonstrated that the crises in postwar Italy directly contributed to the growth of charismatic perceptions of

24. For detailed treatments of the rise to power of Mussolini and Fascism, see: F. L. Carsten, *The Rise of Fascism* (Berkeley: University of California Press, 1969), pp. 45–66; Adrian Lyttelton, *The Seizure of Power: Fascism in Italy, 1919–1929* (London: Weidenfeld and Nicolson, 1973), pp. 30–80; Christopher Seton-Watson, *Italy From Liberalism to Fascism, 1870–1925* (London: Methuen, 1967), pp. 503–602; and Ivone Kirkpatrick, *Mussolini: A Study in Power* (New York: Hawthorn Books, 1964), pp. 99–152.

Mussolini. For Mussolini was the acknowledged leader of Fascism from the time of its founding, although his leadership at times was challenged; but he was not yet perceived in charismatic terms by any significant segments of his Fascist followers,[25] much less by others, although his speeches were greeted with considerable acclaim.

While the case of Mussolini exemplifies crisis contributing to political power but not precipitating political charisma, that of Castro illustrates the development of charisma without the aid of a prior crisis.

No economic or social crisis heralded Fidel Castro's first dramatic move against the Batista regime, his attack on Moncada in 1953. Batista's assumption of the presidency by coup the year before had not been unprecedented in Cuban history and had not been widely viewed as a political crisis. Despite a lopsided economy and considerable poverty, Cuba's per capita income and level of development were among the highest in Latin America. Moreover, there was relative prosperity during the 1950s.[26]

No crisis developed during Castro's exile or immediately after his return to Cuba in 1956 to continue his struggle from the Sierra Maestre. By the time Castro entered Havana in 1959, a large segment of his following was charismatically oriented to him. Yet the only crisis had been that precipitated by his campaign and its effects on Batista.

The case of Castro and even more the cases of Gandhi and Sukarno raise the question of distinguishing types of crisis in attempting to assess the role of crisis in the generation of political charisma. The Weberian formula implies the existence of crisis as a factor independent of the role of the leader and probably antecedent to the prominence of the latter, represented as: crisis → distress → leader + doctrine → charisma. People are susceptible to the leader and his claims in large part because of the crisis. A crisis induced by a leader, however, changes this causal explanation in placing priority and emphasis on the element of leader-

25. The numerous studies, journal articles, and English language newspapers consulted did not yield evidence of charismatic responses to Mussolini during this period. Moreover, Dr. Benjamin F. Brown, my consultant on Italian history for this period, is also of the opinion that any pronounced charismatic perceptions of Mussolini developed after he gained power.

26. Maurice Halperin, *The Rise and Decline of Fidel Castro* (Berkeley: University of California Press, 1972), p. 5; Wyatt MacGaffey and Clifford R. Barnett, *Cuba* (New Haven: Human Relations Area Files Press, 1962), pp. 26, 60.

ship, that is, leader + doctrine → crisis → distress → leader + doctrine → charisma. Whereas in the first formula, the element of leadership is in part outcome and in part precipitant of the final result, in the second one, the leader is catalyst for the whole process.[27]

In the cases of Gandhi and Sukarno it is difficult to pinpoint major crises that were externally generated and not in part attributable to the actions of these leaders or to the responses to these actions by other authorities against whom they were taken. What came closest to a classic crisis in Gandhi's case was the action of the Transvaal government in 1906 that precipitated Gandhi's first attempt at mass political action (see chap. 5). In the case of Sukarno the Japanese occupation of Indonesia might fit this category. But Sukarno had generated charisma years earlier.[28]

The classic notion of crisis I take to refer to a sharp and major disturbance in the social, economic, and/or political order(s), whose effects are or threaten to become deprivational or dangerous and whose outcome is unpredictable. This notion is not easy to deal with in the context of a prolonged anticolonial struggle. One cannot regard the latter as constituting a single political crisis, for in reality most prolonged struggles for national independence have been marked by periods of quiescence alternating with periods of crisis. More significantly, however, in terms of the psychic distress presumably generated by crises, there may well be a difference in the subjective reactions of people caught in a crisis not of their making and those of people purposively involved in helping to create a crisis.

The preceding cases therefore suggest that preconditions of exogenous social crisis and psychic distress are conducive to the emergence of charismatic political leadership but that they are not necessary. If we extend the notion of crisis to include those largely generated by the actions of the leader, greater weight can be attached to crisis as an explanatory factor. In these instances, however, the locus of the explana-

27. In a variant of the first formula the leader is active prior to the crisis but does not significantly gain followers until the crisis, thereby coming into prominence mainly by virtue of it.

28. That there were some charismatically oriented perceptions of Sukarno as early as 1931 has been documented by Bernard Dahm in *Sukarno and the Struggle for Indonesian Independence* (Ithaca: Cornell University Press, 1969), p. 133.

tion is shifted to the element of the leader and his ability to create crises that contribute to his charisma.

Psychological Susceptibility

A complementary approach to explaining the generation of political charisma relies less on the element of social crisis than on the analysis of the psychological predispositions and personality structures of people that render them susceptible to the appeals and domination of a political leader.

Adherents of this approach have derived their analyses mainly from psychoanalytic theory and principally from Freud's *Group Psychology and the Analysis of the Ego* as they have interpreted it.[29] They apply to the charismatic relationship the dynamics described by Freud for groups generally, which will not be recapitulated here. They view charismatic conversion on the part of the followers as a regression to an infantile state. When internal conflict between the ego and the superego becomes too great or when crisis triggers extreme anxiety, individuals "regress to a state of delegated omnipotence and . . . *demand* a leader who conforms to infantile ideas of adult behavior."[30] The leader becomes a surrogate all-powerful father through a process of identification similar to that by which the infant identifies with the parent.

The follower susceptible to charismatic conversion is therefore hypothesized to be either someone with relatively weak psychological integration in general or someone whose integration cannot be sustained under conditions of crisis. Another hypothesis, derived from Erik Erikson's work on identity, suggests that the follower's sense of personal identity is not securely established and that the leader becomes "a substitute for an underdeveloped ego-ideal."[31]

However useful these hypotheses may be in illuminating the possible

---

29. Devereux, "Charismatic Leadership," pp. 149–50; Downton, *Rebel Leadership*, pp. 221–30; Ralph P. Hummel, "Freud's Totem Theory as Complement to Max Weber's Theory of Charisma," *Psychological Reports* 35 (1974), 683–86, and "Psychology of Charismatic Followers," *Psychological Reports* 37 (1975), pp. 759–70; Irvine Schiffer, *Charisma: A Psychoanalytic Look at Mass Society* (Toronto: University of Toronto Press, 1973).

30. Devereux, "Charismatic Leadership," p. 150.

31. Downton, *Rebel Leadership*, p. 228.

psychodynamics of follower conversion, it is probably premature to give them too much weight. To the best of my knowledge, there have not been clinical studies of charismatic converts or, if there have, the results of such studies have not been publicly available. Therefore, it is difficult to generalize with confidence concerning a type of personality structure or specific personality variables of followers susceptible to charismatic conversion.[32]

Psychoanalytic theory may generally equate balance and maturity with an autonomous ego and therefore equate adult submissiveness to and dependence upon external authority with weak or insufficiently developed egos or regressive states. However, it is not difficult to posit conditions or situations under which a quasi-charismatic dependence upon leadership may be a rational adaptation mechanism of a normal ego. Among peasant strata of traditional or preindustrial societies, what may seem to be excessive dependence on and unquestioning loyalty to a leader may actually be an extension or a transfer of a traditional patron–client relationship.[33] Or it may represent complete trust in a particular leader who is recognized to possess the relevant skills and experience to analyze and cope with the demands and pressures of a changing external environment with which the peasant feels helpless and unequipped to deal.[34]

Unlike peasants, who have been considered, rightly or wrongly, especially prone to charismatic followership, highly educated professionals and intellectuals have not been so considered. It is too frequently

---

32. Thus, Downton's illustration of the weak ego theory with the case of Joseph Goebbels's charismatic attachment to Hitler (*Rebel Leadership*, pp. 43–49) is inconclusive, given the contrasting case of Albert Speer, another noted and charismatically oriented Hitler lieutenant. Similarly, Peter Loewenberg's argument that German children deprived of adequate nutrition and of their fathers during World War I developed weakened character structures and susceptibility to charisma during later crises ["The Psychohistorical Origins of the Nazi Youth Cohort," *American Historical Review* 76 (Dec. 1971), 1457–502] raises questions concerning English children similarly deprived. Attempts to relate personality structure to charismatic predisposition are still in the realm of theory and speculation, and paired comparisons are likely to suggest the limitations of explanations derived from the most studied German case.

33. I owe this point to Dorothy Willner.

34. I have observed a number of instances of this among Indonesian peasants, especially among those who have entered industry and depend heavily upon their union leaders for direction in a number of spheres of life.

assumed that they tend to perceive and relate to political leaders in terms of such criteria as expertise and stands on issues of concern to them. Members of these strata are probably more work oriented and more pressed for time than those of many other occupations. However greater may be their training and inclination to process and analyze carefully the information available on political issues, many do not have the time to do so. The overload becomes too great. If they find an individual or a leader with whose orientations on one or two crucial issues they are in complete accord, they will unquestioningly accept his judgments on a range of issues, including those out of his area of competence.[35]

I cannot call the above instances of a quasi-charismatic attitude toward political leaders hypothetical, since I have encountered examples of individuals in both the above categories and in others as well who manifested a tie to a leader that was close to charismatic. Most of them did not show signs of inner disturbance detectable to my clinically untrained eye. But it is not difficult to imagine that nearly charismatic ties to a leader can easily become charismatic ones, given a crisis condition and/or the stimuli discussed in the following chapters.

Even if clinical or other empirical evidence were to substantiate the thesis that charismatic susceptibility is directly and primarily related to personalities with congenitally weak or situationally weakened egos, this would have only limited explanatory power with respect to the genesis of political charisma. The former group could be said to exist in a chronic state of "charismatic readiness," consciously or unconsciously searching for a figure upon whom to project their ego insecurities and conflicts. Yet why does one rather than another of a pool of available leaders come to be seen as their savior and the solution to their problems? If their state itself is really the prime cause of their charismatic conversion, they should be susceptible to the appeals of almost any strong leader or even a succession of them.

The other group is comprised of those potential followers whose state of readiness is not chronic but latent. What presumably precipitates the transformation from latency to activity is a crisis. Yet what about cases of charismatic conversion, such as those noted above, that have not been preceded by crises? Moreover, if these psychic states, preceded or not by

35. I am indebted for this observation to Dorothy Willner.

crises, were a sufficient cause for charisma, the latter phenomenon would probably be more frequent. Collective psychic disorientation was apparently at least as great in Germany immediately after World War I and for a brief period in 1923 as it was in the years that Hitler came to power, but at those times there were no notable charismatic conversions.

The susceptibility induced by certain psychological states is certainly conducive to charismatic conversion, but it appears that the catalyst must be found elsewhere than in the psychic states of followers.

Doctrine, Message, or Mission

Because the role of chief precipitant of political charisma cannot with certainty be assigned to either crisis or psychic susceptibility, several alternatives remain to be considered. One is that of the leader himself, his attributes and actions. Another is the element variously termed doctrine, mission, or message. A third possibility is a combination of these two, since there are situations in which it is difficult to distinguish a doctrine from the leader who originates or espouses it. For example, those exposed to a doctrine almost entirely through the speeches of a leader may be responding as much to his oratorical style as to the ideas he communicates.

When charismatic conversion follows upon crisis and distress, it would seem logical for the doctrine to be the major catalyst, for doctrines of the charismatic leaders who have propounded them have had characteristics attractive to those caught in and confused or angered by crises. These doctrines tend to define the situation in fairly simple terms, thus diminishing the sense of confusion. They absolve people of blame and guilt for the situation in which they find themselves. Instead, blame is projected on agents external to them, on one or several scapegoats, thus also providing them an enemy against whom to direct their anger. Hitler's doctrine is an outstanding example of this, blaming Jews, Marxists, the Allies, and the Weimar leaders.[36]

36. Bullock, *Hitler*, pp. 459–60; Cantril, *Psychology*, pp. 238–45; Fest, *Hitler*, pp. 277, 329–31; Ernst Nolte, *Three Faces of Fascism* (New York: Holt, Rinehart & Winston, 1966), pp. 402–25.

More importantly, the doctrine, especially if it is the "charter myth"[37] of a movement, offers a vision of a future, generally rosy and utopian, that can rekindle hope for the despairing. It frequently sets out specific goals and activities to which followers can commit themselves and from which they can regain direction. Therefore, the doctrine can serve to restore a sense of purpose, of involvement, and of personal importance to those who may have been stripped of them or who may never have sufficiently developed them.

Conversion and strong adherence to a doctrine, however, do not necessarily result in charismatic commitment to its chief proponent. It is admittedly conceivable that an individual encountering a doctrine for the first time may undergo such an exhilarating shock of recognition and discovery that his response to its ideas is straightway transmuted into charismatic recognition of their propounder. To test this notion that the doctrine, rather than another factor, is the chief vehicle for charismatic conversion might require evidence of exposure to the doctrine without the intermediary of the leader or of crowd contagion in the presence of the leader.

The admittedly limited data available on individual conversion do provide some examples of this. One of the Abel respondents recorded that as a result of reading and hearing about Hitler, "his words went right to my marrow,"[38] a phrase suggestive of charismatic import. But the Abel material as a whole seems to support doctrinal conversion and charismatic conversion by means of doctrine as resulting primarily from exposure to the leader. If in many cases, as Merkl notes, "hearing Hitler was all it took to motivate a person to join the party,"[39] in some it was also enough for charismatic conversion to occur.[40] A number of autobiographical accounts of this type of conversion mention the stunning impact of Hitler's ideas or what one refers to as his "sacred truth." However, such accounts make no mention or hardly any mention of the contents of the speech or of any idea in it.[41]

---

37. This term is taken from Barrington Moore's *Political Power and Social Theory* (Cambridge: Harvard University Press, 1968), p. 10.
38. Merkl, *Political Violence*, p. 89.
39. Ibid., p. 537.
40. Ibid., pp. 537–41, 354.
41. Fest, *Hitler*, p. 154; Merkl, *Political Violence*, p. 105.

This suggests that it may be less the content of a doctrine than how it is clothed and delivered that has bearing on the development of charismatic perceptions. Moreover, one has to consider that if the ideas themselves had charismatic potential for whatever leader delivered them, then several leaders whose speeches introduced followers to the doctrine should thereby have gained charismatic responses directed to them. In Germany, Josef Goebbels and Gregor Strasser gave numerous speeches propagating the Nazi doctrine, the latter especially during 1925–26, when Hitler was prohibited from public speaking. They made numerous converts to the cause but apparently did not generate toward themselves the responses Hitler's speeches did toward himself.

There are other reasons that make it difficult to credit doctrine alone with the prime power to produce political charisma. While it is conceivable that some intellectuals, thrown into transports by a doctrine or an idea read or heard, should transfer those transports to the person credited with the doctrine, it would seem unlikely for others. However much a doctrine itself may move masses of people, something else would seem needed to move them to charismatic adulation of an individual.

Finally, one has to account for the instances of charismatic conversion in the absence of doctrine. In the strict sense of the term, Castro did not have a doctrine until after he had gained charismatic acclaim from thousands of Cubans at the end of 1958. Similarly, if one can speak of a doctrine of New Dealism, it did not become manifest until after the initial appearance of charismatic response to Roosevelt shortly after his inauguration in 1932. In the case of Mussolini there were too many doctrines during his rise to power and, as he himself admitted in 1921, no single coherent one.[42] At any rate, this was not the period when he generated charismatic responses, as was noted above.

Nonetheless, it can be argued that the notion of doctrine need not be strictly construed and that the surrogate notions of mission or message might better explain some part of charismatic conversion. A message projected merely as a slogan, such as the independence slogans, "Mer-

---

42. According to Herbert Matthews in *The Fruits of Fascism* (New York: Harcourt, Brace, 1943), p. 16, Mussolini wrote in 1921: "We permit ourselves the luxury of being aristocrats and democrats; conservatives and progressives; reactionaries and revolutionaries; legalitarians and illegalitarians, according to the circumstances of time, place and atmosphere."

deka," "Uhuru," and "Freedom Now," can be held to attract a charismatic response to its originator. Similarly, it might be claimed that Castro had a widely known mission: the destruction of the Batista regime and the restoration of constitutional order on the one hand and agrarian and other economic reform on the other.

The same objection can be raised against this argument as against the parallel one concerning doctrine, that is, what about the "others" with an identical or similar message or mission? Messages and slogans of movements tend to become quickly echoed and reechoed by many leaders. Therefore, if charismatic potential is latent solely in the content of the message, many communicators should be able to arouse it. If the message is linked in people's minds primarily to the leader who becomes charismatic, it is because something else about him or something that he does with the message causes him to be seen as its embodiment.[43]

There were others who shared at least part of Castro's mission, the leaders of about seven groups arrayed against Batista in 1957. Although it is true that Castro had been the earliest opponent, some of the others courted greater danger that year in Havana than he did in the Sierra Maestre. Therefore, while his mission may well have been a factor in generating his charisma, a stronger factor was probably his manner of carrying out that mission.

Thus it appears that a doctrine or mission is only somewhat more likely to cause charisma than the other elements but is not the chief catalyst. What may have made it seem so is the fact that many charismatic political leaders have been outstanding orators who aroused crowds to hysterical frenzies.

The Leader as Catalyst

It appears, therefore, that the conventional formula falls short of adequately explaining the generation of political charisma. Crisis may be

43. A radically new message is not likely to be accepted unless it comes from a leader who already is charismatic or unless the ground has already been prepared for it. In the case of Hitler the ground was well prepared, as has been documented by George L. Mosse, *The Crisis of German Ideology: The Intellectual Origins of the Third Reich* (New York: Grosset & Dunlap, 1964). Neither Gandhi nor Sukarno was the first leader in his country to carry the message of national independence to his countrypeople.

highly conducive to it but is neither a necessary nor a sufficient cause. Psychological propensities in people that disorient them or render them otherwise susceptible to a felt need for a strong leader are also conducive factors but may not be necessary and are not sufficient.[44] An impressive doctrine, message, or mission may be most conducive but is similarly neither necessary nor sufficient to catalyze charisma.

Even if all these elements were present in all known cases of mass charismatic conversion, there would still be the question of why one rather than another of the available political leaders becomes the object of that conversion. Sukarno initially shared leadership of the Indonesian nationalist movement with Hatta and Sjahrir, both of whom were exceedingly admired and popular. Balbo and Grandi were almost as visible as Mussolini in the rise of the Fascist movement. Gregor Strasser, as was earlier noted, gave hundreds of speeches when Hitler was legally prohibited from speaking. He became such a strong rival of Hitler in the public eye that as late as 1930 at least one newspaper predicted that he would soon overshadow Hitler and take control of their party.[45] Yet only Sukarno, Mussolini, and Hitler became nationally charismatic.[46]

It therefore seems that the prime precipitant of political charisma must be the element of the leader himself or his leadership. Some attributes or actions of the leader, some combination of attributes and actions, and/or some mode of presenting these to the public serves to catalyze charismatic perceptions.

Investigation of seven charismatic leaders discussed here and of a

44. In the conventional formula, psychological susceptibility is the element whose validity and relative importance can least be proved or disproved, given the relative lack of clinical or experimental evidence.

45. Fest, *Hitler*, p. 282.

46. The possibility might be considered that the "rivals" may have received some charismatically oriented responses that have escaped notice from chroniclers and historians who generally focus on the winners. There is a further possibility that latent charismatic rivals may have loyally redirected sentiments originally directed to them. My consultants on German and Italian history do not subscribe to the first possibility and, in the case of Indonesia, I can state from personal observation that Hatta did not and probably could not have aroused charismatic responses. Sjahrir probably could have done so but actively discouraged his followers and declined active rivalry with Sukarno for what he perceived to be the good of the country. Yet even if a "rival latent" charismatic leader defers to the one who becomes preeminent, the final explanation would logically be found in the differences between the motivations and actions of leaders in the same ideological camp rather than in the content of the message.

number of others who were probably charismatic has yielded a cluster of four catalytic factors shared by all or most of them. Each of these is also logically linked to the content of charismatic perceptions. The first factor is the assimilation of a leader to one or more of the dominant myths of his society and culture. The second is the performance of what appears to be an extraordinary or heroic feat. The third is the projection of the possession of qualities with an uncanny or a powerful aura. Finally, there is outstanding rhetorical ability.

Although each of these is explained in considerable detail in one of the following chapters, with illustrations from one or more of the seven leaders, no attempt is made to relate each leader to each factor.[47] Moreover, because the material on the individual leaders is meant to be primarily illustrative of processes, not all of it is tied to the same stages in their careers. Over a period of time, a leader may generate charismatic perceptions among other or different segments of a population than he did earlier. The illustrative material on Sukarno, for example, comes from a later period in his career, although he did have some charismatic followers significantly earlier. The same is true with Hitler. The material on Roosevelt deals with his initial achievement of charismatic acclaim. Finally, the chapter on rhetoric is illustrated with only one case because of the problems involved in attempting to ascertain and explain the meanings of symbols and their associations in other cultures.

47. Since these cases are meant to illustrate, rather than to test, the theory, exhaustive illustration would be redundant. Because the theoretical explanation was derived in part from an examination of these cases, the theory would more appropriately be tested by cases of other charismatic political leaders.

4
Charismatic Legitimation: The Invocation of Myth

The roots of charismatic belief and emotion lie deeper than the levels of grievance a leader can exploit or of doctrine he can propound. In nearly every movement begun by, or from which there has emerged, a charismatic political leader, there have been other leaders or potential leaders capable of expressing group grievances and doctrine. The question then becomes why one rather than another of a pool of actual and potential leaders succeeds in stimulating and directing charismatic susceptibilities toward himself.

The deeper sources of charismatic conversion and attachment to a leader can be found in the common denominators and common symbols of a shared cultural heritage. They can be found in the myths that are transmitted from generation to generation in a particular culture. The leader who becomes charismatic is the one who can inadvertently or deliberately tap the reservoir of relevant myths in his culture and who knows how to draw upon those myths that are linked to its sacred figures, to its historical and legendary heroes, and to its historical and legendary ordeals and triumphs. He evokes, invokes, and assimilates to himself the values and actions embodied in the myths by which that society has organized and recalls its past experience.[1]

---

1. For a somewhat more detailed presentation of this line of analysis, see Ann Ruth Willner and Dorothy Willner, "The Rise and Role of Charismatic Leaders," *Annals of the American Academy of Political and Social Science* 358 (Mar. 1965), 82–84.

At a time of transition and crisis, some aspects of a given cultural configuration may lose their significance or be in danger of dissolution. Concomitantly, and even perhaps because of the climate of uncertainty, other beliefs and symbols not only will retain their meaning but will probably gain renewed or added power to move the minds and emotions of people. Inadvertently eliciting or consciously calling upon such beliefs and symbols, the charismatic leader legitimizes himself and his claims by linking them to that which remains sacred to or laden with emotion for the members of his society.

In so doing, the charismatic leader becomes associated in the thoughts and emotions of his followers with the sacred beings, venerated historical figures, or legendary and folk heroes of their culture. He seems to them to embody and express in his person and/or through his actions some of the characteristics that their traditions, transmitted through early socialization, have attributed to divinities and to historic or mythic heroes. He is seen as the contemporary personification of one or more of the pantheon of dominant culture heroes and in turn he becomes a culture hero.

Before discussing further and illustrating this process of charismatic legitimation, I wish to stress that societies tend to differ in their cultural definitions of leadership roles. The same traditions that may be tapped and exploited by an aspirant leader also determine in part who can successfully tap them and how he can do so. The margin for individual interpretation and expression between what is culturally acceptable and what is culturally prohibited in a leader or in leadership behavior may be widened in a society by a leader. However, the culture of a society sets limits upon the selection and sphere of operations open to a leader.[2]

Aspects of appearance, manner, temperament, speech, style of action, ideas expressed, or action advocated that are capable of producing charismatic affect in one culture may have little relevance for another. It is difficult to imagine DeGaulle as a successful political leader in the United States and even more difficult to imagine Gandhi arousing Germans to mass passive resistance. Therefore, as has been earlier mentioned, attempts to find sufficient similarities in the personal attributes

2. See Dorothy Willner, *Community Leadership* (United Nations Series ST/SOA/Ser. 36, 1960), pp. 11–12.

of charismatic leaders to elicit a composite charismatic personality type may be suggestive but are not likely to prove definitive.

It is possible that the phenomenon of charismatic political leadership can emerge in a society only if it is somehow sanctioned by the culture of that society. It is conceivable that such leadership cannot be generated in a society whose cultural definition of leader–follower relations precludes strong personal authority and impassioned personal loyalties to a leader. An individual who might begin to generate such an affect would soon be immobilized as intolerably deviant and dangerous. Ruth Benedict has observed that among the Zuni personal authority is the most vigorously disparaged trait and men striving to become leaders have often been persecuted for sorcery.[3]

The process by which the charismatic leader evokes or draws upon himself the aura or mantle of myth is not easily susceptible to logical analysis, because it is essentially a process of metaphor. Some aspects of a leader or of his actions serve as stimuli to evoke whole complexes of meaning and emotion, just as metaphor in language and thought can evoke the totality of what it symbolizes.[4] In the metaphoric process, two items or individuals need share only several attributes or even one extremely prominent attribute for a linkage to occur such that one can stand for the totality of the other. Let us consider the total attributes or perceived total attributes of a legendary hero in a society as set A; let the totality or perceived totality of the qualities of a contemporary leader in that society be set B. The subset that is formed by the intersection of both

3. Ruth Benedict, *Patterns of Culture* (New York: Houghton Mifflin, 1955), p. 90.
4. For analyses of metaphoric processes, see the many works of literary critics such as I. A. Richards, William Empson, and Kenneth Burke. See also Ernst Cassirer, *Language and Myth* (New York: Dover, 1946), pp. 91–92: "In mythico-linguistic thought . . . we find in operation a law which might actually be called the law of leveling and the extinction of specific differences. Every part of the whole is the whole itself; every specimen is equivalent to the entire species. The part does not merely represent the whole or the specimen in its class; they are identical with the totality to which they belong not merely as mediating aids to reflective thought but as genuine presences which actually contain the power, significance and efficacy of the whole. Here one is reminded of the basic principle of verbal as well as mythic 'metaphor'—the principle of *pars pro toto*." With reference to the notion, referred to in chapter 1, that magicoreligious metaphoric thought is peculiar to parts of Asia and Africa, Ignazio Silone, in *The School for Dictators* (New York: Atheneum, 1963), pp. 93–96, provides a highly diverting rebuttal in the account of a Papuan who was moved to record his observations of the astonishing superstitions of European tribes.

sets, that is, the group of attributes shared by both A and B, is sufficient for B to be seen as A. This process will be illustrated here primarily with the cases of Sukarno and Castro.

Aspects of a leader that can precipitate the process of metaphoric identification include physical appearance, gestures and mannerisms, speech patterns, style of life, and feats or actions. One might distinguish analytically between those attributes and actions of a leader that fortuitously contribute to the linkage with cultural myths and symbols, a process that can be termed charismatic *evocation*, and those attributes and actions they consciously and deliberately adopt and perform, which can be termed charismatic *invocation*. I mentioned earlier that some Cubans saw Castro as Christlike. This image may have been evoked by his beard and his reputation as a young attorney for defending the poor without a fee.[5] However, as will be noted later, Castro deliberately invoked the memory of José Martí, the father of Cuban independence, by the mode of his return to Cuba in 1956. Sometimes, the distinction between evocation and invocation can become blurred in reality. Thus, the manner of John Kennedy's death, by assassination, tended to evoke the memory of Lincoln, an association that was further strengthened by the deliberate invocation of Lincoln in some elements of the funeral, both then contributing almost simultaneously to Kennedy's postmortem accession to charisma in part through the aura of the Lincoln legend.[6]

Sukarno as Mythic Warrior and Semidivine Lover

The identification of a political leader with a sacred and legendary figure is exemplified by the association of Sukarno with Bima, legendary hero and demigod of Javanese and Balinese mythology. Bima is one of the five Pandawa brothers, warrior heroes of the ancient Indian epic, the *Mahabharata*. During the period of the dominance in Java of the Indian religions of Shivaite Hinduism and Buddhism, which are still dominant in Bali, this as well as other vehicles of Indian religious belief and sacred

---

5. Richard R. Fagen, "Charismatic Authority and the Leadership of Fidel Castro," *Western Political Quarterly* 18 (June 1965), 277–78; Robert Taber, *M-26: Biography of a Revolution* (New York: Lyle Stuart, 1961), p. 51.

6. Dorothy Willner, "Ritual, Myth," pp. 406–08.

lore entered into Javanese and Balinese traditions and became a major part of their literature, art, temple sculpture, and oral tradition.

Even more important was the impact of the *Mahabharata* (and another Indian epic, the *Ramayana*) on Javanese and Balinese theater. For over a thousand years in Java, theater has been one of the principal vehicles from which the unlettered have derived many of their beliefs and values and their notions of history. The legends recounted and acted out in the *wayang kulit*, or shadow puppet play, probably the most widespread and popular form of drama, are believed by rural villagers and the less literate of the towns to be history.

Episodes derived from the *Mahabharata* became the nucleus of many of the *lakons*, or basic scripts, of the *wayang* theater, especially *wayang kulit*. These episodes deal with the rivalry of the five Pandawa princes and their cousins, the ninety-nine Kurawas, who grew up together at the court of Astina. This kingdom was wrested from its designated heir, the eldest Pandawa, by the Kurawas. The Pandawas then went into exile, where they had many adventures in forests and neighboring kingdoms. Ultimately, they recovered their kingdom after a great war in which they defeated their cousins. Over the centuries, various *dalangs* or puppet-masters modified, expanded, and added to the basic *Mahabharata* theme until what has come to be known as the Pandawa cycle contained almost 150 recorded scripts. Some plays recount the stories of the gods, ancestors of the Pandawas; in others, the major hero protagonists are the sons of the Pandawas, one of whom is held to be the ancestor of the historic rulers of the old Javanese kingdoms. Some deal with domestic themes, such as the search for a long lost son or daughter or the rescue of a princess abducted by an ogre; others concern dynastic rivalries, problems that plague a realm or other matters of state.[7] Whatever their subject, the plays always contain scenes of battle, usually between the royal heroes and giants or ogres.

In the battle scenes, Bima often stands out. Of the five Pandawa princes, their advisers, and allies, including Kresna, who is the god Wisnu in human form, Bima is the strongest and staunchest warrior.

---

7. James R. Brandon, ed., *On Thrones of Gold* (Cambridge: Harvard University Press, 1970), and Claire Holt, *Art in Indonesia* (Ithaca, N.Y.: Cornell University Press, 1967) contain summaries and basic scripts of some of the *wayang* plays.

Among the names given him are "King of the Warriors," "Pillar of the State," and "Constant Victor."[8] Sukarno never commanded a military force, much less won a battle or a war. He never saw military service and, in fact, was captured by the Dutch in the course of the Indonesian war for independence. In view of this, it is interesting that he was seen by many Indonesians as wearing the mantle of Bima.

This phenomenon can be explained by the process of metaphoric association discussed above and also by the belief of Indonesians in the power of words and symbolic action to shape the course of reality. Sukarno was seen to have shared a number of attributes with Bima, two of which were bravery and a strong or stubborn will. A Javanese school-teacher described Bima's character to an American anthropologist as follows: "If he has an intention he follows it out straight to its conclusion. . . . he doesn't look aside. . . . He always advances and never looks back. Once he has an idea and feels he is capable of carrying it out, he is brave to the end and will not listen to anyone or anything. He is single-minded and fears no one."[9]

In a survey on perceptions of leadership I conducted in 1967 among largely working-class inhabitants of Jakarta and its environs, there was an item asking respondents to name those they considered to have been Indonesia's greatest postcolonial heroes and to list the qualities for which each of them was admired by the respondent.[10] The most frequent response concerning Sukarno was that of eloquence in oratory. Second was bravery and third was determination. Those who elaborated upon the response of bravery most often mentioned the issuing of the Proclamation of Independence in 1945. Detailed answers in the category of determination included such descriptions as "perseverance in the struggle for freedom," "stubbornness," "unyielding towards opponents," "a man with a very strong will."

Interviews with members of the political elite also yielded admiring perceptions of Sukarno as brave and stubborn, even during this period

8. Brandon, *On Thrones*, pp. 291, 330.
9. Clifford Geertz, *The Religion of Java* (Glencoe, Ill.: Free Press, 1960), p. 272.
10. There were roughly 200 respondents drawn from a random sample of the greater Jakarta area districts. Despite the fact that this was the period of the height of the campaign by the new Suharto regime to discredit Sukarno, about 70 percent of the respondents listed Sukarno first among Indonesia's heroes.

when it was inadvisable and even dangerous to express admiration of Sukarno. One informant said, "He dared to play with power and to take risks." An opponent stated that he "often dared to do that which none of the rest of us would dare do." Another longtime opponent, a political leader who had been imprisoned by Sukarno during the period of Guided Democracy, felt that Sukarno had never been intrinsically brave, but that once he had decided upon a course of action, he could appear brave in implementing it. All informants agreed that Sukarno had a strong will and wanted his own way.

Several stances of Sukarno in the course of his career contributed to the creation and maintenance of perceptions of him as extraordinarily brave and stubborn. First was his paramount role in the anticolonial struggle against the Dutch during the prewar and preindependence period. Sukarno had become a nationalist while still a student and soon began to write and publish articles and to deliver speeches on behalf of the nationalist cause. He paid little attention to the warnings of colonial authorities and was arrested, tried, and imprisoned. After his release, he resumed his political activities, well aware of the risks he was running. Again he was arrested and this time exiled to an outlying island.[11] The aura of bravery and persistence began to surround him fairly early in his career.

When Sukarno read the Indonesian Declaration of Independence in Jakarta in August 1945, most Indonesians did not know of the events immediately preceding, and many still do not. These included Sukarno's disbelief that the Japanese had surrendered in the Pacific and his hesitance to take any action, despite urging by other nationalists, until he knew for sure. They also included a "kidnapping" of Sukarno and Hatta, another leading nationalist, by youth groups in an effort to persuade them. The Japanese were much in evidence in Jakarta and were armed. When Sukarno addressed a large audience in the central square, they were present and apparently in control. Thus, the very acts of having declared independence and daring to speak to an audience as he did added to Sukarno's reputation for bravery.[12]

11. Dahm, *Sukarno*, pp. 69–174.
12. Benedict R. O'G. Anderson's *Some Aspects of Indonesian Politics Under the Japanese Occupation, 1944–45* (Ithaca, N.Y.: Modern Indonesia Project, Southeast Asia Program, Cornell University, 1961) contains extensive details of these events on a close to day-to-day basis.

Stubbornness and single-mindedness were consistently displayed in Sukarno's twelve-year-long campaign to obtain West Irian, the territory that had been Netherlands New Guinea. The issue of this territory had been left ambiguous and unresolved in the Dutch–Indonesian settlement of 1950. Soon after this independence settlement was arrived at, Sukarno began to challenge the Dutch on this issue. In four successive Independence Day addresses, he commenced by greeting his audience as Indonesians "from Sabang to Merauke." Sabang is the town at the tip of western Sumatra, the westernmost outpost of the Indonesian Archipelago; Merauke is the Indonesian name for what was the capital of Netherlands New Guinea.[13]

Sukarno spent a good portion of these speeches agitating on this issue. His repeated theme was that independence was not complete until Irian came under the authority and administration of Indonesia and that this could be accomplished only through struggle, not by requesting or by pleading or through diplomatic negotiations. The belligerent tone of Sukarno's speeches, in his travels throughout the country as well as in his Independence Day addresses, was congruent with the ferocity of Bima's challenges to his opponents as traditionally presented in the *wayang* plays.

In this stance Sukarno was at odds with several of his cabinets, particularly the Natsir cabinet of 1950–51, which favored negotiations and tried to restrain Sukarno's public advocacy of economic sanctions against the Netherlands and the abrogation of the Round Table Agreement with that country. In the Independence Day address of 1951 Sukarno defied his critics: "There are people who have called me a 'troublemaker over the problem of Irian.' Hah! These words I shall write in letters of gold upon my breast!"[14]

In physical appearance, Sukarno differed from many of the prominent Indonesian leaders, especially his fellow Javanese, just as Bima in the puppet theater differs from the other princes. The shapes of the leather puppets that represent four of the Pandawa brothers and other highly esteemed figures in the *wayang* are delicate, small, and graceful. This is

---

13. For details, see Herbert Feith, *The Decline of Constitutional Democracy in Indonesia* (Ithaca, N.Y.: Cornell University Press, 1962), and John D. Legge, *Sukarno* (New York: Praeger, 1972).

14. Sukarno, *Dari Proklamasi sampai Resopim* (Jakarta: n.d.), p. 120.

in accordance with traditional Javanese notions of *aloes,* or refinement, for those of noble birth. At the other extreme are the figures representing the giants and ogres, gross in size and crude and ugly of feature. The Bima figure is closer to that of the ogres than to that of the other Pandawas. It is a large muscular figure, although not distorted and ugly. According to the narrative description in a standard script, Bima's is a "rugged handsomeness."[15] Sukarno also did not resemble the aristocrats among Indonesia's leadership, especially those from the courts of Java, who tended to be slight, graceful, and fine-featured. By Javanese standards, his too was a rugged handsomeness.

In voice and speech an association can easily be made between Bima and Sukarno. In *wayang,* the puppeteer varies his voice tone and pitch, depending upon which puppet is presumably speaking. For the other Pandawas and for similar noble characters, he uses controlled and relatively high-pitched tones. For Bima his voice booms like thunder. In his public addresses, Sukarno frequently eschewed the measured, quiet cadences of the classic speech of Indonesia's dominant cultural groups. He often used thundering tones, especially at the climax of a series of repetitive phrases. Bima is also exceptional in his mode of speech. In Javanese it is customary for the speaker to employ levels of language in accordance with the rank of the person addressed relative to his own. But Bima speaks low Javanese to all—even the gods. As early as 1921 Sukarno was referred to as Bima because of his insistence upon addressing a youth meeting in low Javanese.[16]

Bima's style of combat and movements also differ from those of his brothers and other royal characters. Whereas they move slowly and deliberately, gracefully sidestepping an opponent's blows, he rushes into battle, absorbing blows, and often crushes his opponent against a rock. Sukarno's verbal style could often be seen as symbolically that of Bima, as illustrated by the following: "Now we pursue the politics of confrontation against the Dutch. I shall even use the boast of the 'Jogja fellow.' What is this boast? 'Here am I! Where are you?' (thumping his chest with his fists) Where is the chest of the Dutch? You want what? What do you want? An economic confrontation? We are ready! You want a political

15. Brandon, *On Thrones,* p. 291.
16. Dahm, *Sukarno,* pp. 40–41.

confrontation? We are ready! You want a military confrontation? Again we are ready!"[17]

Sukarno was linked to Bima by another attribute—the color black. To the Javanese, colors symbolize qualities and black is generally taken to symbolize strength. Especially during the major battle scenes, Bima is represented by a black-visaged puppet. Sukarno invariably carried a black baton, which some Indonesians saw as a repository of sacred power, a *pusaka* similar to the magically endowed relics prized by the ancient monarchs. Among the magically potent objects he was rumored to possess was a large black stone given to him by a holy man in Bali. Sukarno himself was considered by some to have *sekti*, supernatural power to affect or mold the environment. This is not surprising, in view of the fact that Sukarno ultimately obtained West Irian not through battle but because of psychological and diplomatic warfare and threats to undertake action. The symbolic warrior achieved concrete results, and for a people steeped in symbolism he could truly wear the mantle of Bima.

If Sukarno was seen as Bima by many Indonesians, there were others who saw him as Arjuna, third and probably best beloved of the Pandawas. Some, indeed, saw him alternately as either, depending upon the association evoked by a particular action at a given moment. Arjuna, who is also an incarnation of the god Wisnu and in legend the ancestor of Java's historical rulers, has many attributes, including a firm sense of justice, cool control, and extreme refinement. He is the epitome of the Javanese ideal of the noble knight. He is also so handsome and charming that all women feel drawn to him. In legend he is the husband or lover of countless women.

Sukarno was linked to Arjuna in the minds of many Indonesians I knew by virtue of his many marriages and countless love affairs. Stories circulated to the effect that on his travels men brought their daughters to him, that no woman could resist his charm, that when he pointed his black baton at a woman as an indication he desired her, she was irresistibly impelled toward him. With the exception of some devout Muslims and the modernized women who disapproved of this aspect of his life,

17. Sukarno, Address to the Student Body of Gadjah Mada University, Jogjakarta, Apr. 7, 1961 (mimeo.), p. 8.

Sukarno's reputation among the people gained added political luster from such stories. For in traditional Java, the ruler was not only regarded as the symbol and personification of the welfare and greatness of the realm. He was also regarded, particularly by the peasantry, as the symbol of the land and the soil. Thus, he became symbolically the generator of fertility for the realm as a whole. His own sexuality and procreativity were seen to bear a direct relationship to the potential fertility of the soil.[18] Sukarno's sexuality contributed in other ways to charismatically oriented perceptions of him, as will be discussed in a subsequent chapter.

Castro as the Apostle Returned

The generation of charismatically oriented perceptions of a political leader through the mechanism of metaphoric association with myth and symbol is not restricted to cases of similarities or perceived similarities of the leader to religious or mythic figures. It can also take place when a leader becomes assimilated in the minds and emotions of followers to a historic figure of outstanding stature, especially to one whose life has taken on the lineaments of myth in a society. José Martí was such a figure in Cuba, long idolized and revered by Cubans as "the Apostle" of Cuban independence.[19] In discussing the "cult of Martí," one Cuban has written that a figure in the United States with the stature and devotion comparable to that of Martí in Cuba would have to be "a composite of Washington, Jefferson and Lincoln, supplemented by the best of Henry James, Emerson and Twain."[20] Part of Castro's charisma can be attributed to the identities and similarities of his career to that of Martí.

José Martí did not live to see the independence of Cuba from Spain, although most of his life was spent in tireless struggle for this cause and he is viewed as the man whose inspiration was most responsible for its

18. Dr. C. C. Berg, the noted specialist on medieval Java, described in a personal communication the story of the ruler whose subjects were so apprehensive because he had only one wife and one child that they threatened to force his abdication or removal.

19. For details of Martí's history and of Cuban attitudes toward him, see Richard Butler Gray, *José Martí: Cuban Patriot* (Gainesville: University of Florida Press, 1962).

20. Ramón Eduardo Ruis, *Cuba: The Making of a Revolution* (Amherst: University of Massachusetts Press, 1968), p. 59.

achievement. Martí was the son of Spanish immigrants. While still in adolescence, he wrote and distributed pamphlets against Spanish rule. At the age of seventeen he was imprisoned and subsequently deported to Spain. After sojourns in Mexico and Guatemala, he was permitted to return to Cuba, but within a year he was banished again for seditious activities.

Martí's second exile was spent in the United States, largely in New York. He earned a living as a journalist, and his writings were voluminous. Much of his time was spent in organizing support and raising funds for the Cuban nationalist cause. In 1895 he organized an expedition of fellow Cuban exiles to invade the island and take part in a new insurrection against the colonial authorities he had helped to plan. With the money they collected, they purchased a boat and landed on the southern shores of the Oriente, the eastern corner of Cuba. Martí proceeded inland to join a band of guerrillas and was killed five weeks later.

Part of Castro's life evokes the memory of Martí through apparently fortuitous resemblances. Through his father, Castro is also the son of a Spanish immigrant. Castro also engaged in antigovernment activities in his youth. He was also imprisoned after he and his group attacked the Moncada barracks in 1953 in protest against the Batista regime. He too went into exile after his release. Castro spent a few months in the United States, although his place of residence was Mexico, raising money for his cause from Cuban exiles, as had Martí.

Castro also deliberately exploited the memory of Martí and strove to surround himself and his cause with the aura of "the Apostle," in what has been termed here charismatic invocation. In his now famous defense speech at his trial after the attack on Moncada, "History Will Absolve Me," he mentioned Martí or quoted him at least ten times.[21] He also noted that this was exactly a century after the birth of Martí. A photograph of Castro's headquarters published in a Havana journal in 1956 showed a statue of Martí in the background.[22] In November 1955 Castro stated in a speech in New York to Cubans from whom he was trying to raise money: "We are doing what the Apostle taught us to do when he was in a similar situation."[23]

21. Ibid., p. 58.
22. Gray, *José Martí*, p. 170.
23. Halperin, *Rise and Decline*, p. 7.

The action that probably associated Castro most dramatically with Martí and appeared designed to do so was Castro's return to Cuba in 1956. Castro had earlier stated that he would be back before the end of 1956. The fact that he was training his people in Mexico was hardly a well-kept secret. Castro bought a small boat, the *Gramma*, and squeezed eighty-two men into it. It soon became clear that his plan to land on the southeast coast of Cuba was also no secret. However, despite the risk involved, he kept to the plan and landed not too far from where Martí had landed sixty-one years earlier.

Sukarno as Universal Monarch

Charismatically oriented perceptions of a political leader need not necessarily be tied to specific religious or historic figures. They can be linked to a generalized cultural ideal of heroism or superhuman endowment, a stock type in the cultural repertoire embodying some of the characteristics most esteemed or idealized by the members of a society.

In Java, as well as in other parts of Indonesia and Southeast Asia, such a stock type has been the ideal ruler, the universally honored monarch who is seen to be the center of the universe as well as of his realm. The tradition of stating or suggesting the world-shaking power of a given ruler and the glory of his realm seems to be related to the Buddhist conception of the coming of a *chakravartin*, or ideal universal monarch, referred to in old Javanese variously as the *njakrawati*, *tjakrawati*, or *eruçakra*. In accordance with the belief that words have a reality-molding magic of their own, Javanese rulers invoked this concept and strove to associate themselves with it through the literary works of court poets and chroniclers, inscriptions of themselves and their domains, and the titles they assumed. The *Nagarakertagama*, written in the fourteenth century to celebrate the monarch of the Majapahit Empire, Hayam Wuruk, refers to him as a "universe-swaying" emperor whose praises were sung by the entire world.[24] The tradition continued after Java's rulers were converted to Islam. In the early seventeenth century the

---

24. Prapantja, *Java in the 14th Century: A Study in Cultural History* (*The Nāgara-Kĕrtāgama* by Rakawi Prapañca of Majapahit, 1365), ed. with notes, translations, commentaries by Theodore G. Th. Pigeaud, 5 vols. (The Hague: M. Nijhoff, 1960–63), 4, p. 80.

Muslim ruler of the Mataram Empire took the title of Pakubuwana, which can be translated as "pivot of the world" or "axis of the world." Later in that century the Dutch divided Mataram into two principalities, Surakarta and Jogjakarta. The ruler of the former retained that title and the monarch of the latter assumed the title of Hamengkubuwana, meaning "he who controls the world."[25]

Only a few of Sukarno's subjects were familiar with ancient inscriptions, the court literature, or even the works of contemporary Indonesian historians that often echoed the myths of the court literature.[26] Most of the Javanese, however, had been socialized by the *wayang*, other forms of theater, and oral traditions to see the greatness of a ruler and his realm validated by the honor and tribute tendered by other rulers from distant realms. The standard prologue to a *wayang* performance describes the kingdom in which the initial action takes place with a standard formula. It can be translated briefly as "far-reaching is its fame, high is its prestige."[27] A more elaborate version might run as follows: "The Kingdom stands firm over the earth. Its torch is high, illuminating all the world with its radiance. . . . Not only on Java do countries submit themselves to its rule, but kings from afar proffer allegiance."[28]

Sukarno frequently invoked this formula as he described to his domestic audiences the reputation of Indonesia abroad. Thus, to a peasants' congress in 1962, he quoted it and then listed the capitals in which the name of Indonesia was highly spoken of, such as Moscow, Peking, New Delhi, and Cairo. He told the audience that Indonesia was the country asked to intervene to settle the conflict between China and India.[29]

In his speeches Sukarno used his tours abroad to emphasize to his people the reputation he had abroad. Although his initial references to

25. B. H. M. Vlekke, *Nusantara: A History of Indonesia* (The Hague and Bandung: Van Hoeve, 1959), p. 425, n. 23.

26. C. C. Berg, "The Javanese Picture of the Past," in *An Introduction to Indonesian Historiography*, ed. Soedjatmoko et al. (Ithaca, N.Y.: Cornell University Press, 1965), pp. 87–117; Laura Lord, "The Uses of History in Indonesia" (M.A. thesis, Cornell University, 1958).

27. Soemarsaid Moertono, *State and Statecraft in Old Java* (Ithaca, N.Y.: Modern Indonesia Project, Southeast Asia Program, Cornell University, 1968), p. 61.

28. Brandon, *On Thrones*, pp. 86, 177, 275. The *dalang*, or puppetmaster, works from a brief outline of the scenario and develops the dialogue and selects the words according to his individual preferences.

29. Speech before Peasants' Congress at Semarang, Dec. 20, 1962 (mimeo.), p. 7.

his first foreign tours were modest, Sukarno soon adopted the stance of a great world leader whose visits were sought after and whose presence was seen as conferring honor and enlightenment upon those he visited. How he did this can be illustrated briefly from his address at the University of Jogjakarta in April 1961, in which he described his forthcoming world trip in great detail. "President Kennedy said," he told his audience, "'At the beginning of my administration, I wish to speak with President Sukarno.'" He proceeded to explain that this was because President Kennedy wished to obtain from him a broad understanding of the problems of Indonesia in particular and of Asia in general.[30]

He then listed his itinerary, state by state, capital by capital through Latin America, Africa, and Europe. He mentioned the names of his hosts who were likely to be familiar to his hearers, such as Nkrumah, Nasser, Brezhnev, and Khrushchev. Sukarno's final remark on his trip, casually tossed to his audience almost as an aside, like the skilled actor he was, neatly and climactically underlined his supremacy on the world scene. "Last week I received an urgent request from Chairman Liu Shao-ch'i and Mao Tse-tung to visit," he said. "If there is time, if Allah wills, I shall visit Peking. But if time is short, I shall straightway return."[31]

Probably Sukarno's most effective ploy for invoking the image of himself as the ruler of world renown was by way of demonstration, with foreign ambassadors as his instruments. Sukarno frequently invited ambassadors to accompany him on his speaking tours around the islands of Indonesia. Obviously, such invitations could not easily be refused, and many ambassadors may have welcomed the opportunity to travel with Sukarno. In his memoirs, the former American ambassador, Howard Palfrey Jones, refers to Sukarno's custom of presenting each ambassador to his audiences as a means of building national pride in showing that other countries recognized Indonesia.[32]

Jones apparently missed the whole point of the ritual, for Sukarno's scenario did not place the foreign ambassadors in the position of honored guests being introduced to his audiences. His presentation of them

---

30. Address at Jogjakarta, p. 1.

31. Ibid., p. 2.

32. Howard Palfrey Jones, *Indonesia: The Possible Dream* (New York: Harcourt Brace Jovanovich, 1971), pp. 223–24.

was designed to convey the impression that they were members of his retinue. They were cast in the roles of emissaries sent by vassal states to show obeisance and render symbolic tribute to a mighty overlord.

Sukarno accomplished this partly by the language he employed and partly by his demeanor and gestures toward the ambassadors. For example, he asked an audience in Pontianak, Kalimantan (formerly Borneo), whether they had ever seen an ambassador. When they replied in the negative, he said: "Well, this time I come to Pontianak bringing ambassadors."[33] He told his audiences that he was "followed by" foreign ambassadors and his choice of words was subtle but significant. The obvious term in Indonesian for "accompanied by" is *disertai oleh*. Sukarno, however, did not use this, but employed instead the words *diikuti oleh*. Although this phrase also has a subsidiary meaning of "accompanied by," its primary and most common meaning is "followed by" or "obeyed by."

Sukarno generally summoned each ambassador in turn to the rostrum to be introduced. To them he addressed requests politely in English. But these were sometimes preceded by what could be taken as a peremptory command in Indonesian. To a mass meeting in Bontain, Sulawesi (formerly Celebes), he said: "Now I will show you the ambassadors who follow me . . . will the ambassadors come here."[34]

Sometimes Sukarno was less subtle in making his point. At a mass meeting in Lombok, he concluded the round of introductions with these words: "You see that in my journey I am followed by ambassadors and ministers and foreign as well as Indonesian journalists. So it can be said that my journey is followed by the whole world, by the whole world!"[35]

Sukarno also used such occasions to suggest his ability to sway the world. For example, he told an audience in Pontianak: "It is not only that Bung Karno comes here bringing ambassadors from great countries. Where else in the world can you see the American Ambassador together with the Ambassador of the Soviet Union side by side in an atmosphere of friendship? Only in Indonesia."[36] To people who knew little if any-

---

33. Speech to Mass Meeting, Pontianak, West Kalimantan, Mar. 25, 1961 (mimeo.), p. 1.
34. Speech to Mass Meeting, Bontain, South Sulawesi, Jan. 7, 1962 (mimeo.), p. 2.
35. Speech to Mass Meeting, Lombok, Nov. 11, 1958 (mimeo.), p. 2.
36. Speech at Pontianak, p. 2.

thing of diplomatic protocol, it could certainly appear that Sukarno had accomplished the remarkable feat of reconciling the representatives of two of the world's most powerful contending countries.

The Ayatollah Khomeini and the Once and Future Imam

The most recent and dramatic example of political charisma stemming largely from association with myth is that of the Ayatollah Khomeini of Iran. To the world outside Iran it seemed incredible and inexplicable that an elderly and long exiled cleric could have gained from a distance such a clearly charismatic hold over the minds and emotions of millions of his countrypeople. Yet this incredible phenomenon can be explained in great measure by Khomeini's identification with myths over a thousand years old, the cardinal myths of Shi'a Islam.

Khomeini's antagonist, Riza Shah Mohammed Pahlevi, had also sought to associate himself and his reign with age-old myths and symbols, those recalling the power and splendor of past Iranian empires and their rulers. On one level, the conflict between the cleric and the king was waged in the contemporary political idiom of issues and the uses and abuses of power and policy. At a deeper level, however, the struggle was between the personal charisma of Khomeini, generated by myth, and the institutionalized royal charisma of the Shah, supported by myth. And at this level, the outcome was determined by their respective abilities to assimilate to themselves the myths they drew upon and by the circumstances that aided or hindered the processes of evocation and invocation.

At this level, the Shah would appear to have had an advantage, for in being the king, he automatically inherited some of the charismatic aura that universally surrounds the institution of kingship.[37] This institution had a very long existence in Iran, one of the longest in the world in both history and legend. From 546 B.C., when Kurush, better known to the West as Cyrus the Great, unified the Persian tribes, there have been 33

---

37. In addition to original or "pure" personal charisma with which this study is concerned, Weber discerned and discusses various types of depersonalized charisma that in attenuated form become attached to the lineages, dynasties, and institutions of charismatic founders. See Weber, *Economy*, 1, p. 248, and 3, 1141–43.

main dynasties and more than 400 rulers governing Iran, one of the oldest monarchies on earth.[38]

The charisma of kingship in Iran was reinforced by recapitulation, in schoolbook and story, of the exploits of the great founders and restorers of empire. The Achaemenid Dynasty (546–330 B.C.) created the most extensive and powerful empire the world had seen. Cyrus conquered the kingdoms of Medea, Lydia, and Babylon. His son, Cambyses, added Egypt. When Darius I extended his domain to the Aegean, the Persian or Iranian Empire covered most of the known world from India to the Aegean and was "an example of political organization only parallelled by the Roman Empire."[39] The Achaemenid rulers not only excelled in the construction of roads, palaces, and cities as well as administrative systems. They also treated subject peoples with hitherto unknown racial and religious tolerance.

Names such as Ardashir and Shahpur, borne by contemporary Iranians, evoke the history and legends of the next prominent dynasty, that of the Sassanians (A.D. 211–642). The first Ardashir and his son, the first Shahpur, were also warrior kings. In attempting to restore a diminished empire, they came into conflict with Rome, and Shahpur defeated and captured the Roman emperor Valerian. Their successors continued to be militarily engaged with Rome and also with Byzantium. Among the later Sassanian monarchs was the Iranian ruler whose memory is perhaps the most revered, Khusru I, known as Anushirvan the Just (A.D. 531–89). A social reformer as well as a warrior, he was known far and wide for his wisdom and interest in philosophy. Noted philosophers and scholars from the West traveled to his court.[40]

Knowledge of Anushirvan the Just and of other rulers of the old dynasties as well as legends of primordial rulers and heroes have been disseminated to countless Iranians for hundreds of years through the great Iranian epic poem, *Shah Nama*, or *Book of Kings*. Written in the eleventh century by the poet Ferdausi, this work has been read and recited in

38. Donald N. Wilber, *Iran Past and Present* (Princeton: Princeton University Press, 1975), p. 74.

39. J. H. Illife, "Persia and the Ancient World," in *The Legacy of Persia*, ed. A. J. Arberry (Oxford: Oxford University Press, 1965), p. 6.

40. L. Lockhart, "Persia and the West," in Arberry, *Legacy*, pp. 336–37.

whole or in part in court and in hamlet. Wilber notes that illiterates learned long passages by heart from hearing frequent repetitions and that "even today thousands of uneducated people can repeat long passages of the poem."[41]

The standards set for great kings and heroes are not difficult to discern from the *Shah Nama*, for they are repeated in the descriptions of those held up for admiration. They include an impressive physique and boldness and courage in demeanor. Rostam's stature is that of "a noble cypress"[42] and Shahpur I is cypress-like in height and with the broad shoulders shared by other heroes.[43] Darius, Darab in the epic, is addressed as "Lion-hearted man" and Shahpur termed "the Lion."[44] Heroic figures are presented not only as strong and bold but also as generous and openhearted.

Those of royal origin are early recognized by their possession of *Farr*, a nimbus or halo of light. Although the *Shah Nama* was written after Islam had come to Iran, it reflects the ancient Asian belief that royalty is divinely selected and made known by signs. The association of royal charisma with light or the sun stemmed from the early Aryan and much later Zoroastrian worship of Mithra, the sun-god and the god of light as well as of war. Outstanding rulers and heroes are generally described in the *Shah Nama* as sun-visaged, "brilliant as the sun," protected by their *Farr* and occasionally deserted by it.

If the admired ruler is primarily a warrior, an expander and a protector of the realm, he is also pictured as building cities, causing wasteland to be brought into cultivation, and otherwise overseeing the general welfare. But most esteemed is a capacity for justice. The legendary Key Khosro's rule "spread justice abroad in the world and tore out of the ground the roots of tyranny."[45] Ardashir, upon ascending the throne, tells the multitude that "my treasure is justice" and is later described as "disseminating benevolence and justice in every direction."[46] Of

41. Wilber, *Iran*, pp. 78, 79; see also A. J. Arberry, *Classical Persian Literature* (London: Allen & Unwin, 1958), p. 47.

42. Ferdowsi, *The Epic of the Kings*, trans. Reuben Levy (Chicago: University of Chicago Press, 1967), p. 48.

43. Ibid., pp. 273, 277.

44. Ibid., pp. 227, 275.

45. Ibid., p. 104.

46. Ibid., pp. 270, 278.

Anushirvan, it is said: "The Shah covered the face of the earth with his justice. . . . Any man, small or great, could lie down to sleep in the open, and to the water-hole there came the ewe as well as the wolf."[47]

Unlike his father, Reza Shah, Mohammed Shah did not boast the physical appearance and military exploits that could be associated with those of the warrior kings of Iranian history and legend. But, like his father, Mohammed attempted to develop symbols of continuity with them. Reza had substituted the old name, Iran, for Persia, the name by which the country had come to be known, and had adopted a calendar dating back to the time of Cyrus. Moreover, he had taken as the name of the dynasty he established that of Pahlevi, a term for the ancient language.

Iranian rulers of the past had borne a number of presumably awe-inspiring titles, some assumed and some inherited from forebears. One of the famous inscriptions of Darius began: "I am Darius, the great King, the King of Kings, King of lands peopled by all races."[48] An inscription of Shahpur I began: "I, adorer of Mazda, the god Shapur, King of Kings of Iranians and non-Iranians, of the race of gods. . . ." Shahpur II addressed a letter to the Roman Emperor Constantine as follows: "I, Shapur, King of Kings, partner with the stars, brother of the Sun and Moon. . . ." And Shah Abbas of the later Safavid Dynasty added to his titles "the splendor of Darius."[49]

Among his titles, Reza took from earlier dynasties that of *Shahanshah*, King of Kings. Mohammed added that of *Aryamehr*. This was derived from the old Iranian *Arya-Mithra* and can be translated as "Sun of the Aryans." It was apparently meant to suggest the divine royal radiance, or *Farr*.[50] Mohammed Shah also named and modeled his imperial guard after the guard of Cyrus the Great, known as the Immortals. The crown for his coronation was copied after the crowns of the Sassanid Dynasty.[51]

Perhaps the major and most publicized attempt to invoke the glories

47. Ibid., p. 325.

48. Arberry, *Persian Literature*, p. 223.

49. Wilber, *Iran*, pp. 34, 77.

50. This is a variant of the term *khvarenah*. See Pio Filippani-Ronçoni, "The Tradition of the Sacred Kinship in Iran," in *Iran Under the Pahlevis*, ed. George Lenczowski (Stanford, Calif.: Hoover Institute Press, 1978), pp. 57–62.

51. Gerard de Villiers, *The Imperial Shah* (Boston: Little, Brown, 1976), p. 279.

of the past and link them to himself was the Shah's 1971 celebration of the twenty-five-hundredth anniversary of the founding of the first empire by Kurush (Cyrus). While every village and urban neighborhood was called on to hold its own celebration, the national commemoration was held with lavish splendor among the ruins of Persepolis, the vast palace-city complex built by Darius I. Preparations for the elaborate celebration included importing from France materials and workmen for the building of an entire tent city, luxurious furnishings and trappings, and chefs and food. The guests included royalty, heads of state and government, and celebrities and journalists from around the world.[52] In the course of the proceedings the Shah made a pledge at the tomb of Cyrus the Great at nearby Pasargadae. Units of the Iranian army marched in copies of the raiment of their Achaemenid forebears and there were other such evocative touches. Films of the Persepolis fete were required to be shown at film theaters for weeks and months after the event.[53]

Not all the titles borne by Mohammed Shah evoked the old Achaemenid and Sassanian empires. Some titles, such as Shadow of God on Earth, derived from the conversion of Iran to Islam during the Safavid Dynasty and referred to the ruler as defender and promoter of Shi'a Islam. Mohammed Shah seems to have given little more than ritually dutiful attention to this aspect of his role. In comparison with the strong emphasis he placed on the symbolism of early Iranian royalty, this shah seemed barely interested in the symbolism of Islam. Yet at the end of his reign he had come to be seen by many of his subjects as the contemporary incarnation of a central figure in the cardinal myth of Shi'a Islam, the figure of its arch-villain. His being perceived this way was partly the doing of the Ayatollah Khomeini, who had come to be seen as the contemporary incarnation of the hero of the myth.

The Husein or Kerbala myth stems from the death of the Prophet Mohammed in 632 and the conflicts concerning succession to his authority over the world of Islam. He had not clearly designated a successor. Ali, who was his cousin and his son-in-law and who had been his first convert and closest to him, seemed to some to have the strongest claim to be leader or successor (*khalifa, imam*). However, Umar, one of the

---

52. Ibid., pp. 282, 285.
53. From Iranian informants who prefer anonymity.

oldest and most influential of Mohammed's companions, persuaded others to recognize Abu Bakr, Mohammed's father-in-law. And Abu Bakr, two years later on his deathbed, designated Umar to succeed him. After Umar's assassination a decade later, Uthman, another son-in-law of Mohammed, was chosen over Ali to succeed him.

Ali had maintained his claim but refrained from pressing it actively in order not to split the community. But with Uthman's accession there also arose opposition to Uthman from other factions and on grounds other than legitimacy. The selection of Uthman transferred leadership from Mohammed's clan, the Hashimi, to Uthman's clan, the Umayya, and exacerbated traditional rivalries between the two, as well as political and economic rivalries resulting from the rapid spread of Islamic rule over surrounding areas.

When Uthman was killed in the course of a revolt, Ali finally achieved the caliphate. His legitimacy was contested by the new head of the Umayyads and he in turn faced civil war and was assassinated by former supporters opposed to his willingness to arbitrate with Mu'awiya, the Umayyad claimant.

This was the beginning of a long struggle between the Alids and the Umayyads over the caliphate/imamate and the nature of legitimacy in Islam, a struggle that ultimately produced two main branches of Islam, the Sunni and the Shi'a. From the Alid faction stems the smaller Shi'a branch, which holds that the right to rule and guide the community of Islam is vested in the descendants of Muhammed, most specifically those in the line of his daughter, Fatima, and her husband, Ali. Shi'a doctrine attributes to these descendants some share of that spiritual power and grace with which Mohammed was endowed.

Of these descendants, it is Husein, the second son of Fatima and Ali, whose ordeal has become the cardinal myth of Shi'a Islam in Iran. Husein's elder brother, Hasan, refrained from disputing Mu'awiya's claim to the caliphate after the death of their father. According to Shi'a tradition, he did this because he wished to avoid further bloodshed and because Mu'awiya agreed to cede back the caliphate as of his death. However, Hasan died within the decade, poisoned by Mu'awiya's agents. And Mu'awiya declared his son, Yazid, successor and sought by fair and foul means to gain agreement with this decision.

After Mu'awiya's death in 680, Yazid tried to force recognition from

Husein and others whose preeminence was such that their denial of his claim could threaten his authority. Meanwhile, Husein was again urged by the people of Kufa in southern Iraq to come and lead them in a revolt against the illegitimate caliph, a request he had earlier refused because of his brother's agreement with Mu'awiya. Having established the depth of this sentiment through a cousin, he decided to respond to the call.

Husein's friends and supporters warned him against going, reminding him that the Kufans had not held firm under pressure in their support of his father and brother and might not do so for him, despite their resentment of the tyranny of Yazid. But the Kufans had called upon Husein to be their imam, a call he felt he could not refuse as grandson of the Prophet and thus symbol of a faith still young and endangered. He therefore left for Kufa with his family and a small party of men, having discouraged more followers from accompanying him into danger.

In the midst of his journey Husein received news that Yazid had sent one of his most ruthless subordinates to take control of Kufa and quell the support for Husein. This man had executed Husein's cousin, the latter's host, and a messenger from Husein and thoroughly intimidated the Kufans.

Husein nonetheless decided to proceed, advising his followers to turn back. Few did and as the party reached the desert plain of Karbala, they were confronted by a detachment of troops soon followed by an army of thousands. As the commanders sought Husein's surrender to Yazid, his party, including the women and children, were subjected to severe ordeals. For days, they were prevented from obtaining water.

In the battle that followed, Husein, his children, and all but two of the males in his party were slain and their bodies mutilated and left on the plain. The women and children were taken to Kufa, where Husein's head was publicly displayed and then sent to Yazid in Damascus.[54]

For Shi'ites, Karbala, the place of the massacre, has become a sacred site and a place for pilgrimage. The tenth day of the Moslem month of Muharram, the day of the massacre, has become a sacred date. Husein

---

54. Major sources for the Shi'a version include: Syed Husein M. Jafri, *Origins and Early Development of Shi'a Islam* (London and New York: Longman, 1978); Muhammad Husayn al-Tabataba'i, *Shi'ite Islam*, trans. and ed. Seyyed Hosein Nasr (London: Allen & Unwin, 1975); and Michael M. J. Fischer, *From Religious Dispute to Revolution* (Cambridge, Mass., and London: Harvard University Press, 1980).

himself has come to represent more than the man who, at great risk to himself, upheld the true faith when it was endangered. For Shi'ites he is one who knowingly and voluntarily sacrificed himself to maintain in the world the consciousness of truth and justice.[55] He symbolizes the duty of right to strive against wrong even when right is weak and wrong is strong. He personifies the obligation of each individual to take action against injustice.

The reenactment and reliving of the martyrdom of Husein take place each year in Iran, commencing with the beginning of the month of Muharram and rising in emotional intensity to the climax on Ashura, the tenth of the month. There are passion plays and ritual mourning processions in which men flagellate themselves to share or repent the sufferings of Husein. There are gatherings at which skilled narrators arouse their listeners to weeping and breastbeating as they painstakingly recount each detail of each episode of the ordeal at Karbala.[56]

Myth, according to Lévi-Strauss, has an operational value in that its pattern is timeless, explaining the present and future as well as the past.[57] Among Shi'ites and especially in Iran, the myth of Husein has held universal and recurrently specific significance. As Algar has noted, Husein's struggle against the Umayyads became an archetype of the struggle between justice and tyranny, and all autocratic regimes were likened to that of the Umayyads.[58] In the last century, religious leaders have drawn such comparisons in opposition to the Qajar Dynasty and to the modernization efforts of Reza Shah Pahlevi.[59]

Thus, the Ayatollah Khomeini acted within a tradition when he publicly attacked Mohammed Shah Pahlevi in 1963, comparing him to Yazid. At that time, Khomeini was one of the three Iranian *mujtahids*

55. A young Iranian informant put it thus: "Husein's death was the water for growing the tree of true Islam."

56. Gustav Thaiss, "Religious Symbolism and Social Change: The Drama of Husein," in *Scholars, Saints and Suffis*, ed. Nikki R. Keddie (Berkeley and Los Angeles: University of California Press, 1972), pp. 349–66, and Fischer, *Religious Dispute*, pp. 170–72, 260–63.

57. Claude Lévi-Strauss, "The Structural Study of Myth," *Journal of American Folklore* 68 (Oct.–Dec. 1955), 430.

58. Hamid Algar, "The Oppositional Role of the Ulama in Twentieth Century Iran," in Keddie, *Scholars*, p. 233.

59. See Nikki R. Keddie, "The Roots of the Ulama's Power in Modern Iran," in Keddie, *Scholars*, p. 212 n., and Fischer, *Religious Dispute*, p. 186, for examples of likening the ruler to Yazid in the 1840s, 1919, and 1935.

(outstanding interpreters of Islamic law) upon whom had fallen the mantle of the recently deceased Ayatollah Burujirdi, the *marja'-i taqlid* (chief interpreter and guide).[60] Of these, he was the most critical of the Shah and most adamant in opposition. This alone might not have sufficed to link Khomeini with Husein in people's minds. But the Shah and his security forces provided the contemporary parallel.

Soon after Khomeini began preaching against the Shah, and after students in Qum, the site of his school and a leading religious center, began to demonstrate, the school was invaded by security police. The attack occurred on the anniversary of the martyrdom of the Sixth Imam, the one most revered in Shi'a tradition after Ali and Husein. Khomeini's picture began to appear in bazaars around the country as a symbol of opposition to the Shah. The month of Muharram arrived, and the atmosphere was suffused with tension as well as religious emotion.

Just after Ashura, the anniversary of the Karbala massacre and the martyrdom of Husein, Khomeini was arrested and many of his student followers and others among protesting crowds were killed. The catalytic link between Khomeini and Husein was forged.

Shortly afterward, Khomeini was sent into exile.[61] His exile served to link him into another sacred myth of Shi'a Islam, that of the *Imam-al-Zaman* or Hidden Imam.[62] The twelfth imam descended from Mohammed through Fatima and Ali, Mohammed Abûl-Qâsim, was the last. In 872, when his father was martyred, he disappeared and went into occultation or concealment from the material world, according to Shi'a belief. However, he still remains the preeminent authority in the Islamic world and all other authority derives from his. *Mujtahids*, *marjas*, and other religious authorities are seen as his agents or intermediaries.[63]

Moreover, with no recognized distinction between spiritual and secu-

---

60. Algar, "Role of the Ulama," p. 245; Marvin Zonis, *The Political Elite of Iran* (Princeton: Princeton University Press, 1971), pp. 44–45.

61. Sources consulted differ on the details of Khomeini's arrest and exile. Algar states that Khomeini was arrested immediately, whereas Zonis notes that Khomeini was arrested, released, and rearrested and sent into exile later. Khomeini's exile was in the place where Ali was reputed to have been buried.

62. The term *Imam-al-Zaman* literally means the Imam of the Age or the Imam of All Time.

63. Keddie, in Keddie, *Scholars*, pp. 216–17; Reuben Levy, *The Social Structure of Islam* (Cambridge: Cambridge University Press, 1965), p. 181.

lar authority, the Hidden Imam is also seen as the ultimate secular ruler, the true sovereign. Any head of the state is seen as acting in trust for him. The first constitution of Iran, drawn up in 1906, gave expression to this belief in stating that the parliament would be established with the agreement and consent of the *Imam-al-Zaman*.[64]

Shi'a doctrine also holds that the Hidden Imam will emerge from concealment to bring justice to the world. This messianic notion arose from and became interlinked with a prior belief, shared by Sunni Islam, in the ultimate coming of *al Mahdi*, the Guide and Restorer of the Faith.[65]

Neither Ayatollah Khomeini nor his spokesmen explicitly claimed that he was the coming Imam. To have done so would have caused considerable controversy and opposition within Iran's clerical establishment. Yet by the mid-1970s, as the Shah's authority was increasingly challenged, the challengers began to refer to the exiled Khomeini as "Imam" Khomeini.[66]

Myth alone did not account for the Shah's loss of inherited royal charismatic authority and Khomeini's achievement of personal political charisma. That it did not help to sustain the former but strongly served to generate the latter suggests some determinants of the role of myth in charismatic legitimation and political legitimation generally.

The Shah sought to invoke a generalized myth of the heroic age and kings of the Achaemenid period. The evocative power of generalized or composite myths may well pale in competition with that of fairly specific ones such as those tapped by Khomeini.

How closely contemporary circumstances and actors correspond with those of the myth would seem to be significant in achieving identification. At Persepolis the Shah seemed to seek specific association with Cyrus the Great. But there had been little in his own career to correspond with the image of a conqueror and empire-builder. Perhaps his father,

64. Levy, *Social Structure*, p. 288; G. E. Von Grunebaum, *Islam: Essays in the Nature and Growth of a Cultural Tradition* (American Anthropological Association, memoir no. 81, Apr. 1955), p. 12.

65. For details of the revolts and messianic movements led by proclaimed or self-proclaimed *mahdis*, see Jafri, *Origins*, pp. 228–65, and Bernard Lewis, *The Arabs in History* (New York: Harper & Row, 1966), pp. 72–73.

66. Fischer, *Religious Dispute*, pp. 127, 177–78, 212.

Reza Shah, might have seemed credible as a modern mini-Cyrus. However, Mohammed Shah fled his country during a crisis in 1953 and was restored to his throne with the aid of a foreign power. Parallels in pomp and pageantry could not suffice for identification with heroic Achaemenids.

Correspondences between the situation of Khomeini and elements of the versions of the Imam–Mahdi myth were close. Just as the Imam may be hidden from the world but is in communication through a few receiving his word, Khomeini was hidden from the sight of most Iranians but was in communication through a few. In some versions, before the Imam can bring justice, he must lead people in a struggle against tyranny and oppression and in some he cannot appear until a period of great tyranny and oppression has occurred. For Khomeini's followers the times and the man seemed to fit the mythic scenario. For the Husein scenario, the Shah himself, as noted above, provided the parallel.

Finally, myth reinforced by ritual is likely to be more compelling than without such reinforcement. The royal myth of the early rulers of Iran was presented in schoolbook and story and in celebrations such as that at Persepolis. But these could not have given the royal myth the vitality, emotional depth, and timeless reality of the yearly rituals reenacting the myth of Husein, rituals in which people participated and thus felt the myth in the present.

5
Charismatic Conversion: Heroes, Saviors, and Miracles

As Weber noted, one of the characteristics of the charismatic phenomenon is the perception of the leader by followers as a hero or savior.[1] This chapter analyzes the various elements that enter into the creation of images of heroic feats by leaders, of images of actions by leaders that save or seem to save people from distress and disaster, and of deeds performed by leaders that are or seem to be miraculous. These elements and the ways in which they relate to one another are illustrated by brief case studies of some actions and action sequences of some charismatic political leaders that stimulated perceptions of them as heroes and saviors.

I use the term *image* here because in many instances it is not, or at least not only, the intrinsic nature or type of an action that results in its being seen as heroic or miraculous. The conditions prior to its undertaking, evaluations concerning the ease or difficulty of the task with which the action is concerned, the timing and the duration of the act, the mode or style in which it is undertaken, and the protagonists on whose behalf or the antagonists against whom the action is directed are some of the factors that help to shape the ways in which an act or a series of actions is perceived.

The heroic image can be developed by the successful performance of

1. Weber, *Economy*, 1, pp. 241–44; 3, p. 1116.

an extraordinary feat or a deed accomplished to an extraordinary degree. How extraordinary a deed appears in the eyes of the beholders depends in part upon the element of difficulty attached to it. If an act or a task seems to be extremely difficult to accomplish and fraught with obstacles, its execution appears remarkable. If the act or task is one that has been considered impossible to perform, its accomplishment with less than complete success will also appear remarkable, and full success endows the doer with the aura of heroism.

Apart from whatever specific obstacles may be connected with a particular task or deed, there can be another element that enters into perceptions of it as exceedingly difficult or impossible. This is the existence of previous and unsuccessful attempts by others to accomplish the task. The element of contrast can be important in the formation of evaluations of the magnitude of success. It may well be, for example, that a propitious time has arrived for the solution to a hitherto insoluble problem or conflict so that few obstacles remain to confront the latest would-be solver; nonetheless, the fact that the problem or conflict had defied solution in the past, despite many attempts, can easily create the impression that the individual who now solves it has succeeded in accomplishing an impossible task.[2]

Therefore, one element of an extraordinary feat is the existence of a major obstacle or obstacles or the perception of the feat as difficult or impossible to perform. The more insuperable the obstacles to successful performance appear, the more extraordinary the accomplishment will seem. The greater the extent of prior unsuccessful attempts to achieve the same goal, the greater will appear the obstacles and the more extraordinary the successful accomplishment.

A second important element contributing to perceptions of an act as extraordinary or heroic is that of the risk involved or the apparent risk entailed.[3] It almost goes without saying that throughout history and in

---

2. An example of this was Mussolini's signing of the Lateran Treaties with the Pope in 1929, which effected a reconciliation between the Italian State and the Vatican after a dispute that had endured for more than half a century.

3. Risk can be viewed from several perspectives, that of the actor(s) in the situation, that of the observer in possession of all relevant information, and that of other observers. The degree of risk involved in an enterprise may be estimated differently from each of these perspectives. Here the perspective is that of the last mentioned category, observers with imperfect information. Friedland ("Sociological Concept," p. 21) has also emphasized the element of risk in connection with the generation of charisma.

many cultures the notion of heroism has often been associated with daring to do something dangerous against unlikely odds of success.

Aside from the specific circumstances surrounding any particular act that would make it appear hazardous, there are at least three general factors that can contribute to impressions of an act as risky. The first is the existence of prohibitions, legal or otherwise, against the commission of such an act. Closely related to this is the possibility or probability of retaliation or reprisal by those against whom the act may be directed or by those who would consider themselves threatened by the successful completion of such an act. Finally, the degree of perceived risk would depend upon the perceived relative strength of those challenged or threatened compared to that of the individual or group engaged in committing the act.

Thus, the greater the apparent risk, the more likely it is for a successful act to seem to be an extraordinarily heroic feat. The firmer the prohibitions against it and the greater the possibility of retaliation, the more likely it is to seem fraught with risk. The stronger those challenged or threatened by an act appear, the more likely it is to seem full of risk.

The element of challenge, dealt with here in connection with risk, can also be seen as an autonomous element in relation to the development of perceptions of heroism. Leadership acts, including some perceived as heroic, need not necessarily involve struggle against palpable opponents. Impressive feats can be performed in coping with natural elements, fiscal crises, rescue needs, and so forth in which the element of contending human forces is lacking. As will be described later, the case of Roosevelt illustrates an extraordinary accomplishment that did not involve conflict.

However, when a leader issues a challenge or initiates an act that can be seen as a challenge to an opponent or opponents or to a particular system or status quo, this tends to place him in a potent position with respect to the formation of an image of heroism. Apart from the risk that may be involved, the challenger most frequently tends to be weaker than the challenged. In fact, cases in which it is the other way around can generally be excluded from the likelihood of heroic potential. A weaker challenger evokes the image of a David-and-Goliath confrontation and similar images from various cultures that cast weaker challengers defying stronger powers as heroes.

The nature of the challenge, however, is also a factor in the creation of the heroic image. Together with the elements of the difficulty of the task and the risk involved, discussed above, perhaps the third most crucial element contributing to perceptions of an act as extraordinarily heroic is the degree to which the act is perceived as of critical importance to those concerned. There is a substantial difference between a leader's performing an act, however difficult and risky, that is seen to benefit mainly himself or those close to him, and the successful completion of an act whose consequences benefit or seem to benefit a collectivity—a community, a national group, a state.

Obviously, the specific deeds that have been or can be seen to be of benefit to people cannot be listed here. Most of them, however, would probably fall under three or four general categories. One category might be called that of rescue, involving acts that liberate people from intolerable conditions or free them from dangers or threats of danger. A second category is that of restoration, recovering for people something of which they have been deprived and the loss of which they have suffered from or grieved over. A third one that can, but need not, overlap with the others is that of remedying or avenging a flagrant injustice or injury. Finally, there is the act that provides for people some new or unanticipated or hoped for but not expected gain or improvement.

This last category may have less potential for the creation of the heroic image than do the others. The latter include the element of contrast between the state of people prior to the act and after it, a change that is devoutly wished for even if seen as unattainable. Thus, there is likely to be a greater emotional investment in and emotional reaction to the success of the act. The greater the involvement of people in the outcome of the act, the more heroic may seem its accomplishment.

There are some circumstances in which the specific situation of the leader in relation to the type of act can magnify the perception of heroism. If the act is one that appears to involve personal sacrifice on the part of the leader or reflects a stance least expected from someone of his background, it gains an added dimension of valor. The defiance of South Africa's racial policy by a wealthy and successful barrister, Gandhi, the championing of the common man by a member of one of the leading American oligarchical families, Roosevelt, and the organizing of a radical revolution by a middle-class lawyer of the plantation gentry, Castro, made a somewhat different impression, one suspects, than would have been the case had these acts been undertaken by, respectively, a petty Indian trader in Natal, an American president who grew up on a small Minnesota farm, or a Cuban captain who had been a *campesino.* One might think that the latter, of lesser status and more directly vulnerable to the situations the acts were designed to correct, might appear more heroic. However paradoxical it appears, those of privileged status who undertake difficult and dangerous acts on behalf of others in which they have little or nothing to gain and perhaps something or even much to lose can be seen as potentially heroic precisely because it is not in their own interests or even contrary to their interests and they do not have to do it.

One other aspect concerning the nature of the task or act needs to be mentioned. The gain or benefit resulting from the heroic act need not be material or tangible but can be psychic. Thus, a deed of restoration involving the recovery for people of land that once was theirs and was then taken from them is a tangible benefit; restoring their pride and dignity after they have been subject to humiliation is conferring a psychic benefit.

A central element in what I have earlier referred to as the timing and duration of an act is that of suspense. An act undertaken with apparent suddenness and without prior notification to or awareness by a public can have a dramatic effect that heightens the heroic impression produced by the combination of other elements. Probably most dramatic is an act that is played out over a period of time during which suspense is generated concerning the possible outcome. This is especially true when the act involves challenge and confrontation. Suspense can heighten perceptions of the degree of risk and of the possibilities of retaliation. It is possible, although rare, for an act that contains hardly any of the elements discussed above to be nonetheless perceived as quasi-heroic if it dissipates extreme tension or suspense produced by a prolonged crisis.

Finally, a factor already touched upon in its relation to other elements, that of contrast, may come into play. Contrast can play a major role in the formation of images and evaluations of various dimensions of an undertaking. Acts are rarely measured against a priori absolute standards but more generally relative to the state of relevant factors. Thus, whether an act is perceived as miraculous or not or how miraculous it would appear may well depend upon the degree of difference between initial beliefs in the impossibility of its achievement and the extent to which it is ultimately accomplished. As observed earlier, perceptions of the magnitude of success of a leader may be augmented by contrast with the attempts and failures of his predecessor or predecessors to perform the same feat that he has managed to bring off. Most notably, contrast is an important feature in the development of heroic perceptions in a situation of challenge and confrontation. Fidel Castro and a handful of followers in the Oriente had not yet won a single military victory when Herbert Matthews's reports in the *New York Times* dramatized to the world and Cuba the image of a small intrepid group challenging and determined to destroy the infinitely more powerful armed might of Batista.[4] There were, of course, other elements involved in the sudden emergence of Castro as hero, such as perceptions of the Batista regime and whether Castro was already seen by a sufficient number of Cubans as wearing the mantle of Martí. Nonetheless, the very contrast between the situations of Castro and Batista in 1957 was enough to endow Castro with the aura of heroism in the eyes of many.

Although the genesis and development of perceptions of an extraordinary, heroic, or miraculous feat can be explained in terms of the elements analyzed here, there is still an additional factor that can affect these elements and the perceptual responses to them. This is the role of the leader, more precisely the mode or style of the leader in his execution of the act. For example, Roosevelt, as will be described, augmented perceptions of the failure of his predecessor and contributed to the atmosphere of growing crisis and suspense by refusing to work with his predecessor during the transitional period or to indicate what plans he was formulating to cope with the crisis. Gandhi had the habit of notifying the British authorities in advance of the kind, date, and details of a campaign he proposed to launch against them. This was not a tactical threat, although it could be taken as such, but a matter of Gandhi's concern with openness and honesty. However, in so doing, Gandhi magnified the apparent perceptions of risk since the British could be assumed to be preparing countermeasures and reprisals before the onset of the campaign, as indeed they did. Moreover, the element of suspense, whose effectiveness tends to increase with time up to a certain point,

4. *New York Times*, Feb. 24, 1957, and following.

began to be operative earlier, with Gandhi's announcements, than it would be in confrontations conducted in a more orthodox way.

These elements and their interaction in the process of charismatic legitimation through the creation of images of a leader as hero and savior (two heavily overlapping concepts) are elaborated and illustrated by examples of acts performed by Hitler, Gandhi, Roosevelt, and Mussolini. In all but two of the instances concerning Gandhi, these acts took place soon after the leaders in question entered public office. Therefore, for major segments of the populations of the countries they led, these acts may well have been the initial stimuli for the development of charismatically oriented perceptions of them.

These cases are deliberately not parallel in order to indicate that not all the elements detailed above are essential for the development of the belief that a feat is heroic and also in order to emphasize the importance of historical and cultural contexts.

Hitler as Hero of the Rhine

The military reoccupation of the Rhineland by German forces in 1936 at the order of Adolf Hitler, Germany's chancellor, contained nearly all the elements outlined above and made Hitler a hero to many Germans who were not Nazi followers. In addition, the march into the Rhineland included another element, not mentioned earlier—surprise and shock, both of which are capable of heightening the effects produced by the combination of elements I specified as conducive to the development of the heroic image.

Hitler's address to the Reichstag, the German parliament, on March 7, 1936, electrified its deputies, the German people, and much of the rest of the Western world. Apart from announcing an election at the end of the month, Hitler stated that Germany was no longer bound by the Treaty of Locarno and that, while he was speaking, German troops were marching into the demilitarized zone of the Rhineland. He had barely finished the latter announcement when there was a tumultuous reaction in the Reichstag. As one journalist recorded in his diary:

> They spring, yelling and crying to their feet. The audience in the galleries does the same, all except a few diplomats and about fifty of

us correspondents. Their hands are raised in slavish salute, their faces now contorted with hysteria, their mouths wide open, shouting, shouting.[5]

To understand how momentous the march into the Rhineland was for the German people, it is necessary to go back to the peace settlement after World War I. Of the victors of that war, France had been the one whose territory had been invaded by German armies twice in half a century. And France had been determined to secure a settlement that would guarantee it maximum security from another such invasion. Because the Rhine River constituted the only natural barrier, the original French objective had been to make it a permanent strategic frontier, preventing the possibility of German troops being stationed in the Rhineland area west of the Rhine. During the peace treaty negotiations, French representatives had sought to have German territory west of the Rhine detached from Germany and established as a separate neutral buffer state. This had been opposed by the representatives of Great Britain and the United States. A compromise had finally been reached by which France had agreed to settle for a military occupation of the Rhineland by the Allies for fifteen years in return for a promise of an Anglo-American guarantee of immediate military assistance in case of renewed German aggression. This promised treaty, however, had not been formalized, as a result of the failure of the American Congress to ratify agreements made by President Wilson.[6]

Many Germans had strongly resented the occupation, as they had also resented other terms of the Versailles treaty, such as the war guilt clause, reparations, and the disarmament of Germany. The occupation of German soil by foreign forces, however, had probably appeared most onerous to many, since it had been the most visible sign of defeat and humiliation. The occupation had also been tied to Germany's fulfillment of some of the other conditions of the treaty, notably to reparations. Thus, when Germany had defaulted on payment of reparations in 1923, French and Belgian forces had been sent to occupy the Ruhr and France had lent support to separatist movements in the Rhineland.[7]

5. Shirer, *Berlin Diary*, p. 53.
6. G. M. Gathorne-Hardy, *A Short History of International Affairs, 1920–1939* (London: Oxford University Press, 1950), pp. 52–55.
7. Ibid.

During the 1920s there had been negotiations between the leaders of the German Weimar Republic and those of the Allies, as the former sought to renegotiate what had been felt to be the more onerous terms of the Versailles treaty. In some respects they had been successful. Thus, the evacuation of the Rhineland by Allied forces—one of the major objectives of the negotiations—had begun in 1925 and been completed in 1930.

Nonetheless, from the point of view of many Germans, some of the "shackles of Versailles" still remained. For the Treaty of Versailles had provided not only for the temporary occupation of the Rhineland but also for its demilitarization thereafter.[8] This forced demilitarization was seen as constituting a limitation upon Germany's sovereignty, as symbolizing the scars of Versailles, and as disgracing and staining German national honor.

Hitler's audacious action had not been anticipated, except by Flandin, the French foreign minister, and some of his colleagues. Those who had been involved in or closely followed European political and diplomatic affairs in early 1936 did suspect that Hitler might take some sort of step involving the Rhineland. The previous year France and the Soviet Union had signed a mutual assistance treaty, objected to by Germany as constituting an attempt to encircle her. Criticisms in the German press had also carried references to the Rhineland and had increased during the early part of 1936 as the treaty was scheduled to come before the French parliament for ratification. But the general expectation and that of the British and Belgian foreign ministries had been that Hitler would use the ratification of the Franco-Soviet Mutual Assistance Treaty to attempt to renegotiate the Locarno pact status of the Rhineland.[9]

For several reasons, it had not been anticipated that Hitler might move as he did. In the first place, an invasion of the Rhineland by German forces was illegal and, in fact, doubly illegal. It violated not only the

8. Merkl, *Political Violence*, pp. 190, 205, notes that one out of every four of the Abel collection respondents indicated strong sentiments against the occupation and many had been involved in active demonstrations or underground activity in the occupied area. Compared to other respondents, these were more charismatically oriented to Hitler, whom they saw as "savior in the hour of the deepest humiliation of the fatherland."

9. Anthony Eden, *The Memoirs of Anthony Eden: Facing the Dictators* (Boston: Houghton Mifflin, 1962), pp. 373–78; Arnold J. Toynbee, *Survey of International Affairs, 1936* (London: Oxford University Press, 1937), pp. 252–54; *New York Times*, Feb. 26, 1936; Mar. 6, 1936.

terms of Article 43 of the Versailles Treaty but also those of the first article of the Rhineland treaty of the Locarno pact. The Rhineland treaty had been initiated by Germany and cosigned with Great Britain, Belgium, France, and Italy in 1925 at Locarno. It guaranteed the frontiers between Germany on one side and Belgium and France on the other and reaffirmed the demilitarization of the Rhineland in accordance with the Versailles treaty.

Apart from the illegality, however, there had appeared to be a more critical consideration standing in the way of such drastic action, the strong likelihood of retaliation. Hitler had already shown scant concern for legality, having rearmed Germany contrary to the provisions of the Versailles treaty. But with respect to the Rhineland, the pact of Locarno contained teeth lacking in that of Versailles. It provided that in case of a flagrant violation by one party, the others would come to the immediate aid of the party against whom the violation was directed.[10] In view of the prior attitude of France, it seemed likely that France and probably Belgium would not only consider a military move into the Rhineland a flagrant violation but would take immediate military steps to counteract it. A final deterrent to such action on the part of Hitler had seemed to be the fact that the French army at this time was substantially stronger than the German army.

Thus, Hitler's move appeared reckless and rash, not least to his own generals. His announcement was greeted in Germany with considerable anxiety as well as jubilation. Otto Tolischus, the *New York Times* correspondent in Berlin, described the "tense suspense . . . which manifests itself everywhere even in the midst of the general satisfaction." He reported that people were "half stunned by the sweep of Hitler's action and half scared by the possible price of such action" and were asking one another and especially asking foreigners whether the French would march.[11]

This was the basis for German apprehension, not concern that the violation of international agreements might bring international condemnation or reprisal. For Hitler had stated in his speech that the Franco-Russian pact violated the Locarno pact and therefore freed Germany

---

10. The text of the treaty can be found in Toynbee, *Survey*, p. 266.
11. *New York Times*, Mar. 8, 1936.

from the latter. Moreover, Hitler had offered to replace Locarno with an agreement for a new demilitarized zone if France and Belgium would agree to have similar zones on their sides of the borders, to conclude a new nonaggression pact, and to return to the League of Nations.[12] As all this was explained to the German people in the German press, it could well have seemed eminently reasonable and even generous on the part of their leader. Furthermore, they were informed that the British people were impressed by these offers.[13]

Some realized, however, that the French were not likely to view the situation in this light. One of the most apprehensive was Hitler's minister of war, who was prepared to withdraw the German troops in the Rhineland the day after they entered it. Generals of the German High Command nervously tended to agree with him. Despite his own apprehensions Hitler vetoed all suggestions for any pullback.[14]

Initially, it seemed highly probable that the French would move militarily and soon. On the day of the coup, French officials declared that although France would appeal to the League of Nations, it was prepared to take military measures, supported by its allies, to force Germany to evacuate the Rhineland.[15] All army leave in France was immediately canceled and more than 50,000 French troops were rushed to the forts on the border, which were already manned by about 100,000 soldiers.[16]

In the midst of the suspense and anxiety, on Sunday, March 8, the day after the momentous announcement and march, Germany observed Heroes' Memorial Day, a holiday created by Hitler to honor the German dead of World War I and of the National Socialist Party. Hitler received "unprecedented ovations" by both the army and the people. Throughout the day the square in front of the Chancery in Berlin was filled by thousands of people shouting for him and "thunderous ovations" greeted his appearances.[17]

The day passed without a military response from France beyond the

---

12. Toynbee, *Survey*, pp. 263–64. During this period Hitler continued to ignore France's offer to submit the treaty to the international court.

13. *Völkischer Beobachter*, Mar. 8, 1936.

14. Gathorne-Hardy, *Short History*, p. 401; William Shirer, *The Rise and Fall of the Third Reich* (New York: Simon and Schuster, 1959), pp. 402–03.

15. *New York Times*, Mar. 8, 1936.

16. Ibid., Mar. 9, 1936.

17. Ibid.

increased mobilization of forces. Anxiety still prevailed. In Cologne, for example, people were frequently heard asking one another what the other countries would do.[18] That evening, Sarraut, the French prime minister, made a nationwide radio speech to his countrypeople that was scathingly critical of the German action. He reported that his government had referred the matter to the Council of the League of Nations and to the Locarno pact powers. However, he implied the possibility of unilateral French military action in stating that his government was not "disposed to allow Strassbourg to come under the fire of German guns."[19]

It was and would be exceedingly difficult to estimate the extent of awareness among the German people of opinion and reactions in foreign capitals, given the controlled German press and the risks of tuning in to foreign broadcasts. In Berlin the *London Times* correspondent reported on Monday, March 9, that Berliners were "anxiously scanning" the foreign press for reactions abroad.[20] Even those Germans who had access only to the controlled domestic press easily could have become apprehensive from reading between the lines. Thus, the *Völkischer Beobachter*, the paper of Hitler's party, gave most of its space, as might be expected, to praising, explaining, and defending Hitler's action. In referring to the speech of Sarraut in a major article, however, it stated that he did not want to understand the German position and that the French government was being rigid.[21] The very tone of its attacks on the latter strongly suggested the existence of a very tense situation.

On Tuesday, March 10, the foreign ministers of the Locarno pact states met in Paris, with another meeting scheduled to be held in London two days later. Even before the meeting it became apparent, from Foreign Secretary Eden's speech to Commons the previous day, that the British position might differ from the French. Eden had condemned the German action but denied that it implied a "threat of hostilities."[22] At the meeting, the French foreign minister, Pierre Flandin, pressed for

18. Ibid.
19. Toynbee, *Survey*, p. 269; Neville Waites, ed., *Troubled Neighbors: Franco-British Relations in the Twentieth Century* (London: Weidenfeld, 1971), p. 164.
20. *London Times*, Mar. 10, 1936.
21. *Völkischer Beobachter*, Mar. 10, 1936.
22. Toynbee, *Survey*, p. 225.

joint action by the Locarno powers, including, if necessary, a resort to force.[23] British representatives favored much less drastic action, such as condemnation of Germany's treaty violations by the League of Nations and the commencement of negotiations with Germany.[24]

For the next few days the issue appeared to be whether France would induce England to take strong steps, including concerted military action (which France appeared reluctant to undertake alone), or whether England would induce France to modify its position, which minimally required the withdrawal of German troops under penalty of sanctions.[25] French public opinion became even more aroused after the Paris meeting as news arrived that more troops were entering the Rhineland. Flandin left for London increasingly determined to obtain the "maximum reparation from Germany and the maximum guarantee of assistance from Great Britain."[26]

In Germany there was still the feeling of triumph as well as the feelings of anxiety and suspense felt in other countries. On the one hand, Germans exhibited pride in Hitler's "master stroke," while hoping that, and wondering whether, he would carry it off. On the other hand, they displayed depression at reports of the meeting in Paris and some fear about the implications of the firm French stand.[27]

Before the London meeting of March 12, the British government tried to secure from the German government a partial withdrawal of troops from the Rhineland and an agreement not to increase their number or build fortifications at least through the period of the Locarno negotiations. As the meeting opened, the German government indicated refusal of the former condition and agreement to the latter.[28] While the British considered this to be something of a gain, the French did not. For on the same day, Hitler gave his first election speech—at Karlsruhe in the Rhineland. He told a wildly cheering audience that "nothing will induce us to renounce this regained sovereignty over the Rhineland zone."[29]

23. Eden, *Memoirs*, pp. 390–97; Waites, *Neighbors*, p. 165.
24. Toynbee, *Survey*, p. 283.
25. Ibid.
26. Ibid., p. 285.
27. *London Times*, Mar. 12, 1936.
28. Toynbee, *Survey*, pp. 285–87.
29. Ibid., p. 286.

At this time, however, extreme uneasiness was reported among the people of Berlin. Press control had succeeded in keeping from a large portion of the general public much of what had been happening. Some of this had begun to seep out, however, and some of the public became almost as aware of the gravity of the situation as official circles had been all along. The *London Times* correspondent reported that for the first time a "breach of treaty" was talked about and many believed that Hitler would not have ordered a move into the Rhineland without the prior agreement of England.[30]

However, at the London meetings of the Locarno countries the French position was not gaining support. While these were in progress, the Council of the League of Nations also began meetings to discuss the charge of Germany's violation of the Versailles treaty. These were marked by disagreements over whether Germany should be represented at the debates, by demands from Germany that Hitler's proposals be discussed, and by threats from France to withdraw.[31]

Meanwhile, Hitler delivered his second major speech in the demilitarized zone, at Frankfurt on March 16. The several hundred thousand people who flocked to Frankfurt for the occasion "frantically acclaimed" him. He asserted that there was no question of Germany's retreating on the decisions made.[32]

By March 18 it seemed clear that the British policy of negotiation with Germany had prevailed in London over the French proposals to press for immediate German withdrawal through threat of sanctions. As a German delegate left on that date for the League Council meetings in London, people in Berlin were described as beginning to believe that the Rhineland coup was successful.[33] Two days later, the *New York Times* correspondent in Berlin reported that the fear of a possible war had passed.[34]

Hitler had indeed won his daring gamble. With Britain acting as mediator rather than as guarantor and enforcer of international treaties, with France unwilling to move alone or with smaller powers, such as

30. *London Times*, Mar. 14, 1936.
31. Toynbee, *Survey*, pp. 294–98.
32. *London Times*, Mar. 18, 1936.
33. Ibid., Mar. 19, 1936.
34. *New York Times*, Mar. 21, 1936.

Poland, which supported France's position, in the face of the British stand, and with other powers willing to do little more than register disapproval, the crisis petered out into weeks and months of proposals and counterproposals.[35]

One of the Locarno meeting proposals envisaged an international police force stationed on a narrow strip of Germany's borders with France and Belgium. In a speech in Breslau on March 22 Hitler dramatically declared that Germany would never "capitulate" to any such demand. He received a "tremendous reception" and there were reportedly no pauses in the "Heils" from those lining the five-mile drive from aerodrome to hall.[36]

Germany was ultimately exposed to nothing more serious than a unanimous vote by the Council of the League that it had committed a breach of treaty. Hitler's views on treaties were expressed in a speech at Berlin on March 24:

> If the rest of the world clings to the letter of treaties, I cling to an eternal morality. If they raise objections about paragraphs, I hold by the vital eternal rights of my people. . . . If they try to read avowals of guilt into such letters and paragraphs, then I . . . must assert the nation's right to live—its honour, freedom, and vital interests.[37]

It is unlikely that Hitler's audience, even the most peace-loving of them, saw the implications for the future in such a statement. In analyzing the relative importance to German voters of the various issues in the forthcoming election, one correspondent stressed the primacy of the abolition of demilitarization and the "complete liberation of German soil."[38] What this correspondent did not mention was the special importance of Rhineland soil to the national consciousness of patriotic Germans. As evidenced in poetry and songs, the Rhineland had long held a special place in the sentiments of many Germans, for whom it symbolized the "heartland" of their country.[39] Thus, in "liberating" this

---

35. Eden, *Memoirs*, p. 407.
36. *London Times*, Mar. 23, 1936.
37. Toynbee, *Survey*, p. 319.
38. *London Times*, Mar. 23, 1936.
39. For example, in a nineteenth-century German songbook, there are three patriotic songs with "Rhine" in the title, "Zum Rhein, übern Rhein!," "Der freie, deutsche Rhein,"

"heartland," Hitler in their eyes performed a glorious feat. That he achieved this without armed conflict in the face of great odds made him even more of a hero. Moreover, many who did not already believe in the infallibility of his judgment began to do so.

Mussolini as Defiant Restorer of Honor

Mussolini's initial accession to heroism in the eyes of his countrypeople can be analyzed in terms of most of the same elements that characterized the case of Hitler and the Rhineland, for example, challenge to world powers and retribution for national humiliation. However, there are some noteworthy differences. In the case of Mussolini one can argue that it was less a single dramatic action of powerful import that gave rise to perceptions of him as heroic than a succession of relatively small-scale actions. This could be termed the "incremental" development of the heroic image. Furthermore, the element of risk did not really exist, although the appearance of it did. For these and other reasons, the case of Mussolini is worth recounting.

Within slightly more than a year after he came to power, Mussolini came to be seen in Italy as the fearless champion of Italian rights and the restorer of Italian honor and prestige on the international scene. This image had been created by his handling of three successive international issues, the Treaty of Lausanne, the Corfu case, and the Fiume dispute. The magnitude of the effects of Mussolini's actions on the perceptions of the Italian people can best be understood against the background of previous Italian efforts at international bargaining and of dominant Italian views concerning their outcome.

At the time Mussolini became prime minister in 1922, many Italians were convinced that their country had been unfairly deprived of the gains expected as its share of victory in World War I and had been most shabbily treated at the Paris Peace Conference three years earlier. Not

---

and "Die Wacht am Rhein," all with strong martial overtones. The last contains the lines: "He looks to the heavens . . . and swears with proud desire to fight: You, Rhine, stay as German as my breast! As long as there is a drop of blood, as long as this hand can heft the sword, as long as this arm can hold a gun, no enemy will tread your banks!" and the refrain "Firm and true stands the watch on the Rhine!"

only nationalists but many others resented what they felt to have been the selfishness of their allies and the weakness of some of their own statesmen. Bitter jokes had been circulating to the effect that Italy had won the war but lost the peace. Between 1919 and 1922 the belief in a "mutilated victory" had gained wide credence.[40]

Italy had obtained little in the postwar settlement in comparison with the territories, reparations, and economic advantages gained by Great Britain and France. Scant attention had been given to Italy's claims for territory and influence in Africa and the Near East as France and Great Britain divided up between them Germany's former colonies and the new mandates. Apart from the substance of the settlement, the treatment accorded the Italian delegation to the Peace Conference by the representatives of the other major allies, especially by Woodrow Wilson and the American delegation, had seemed humiliating and insulting.

The conduct of the negotiations over the disposal of the former Austro-Hungarian territories on the eastern shore of the Adriatic Sea had been particularly galling to Italians. They had long considered the Adriatic as "mare nostrum," that is, "our sea," whose eastern coast was seen as vital to Italy's defense. By the secret Treaty of London in 1915, which had brought it into the war on the side of the Allies, Italy had been promised the province of Dalmatia, along this coast, which contained some old Italian communities among its largely Slavic inhabitants. However, at the conference, Wilson's opposition to secret treaties and his concern for the principle of national self-determination had led him to insist upon the incorporation of Dalmatia into the new state of Yugoslavia.

Vittorio Orlando, Italy's prime minister, had argued that if Italy were to renounce its right to Dalmatia, it should receive in compensation the port of Fiume, which had not been mentioned in the Treaty of London but which was inhabited largely by Italians. Wilson, who had backed Yugoslavia's claim to Fiume, had refused to consider this possibility. Moreover, he had issued a public appeal to the Italian people over the heads of their prime minister and delegation. In angry protest, Orlando had thereupon left the conference and returned to Rome. The Italian

40. Seton-Watson, *Italy*, p. 504; Alan Cassels, *Mussolini's Early Diplomacy* (Princeton: Princeton University Press, 1970), pp. vii, 40, 80.

populace had reacted with outrage and frenzied demonstrations against Wilson, the United States, and the other Allies.

No attempt had been made after this to conciliate Italy or to persuade Orlando to return to Paris. Instead, in his absence alterations in the treaty with Germany had been made to Italy's disadvantage, and the African mandates had been assigned to Great Britain and France. When Wilson, Clemenceau, and Lloyd George had made it evident that they were prepared to sign the peace treaty with Germany and to proceed with the Austrian and Hungarian treaties without Italy, Orlando had inconspicuously returned to the conference in mortification. This pointed indication that Italy carried little weight with its allies had caused great rancor in that country.[41]

Contrasted with this background, Mussolini's first publicized venture into international diplomacy seemed to exact some symbolic retribution for past humiliation. Soon after entering office, Mussolini was scheduled to attend a peace conference on Turkey at Lausanne, Switzerland. He was invited to meet with Curzon, the British foreign secretary, and Poincaré, the French premier, at Lausanne immediately preceding the official opening of the conference. Mussolini replied by telegraphing them to come to meet him instead at Territet, a village on his route close to Italy. He also informed the press that Italy was no longer "the slave of the Allies" and that whether Italy remained in the alliance would depend upon the outcome of the meeting.[42] Poincaré was indignant, but Curzon persuaded him to accede to Mussolini's demand.

From the Territet meeting emerged a communiqué of agreement on the questions to be discussed at Lausanne together with a statement stressing the equality of status of the three allies. Such a statement could easily have been seen as an unnecessary tacit admission of Italy's prior inequality. To the Italian people, however, Mussolini seemed to have scored, not least by having forced Europe's leading statesmen to go out of their way to accede to him at his summons. Moreover, the Treaty of Lausanne confirmed Italy's possession of the Dodecanese Islands in the Aegean, which had long been contested by Britain on behalf of Greece.[43]

41. Seton-Watson, *Italy*, pp. 528–30, 534.

42. *New York Times*, Nov. 20, 1922.

43. Cassels, *Diplomacy*, pp. 14–16; Kirkpatrick, *Mussolini*, pp. 193–95; Seton-Watson, *Italy*, pp. 667–68.

Soon after this, Mussolini dramatically and apparently successfully defied the League of Nations and world opinion. The uneasy relations that had existed for years between Italy and Greece worsened with the Lausanne recognition of Italy's occupation of the Greek-populated Dodecanese Islands. Greek resentment, manifested in anti-Italian press campaigns and demonstrations, precipitated in turn anti-Greek sentiment in Italy. On August 27, 1923, Italians received news of the ambush and murder on Greek territory of the Italian members of a mixed boundary commission engaged in delimiting a frontier. Italian public opinion was reported as "aroused to fever heat," as demonstrations took place in major cities such as Milan and Florence.[44]

Mussolini immediately sent a twenty-four-hour ultimatum to the Greek government containing seven demands. This action was greeted enthusiastically in Italy. In Rome, street corners were reportedly filled with groups of people surrounding those with newspapers, who read out loud the text of the ultimatum as their hearers cheered each demand vociferously.[45]

The Greek government agreed to the demands for military honors and special funerals for the victims but rejected those for an immediate inquiry, execution of the culprits, and an indemnity of 50 million lire. The grounds given for rejection were that since the perpetrators of the crime had disappeared and not been apprehended, there was no real evidence of Greek responsibility for the murders.

Mussolini declared the Greek reply unacceptable and took the dramatic step of sending the Italian fleet on August 31 to seize and occupy the Greek island of Corfu at the entrance to the Adriatic. Token Greek resistance led to a bombardment in which fifteen Greek refugees from Turkey housed in a military citadel were killed. The following day, Greece appealed to the Council of the League of Nations and the dispute aroused considerable international attention and tension in the succeeding days.

The murder of the Italian members of the boundary commission was almost overlooked as world official, press, and public opinion condemned the Italian attack on Corfu. In Italy, however, Mussolini had staunch support for the steps he had taken. He received thousands of

44. *New York Times*, Aug. 30, 1923.
45. Ibid.

telegrams from individuals and groups from all strata of Italian society indicating complete confidence in him and his actions.[46]

As the League Council assembled to discuss the issue, Mussolini declared that it did not fall under the jurisdiction of the League and was a matter of his state's "national honor." The Italian delegation argued that the dispute did not constitute aggression within the meaning of the League Covenant and should be handled by the Conference of Ambassadors at Paris, under whose aegis the boundary commission had been operating.

The issue of jurisdiction was more than a legal technicality. It was recognized that the smaller membership of the Conference would be more likely to favor Italy than would the larger membership of the League. The British delegate to Geneva, supported by delegates of many small countries, strongly pressed for a vote for League jurisdiction. The issue received wide attention, not only because of its substance, but because it was felt that this was a test of League prestige and effectiveness.

On September 4, Mussolini, against the advice of his own diplomats, publicly threatened that if the League Council did vote to deal with the dispute, Italy would withdraw from membership in the League. The League gave the issue over to the Conference of Ambassadors, which, on September 7, presented Greece with substantially the same terms as had Mussolini. Greece submitted to these terms and paid the indemnity and Mussolini ordered the evacuation of Corfu.

There had been some suspicion abroad that Mussolini wished to obtain Corfu as a naval base and had used the massacre as a pretext for something more than a temporary occupation. Mussolini's order for the evacuation was delayed on various pretexts and was given after considerable pressure from Great Britain. This was not known to most Italians, however, who saw the outcome as a complete and unalloyed victory for Mussolini. He had forced the League to withdraw; he had secured the transfer of the dispute to an arena of his choice; he had gained most of what he originally demanded. Above all, he had upheld Italy's national honor and had restored its prestige as a power to be reckoned with in international affairs.[47]

46. *New York Times*, Sept. 2, 1923.
47. For details of the Corfu case, see: Cassels, *Diplomacy*, pp. 91–126; Seton-Watson, *Italy*, pp. 670–73; and *New York Times*, Sept. 1–15, 1923.

During the same period, Mussolini also moved to settle the still unresolved issue of Fiume. Fiume had become the chief symbol in Italy of the "mutilated victory" and of injured national pride resulting from the Wilson–Orlando collision. In 1919, negotiations on the Adriatic settlement had been resumed but had been deadlocked again when, in September of that year, Fiume had been invaded and occupied by a group of Italian military volunteers led by Gabriele D'Annunzio, famed poet, war hero, and long a zealous Italian nationalist. This action had been wildly acclaimed in Italy, not only by nationalists and Fascists but by Italians of other political persuasions.

The government of the period had been helpless to act in the face of such overwhelming sentiment and D'Annunzio and his legionaries had remained in control of Fiume for the next sixteen months. The next government, headed by Giolitti, had been concerned to normalize relations with Yugoslavia as part of its policy of counteracting French influence in the Balkans and Central Europe. It had therefore come to an agreement with Yugoslavia, whose general terms provided for the renunciation of Italy's claim to Dalmatia and for Fiume to become an autonomous state with Italian access to it through a thin strip of coast.

After this agreement had been ratified in Italy, there became public a secret protocol to it, by which Sforza, the Italian foreign minister, had promised Yugoslavia sovereignty over a small part of Fiume. This revelation had stirred up a storm of criticism to the effect that Italian interests had been "renounced" and the "Italian character" of Fiume had been compromised. The Giolitti government had been forced to resign. By the time of Mussolini's March on Rome, the agreements that were to have implemented the original agreement had still not been submitted to the Italian parliament.

Mussolini began with what has been termed "a pacific act of foreign policy . . . covered by bluster for domestic consumption,"[48] supporting the treaty with apparent reluctance and securing ratification of the implementation agreements. In March 1923, a mixed Italo-Yugoslav commission began working out the details of the frontier and of the administration of Fiume. Difficulties soon arose and by July there was a

48. Dennison I. Rusinow, *Italy's Austrian Heritage, 1919–1946* (Oxford: Oxford University Press, 1969), p. 187. Rusinow notes that while the Italian Foreign Office was working toward a friendly alliance with Yugoslavia, Mussolini and one of his cabinet members were assuring the public that Dalmatia would not be forgotten.

deadlock. Mussolini tacitly suggested to Belgrade that the Fiume Free State be dropped in favor of Italian annexation in return for some further Italian concessions. But the concessions asked for by the Yugoslav government turned out to be ones that Mussolini was not prepared to grant. Yugoslavia then suggested that the differences be submitted to arbitration, as had been provided for by the agreements, but Mussolini objected to this.

On August 8, Mussolini gave the mixed commission a two-week ultimatum, threatening a new course of action if the commission could not reach an agreement preserving the "historic and present Italian character" of Fiume.[49] On August 24 he extended the deadline another two weeks. As it drew near, he and his foreign ministry quietly engineered the resignation of the Italian provisional governor of Fiume; he even participated in the drafting of the latter's letter of resignation. These facts were not of course known at the time. What was public was that the governor's letter of resignation stressed the dangerous economic and security situation of Fiume and requested Italian rescue.

While the crisis over Corfu was still occupying international attention, Mussolini on September 16 sent General Giardino to take over Fiume as military governor, ostensibly to restore order. Tension prevailed for several days thereafter. There was fear that this barely disguised annexation might provoke war, especially if Yugoslavia were to join with Greece.

The independence of Fiume, however, appeared to be less important to the government of Yugoslavia, including King Alexander, than securing Italian friendship. The resumption of negotiations between the two governments led in January 1924 to the signing of the Treaty of Rome, to which was added a five-year friendship pact between Italy and Yugoslavia. Fiume was then officially incorporated into Italy.[50]

Thus Mussolini had succeeded where preceding governments had failed. Some had insisted upon Fiume at the cost of continued antagonism with Yugoslavia; others had improved relations with Yugoslavia at the cost of Fiume. Mussolini had obtained the seemingly impossible: both Fiume and alliance with Yugoslavia.

49. Cassels, *Diplomacy*, p. 129.

50. Seton-Watson, *Italy*, pp. 539–47, 577–82, 590–91, 673–76; Cassels, *Diplomacy*, pp. 80–85, 127–45; Rusinow, *Austrian Heritage*, pp. 126–60, 185–89.

The contrast between Mussolini's successes in foreign affairs and the failures of his predecessors was enhanced by his having moved decisively and rapidly on two fronts almost simultaneously. But it was not only the vigor that Mussolini displayed in defense of what Italians felt to be righteous causes that contributed to their perceptions of him as heroic. He also appeared to have shown exceptional boldness in the face of unusual risk.

Mussolini was not seen as having challenged merely smaller and weaker powers than Italy. For behind Greece and Yugoslavia were seen the supportive shadows of Great Britain and France, respectively. Recent history had been replete with examples of powerful countries entering wars to aid smaller allies. The average Italian most likely had not known, as had Mussolini, that France for her own reasons had tacitly supported Mussolini's stand on the League and that the Yugoslavian government had recently ceased to regard Fiume as vital.

Therefore, Mussolini was also seen as having dared to challenge indirectly two of Europe's mightiest powers. In so doing and in succeeding, he had not only redeemed Italy's national honor. In Italian eyes, he had also made Italy a power to be respected and even feared in the international arena.

Roosevelt as Savior from Fear and Want

As indicated earlier in this chapter, the creation of the image of extraordinary heroism does not depend exclusively upon situations involving challenge of or confrontation with human opponents or groups of opponents such as nation-states. An outstanding feat can include delivering people from natural or social disasters or averting impending crises and dangers. Those who perform outstanding feats of this kind, feats in the category of rescue, are frequently referred to as saviors. As is described in the case of Roosevelt, the elements that contribute to making a feat of rescue appear outstanding or miraculous are largely the same as those specified earlier, except that in social, as distinct from natural, disasters, the elements of confrontation and risk are generally not present.

When Franklin Delano Roosevelt was inaugurated as thirty-second president of the United States on March 4, 1933, the state of the nation was harrowing, materially and in the mood of the people. Three years of economic depression had produced widespread joblessness, hunger, apathy, and despair. Moreover, there was panic in the air. More and more banks were closing, and it looked as if the country's banking system and the entire economy would imminently collapse.

There did not seem much to hope for from the incoming president, beyond an impressive smile and a warmly resonant voice, for he "was widely regarded as something of a goodnatured playboy"[51] and was viewed by some political observers as immature in the way he seemed to face the problems before him.[52] Moreover, from the perspective of the millions suffering from the Great Depression, it was probably too much to expect more than token sympathy from someone who belonged to the most privileged social and economic stratum in the country.

For many, hope had drained away as conditions had steadily worsened in the three years from the onset of the depression. In those years, unemployment had practically quintupled. A census of April 1930 had shown more than 3 million unemployed; the figure had doubled by the beginning of the following year; at the end of 1931 it had been more than 10 million; and by March 1933, roughly 15 million, or one-third of those eligible to work, had been unable to find employment.[53]

That many of those still employed were not in comfortable circumstances can be inferred from a few statistics. Total national income had fallen from more than $87 billion in 1929 to about $41 billion in 1932. During this period, wage payments had dropped by 60 percent and salary payments by 40 percent. In the iron and steel industry, for example, wages averaged 63 percent less at the end of 1932 than they had in 1929. Although many industries had complied with President Hoover's request not to cut pay rates, they had reduced the number of working hours and days for their employees, which of course had had the same effect as pay cuts. Others did not maintain rates, and there were numerous instances in 1932 of people receiving less than half the salary or

51. Thomas A. Bailey, *Presidential Greatness* (New York: Appleton-Century, 1966), p. 102.

52. William E. Leuchtenburg, *Franklin D. Roosevelt and the New Deal* (New York: Harper Colophon, 1963), p. 32.

53. Dixon Wecter, *The Age of the Great Depression: 1929–1941* (New York: Macmillan, 1948), pp. 16–40; Leuchtenburg, *Roosevelt*, p. 19.

wages that they had received for the same job several years earlier. There were cases of women receiving 10 and 25 cents an hour.[54]

Unemployment, underemployment, and diminished incomes were only part of the dismal effects of the depression. In those three years, about 85,000 businesses and about 5,000 banks had failed, the latter destroying in their fall 9 million savings accounts. In 1932, 273,000 mortgaged homes had been foreclosed and in early 1933 home mortgage foreclosures were at the rate of 1,000 daily.[55]

Living conditions for many were at the point of bare survival. For example, statistics in October 1932 indicated that one-fifth of the children in New York City public schools were ill with malnutrition. Diagnoses of malnutrition among patients of a Philadelphia community health center had risen 60 percent between 1928 and 1932. Despite municipal soup kitchens and free distribution of bread in many cities, there were numerous cases of people eating garbage and fighting over garbage in city dumps. In many communities there were children who could not attend school for want of clothing. In some places, families evicted from their homes lived in tents in the middle of winter. Others lived without heat or light. Throughout the country, well over a million jobless men rode the rails and roamed the roads, hobo style, in search of jobs. They lived in "hobo jungles" of shacks made of tin cans, barrel staves, or boxes, or in abandoned freight cars or factories.[56]

To these victims of the depression, to those on the brink of becoming victims, and to others who foresaw and feared a similar fate, President Hoover had appeared unfeeling, unable to cope, and unable to offer plausible hope of improvement or alleviation. Hoover had not attempted to mobilize the resources of the federal government in the first few years of the depression, for he did not believe in federal intervention except as a last resort. Initially, Hoover had hoped that business would be able to pull itself out of the slump and had held numbers of conferences with business and financial leaders. For the first two years of the depression, his efforts to deal with the problems of unemployment and relief had

54. Wecter, *Great Depression*, pp. 17–18; Schlesinger, *Roosevelt*, 1, pp. 248–49.
55. Wecter, *Great Depression*, pp. 17, 49.
56. Schlesinger, *Roosevelt*, 2, p. 3; Wecter, *Great Depression*, pp. 38–40; Leuchtenburg, *Roosevelt*, pp. 43–47.

consisted largely of encouraging private and voluntary organizations and then local communities to undertake the task of assisting those needing help in their areas. It was not until the middle of 1932, when it was clear that many municipalities and state governments were out of funds or close to that state, that President Hoover had supported the passage of a relief bill and had empowered the recently created Reconstruction Finance Corporation to lend money from the national treasury.[57]

That Hoover had not been able to cope with increasing economic failure or to relieve growing distress may well have contributed to the sense of despair of many Americans. For he had been known as the "great engineer," respected for the prodigious feats he had performed in providing relief for Europeans on the brink of starvation as a result of World War I. To those who may have seen the situations as parallel (which they were not, of course, in the absence of an outside source of aid and funding in the 1930s), Hoover's failure may have suggested the uselessness of any hope.

For some, anger and violence, rather than hopelessness and apathy, had been the response. In 1930 there had been demonstrations of the unemployed in Chicago, Los Angeles, and Seattle; by 1932 there were hunger marches in many parts of the country. Farmers, especially in the Midwest, had used force to stop mortgage foreclosures and to halt deliveries of produce in protest against the low farm commodity prices. In various parts of the country there had been sporadic seizures of public buildings, break-ins and looting of factory buildings, and seizures of food from stores. Leaders of labor and farm groups had testified in Congress about their fear of revolution. In January 1933 the head of the Farm Bureau Federation had predicted to a Senate committee that a revolution would take place in the countryside within a year if the situation of farmers did not improve.[58]

Between Roosevelt's election in November 1932 and his inauguration four months later, three further developments had helped to create an ominous backdrop to his entry into the presidency. A lame-duck Congress had met in these months but had come up with no significant economic measures. Bank failures had begun to accelerate at an alarm-

---

57. Wecter, *Great Depression*, pp. 43–47.
58. Schlesinger, *Roosevelt*, 2, p. 3; Leuchtenberg, *Roosevelt*, pp. 23–26.

ing rate, especially in the western states. Rumors of possible failures had caused people to rush to banks to withdraw savings, which precipitated the very failures they had feared as bank reserves had been unable to meet demands. By the middle of February it had begun to appear that a fatal crisis of the economy was at hand. One after another, governors of states had felt compelled to suspend temporarily all banking operations in desperate attempts to stave off the complete collapse of banks. By inauguration day, banks were closed in thirty-eight states and panic was endemic.

The third factor that had contributed during those months to the growing suspense over the survival of the economy was Roosevelt's low profile. Roosevelt had ignored the many pressures upon him to reveal his plans or give some indication of the directions of his future policies. He had not even made his cabinet appointments known until shortly before inauguration. Moreover, he had declined urgent requests from outgoing President Hoover to join with the latter in making or approving some economic decisions and statements.[59]

Thus, on the day of Roosevelt's inauguration, the economic state of the country seemed as dire as anyone could imagine, and the emotional state of the country ranged from despair and apathy on the part of the long unemployed to apprehension and panic on the part of bankers and businessmen. What would the new president do? What could he do? What could anyone do?

The first thing the new president did was to deliver an inaugural address that struck the notes of assurance and determination. In now famous phrases he told the country that "the only thing we have to fear is fear itself" and promised that, if necessary, he would ask for power "to wage a war against the emergency" equivalent to wartime powers. As is elaborated in the next chapter, Roosevelt's rhetoric in this address, with its religious and martial imagery, could be felt as constituting a call to a crusade.[60] The spirit and tone of the speech were applauded by members of Congress and in editorials of major newspapers around the country as reflecting courage, confidence, and optimism.[61]

---

59. Tugwell, *Roosevelt*, pp. 254–62; Burns, *Roosevelt*, pp. 147–48.

60. Leuchtenberg, *Roosevelt*, p. 42, observes that the message of the most frequently repeated sentence, that on fear, had been stated by Hoover also.

61. Extracts from editorials around the country are contained in the *New York Times*, Mar. 5, 1933.

On the day following the inauguration there began a hectic and an almost uninterrupted round of executive and congressional action that did indeed resemble wartime mobilization and that has since come to be known as the "Hundred Days." Roosevelt, on that day, a Sunday, called a special session of Congress for Thursday, March 9. He also proclaimed a national bank holiday to allow the banks to surmount the crisis. On Monday he issued an order prohibiting the export of gold. When Congress met on March 9, it received the president's message on banking and on the same day passed an emergency banking act giving the president new powers over money and banking. The next day there were another presidential message on the economy and a request for additional executive powers. This measure was also rapidly passed.

Within a week after Roosevelt's inauguration the environment in Washington had changed drastically. Moreover, news about this change was being spread throughout the country and was lifting the spirits of people. Newspaper correspondents seemed hard put to find words with which to communicate their sense of the transformation. Arthur Krock, the *New York Times* Washington correspondent, described the sensation as "like that which a person . . . would experience when he changes from an oxcart to an . . . airplane."[62]

On March 12, Roosevelt gave the first of his "fireside chats" over nationwide radio. He talked about the banking crisis in simple terms and explained the purpose of the bank holiday. He promised that banks would begin to reopen on the following day and asked his listeners for confidence and courage.

The impact of Roosevelt's words was seen the following day when people entered the reopened banks, many to redeposit money they had earlier withdrawn. In fact, in most cities the total amounts deposited were considerably greater than those withdrawn.[63] Another indicator of his impact was the fact that within twelve days from Roosevelt's inauguration, the White House was inundated with more than 14,000 telegrams of praise for his actions.[64]

During the next three months an impressive volume of legislation

62. *New York Times*, Mar. 12, 1933.
63. Leuchtenburg, *Roosevelt*, pp. 44–45; *New York Times*, Mar. 14, 1933.
64. *New York Times*, Mar. 17, 1933.

would be requested by Roosevelt and passed by Congress, including: an agricultural adjustment act to aid farmers, a civilian conservation corps measure to create jobs for young men, an emergency relief bill to supply funds for direct relief to states and municipalities, acts reforming banking and the securities market, an act setting up a federal employment program, measures to save home mortgages, an act creating the Tennessee Valley Authority, and others.[65]

With the exception of an initial spurt in employment, the major economic effects of these measures and other legislation that would comprise the New Deal would not be felt for several years. But the initial psychological impact was immense. The feeling of action was bracing and revivifying.

Gandhi and the Conquest of Self and Other

In 1931 Winston Churchill expressed his revulsion at "the nauseating and humiliating spectacle of this one-time Inner Temple lawyer, now seditious fakir, striding half-naked up the steps of the Viceroy's palace, there to negotiate and to parley on equal terms with the representative of the King Emperor."[66]

The spectacle so revolting to Churchill was that of Mohandas K. Gandhi negotiating with Lord Irwin, the British viceroy of India. Churchill may have perceived it as he did because he recognized that it signified the beginning of what he would refuse to preside over a decade and a half later—the liquidation of the British Empire. The standard pattern of the colonizer dictating terms to or enforcing them upon the colonized had been ruptured. The representative of the world's greatest colonial power was instead negotiating terms with the leader of the colonized in its largest colony. In the eyes of his Indian followers, of other Indians, and of much of the world, Gandhi had accomplished a most remarkable feat. The terms of the so-called Delhi Pact that concluded the talks mattered less to many than the fact that such negotiations could take place.

65. For details of the early New Deal legislation, see: Burns, *Roosevelt*, pp. 166–71; Leuchtenburg, *Roosevelt*, pp. 48–62; and Wecter, *Great Depression*, pp. 61–80.
66. Fischer, *Gandhi*, p. 281; Penderel Moon, *Gandhi and Modern India* (New York: Norton, 1969), p. 165.

The negotiations were the outcome of what had been to date Gandhi's most highly publicized confrontation, the so-called Salt March of 1930 and the months' long civil disobedience campaign that followed it. This feat will be recounted here, in addition to Gandhi's initial one, many years earlier, because it illustrates several aspects of the possible contributions of political achievements to charisma that were not dealt with in the preceding examples.

Gandhi differed from the other charismatic political leaders dealt with here in several ways. He did not hold public office, thus achieving what Rustow has termed "powerful results in the absence of power."[67] Secondly, Gandhi involved his followers in his exploits directly and not merely vicariously, and the type and degree of their involvement had consequences for the generation and diffusion of his charisma. Finally, Gandhi developed a new and potent political weapon that not only augmented the dramatic elements of confrontation with an opponent but also contained within itself features conducive to the generation of charisma.

Although all these factors were present to a limited degree in Gandhi's first campaign as a political leader in South Africa, they were most fully developed in the 1930 campaign. Moreover, the latter illustrates the frequently cumulative and sometimes spiraling aspect of political charisma, for by 1930 Gandhi had already gained widespread charismatic recognition in India. That charisma probably contributed to some of the success of the campaign that in turn further spread and expanded his charisma.

Gandhi's initial campaign began in 1906, when the government of Transvaal, South Africa, drafted an ordinance requiring all Indians, including women and children, to register, be fingerprinted, and carry certificates at all times under penalty of fines, imprisonment, or deportation. For about a decade preceding that year, Gandhi had worked in South Africa as an attorney countering racial discrimination against Indians. Until then he had mainly utilized the courts, petitions, persuasion, and publicity. However, Gandhi saw this ordinance as having such dire implications that, at a mass meeting in Johannesburg on September

---

67. Dankwart A. Rustow, "Ataturk as Founder of a State," in *Philosophers and Kings: Studies in Leadership*, ed. Dankwart A. Rustow (New York: George Braziller, 1970), p. 209.

11, 1906, he sponsored a resolution that Indians refuse to obey this ordinance. One of the others present suggested that they take an oath to do so and 3,000 Indians unanimously swore to defy the ordinance, should it become law.[68]

When the Asiatic Law Amendment Ordinance was passed, Gandhi first went to England to try to obtain a royal veto. A promise he received from the Colonial Secretary that it would not be approved turned out to be misleading. For within a few months the Transvaal ceased to be a British crown colony; the ordinance was reenacted in March 1907 and all Indians were required to register by July.

This was the start of *satyagraha*, a novel concept in the history of political protest and confrontation. Even without this, a Gandhi-led campaign would have had the flavor of a classic confrontation in the David-and-Goliath mold. For a small and weak-looking man defied a powerful antagonist; the situation of challenge involved risks and reprisals; and when, as did Gandhi, the challenger acted as champion of oppressed people in order to remedy injustices against them, the aura of heroism was strengthened by the nature of the cause.

Satyagraha, or "truth force," as Gandhi called it, added several elements to this image. Although it was rooted in a traditional Indian concept of *ahimsa*, or nonviolence, it was something more than mere passive resistance. Gandhi conceived *satyagraha* as a set of principles or a mode of rectifying or overcoming a wrong or an evil situation by finding and holding to the truth and by refusing to submit to the wrong or evil firmly but without violence. If one is subjected to violence by the wrongdoers, one endures stoically, refraining from offering violence to them. Self-control, calmness, and, if necessary, self-suffering in the face of provocation is the stance of the *satyagrahi* and, hopefully, they will convert the wrongdoer.[69]

However idealistic and absurd it might have appeared to many to expect to oppose coercion with nonviolent resistance and convert the coercer, a peculiar logic or rather psycho-logic underlay this technique. Nonviolent resistance on the part of one protagonist confronts the other

---

68. Ashe, *Gandhi*, pp. 96–99; Fischer, *Gandhi*, pp. 81–83.
69. Joan V. Bondurant, *Conquest of Violence: The Gandhian Philosophy of Conflict* (Princeton: Princeton University Press, 1958), pp. 15–35; Ashe, *Gandhi*, pp. 100–01.

with the choice of either conceding or of escalating the latter's own violence. Depending upon the contexts and the value systems of those involved, the intensification of violence against nonresisters can have its drawbacks. It can lead to feelings of discomfort, guilt, and even self-loathing by those applying and intensifying violence.[70] Moreover, in the eyes of observers it can seem to be unjustifiable and indefensible cruelty.

Apart from the elements of drama mentioned as inherent in an unequal David-and-Goliath confrontation, a *satyagraha* campaign had its own dramatic element in addition. While stoically submitting to punishment may have initially seemed "unnatural," especially to the British and the martial subcultures of India, it came to be seen as unnaturally heroic, requiring as it did the exercise of extreme determination, self-control, and will power. To the usual suspense concerning the outcome of a struggle, there was added the suspense over the length of time and the degree to which *satyagrahis* could endure provocation and avoid the temptation to strike back or flee.

The suspense and drama that characterized the later campaigns were hardly present in the early stage of the South African campaign. This was actually a series of campaigns on several issues that lasted about seven years and that involved periods of relative quiescence as well as of mass organized activity. The first began immediately after the passing of the registration ordinance in 1907. A Satyagraha Association was formed and Gandhi gave directives to its members and others in the pages of *Indian Opinion*, a publication he had begun in 1903 and for which he regularly wrote. The first action involved volunteers picketing the government registration office in order to dissuade the Indians who did appear at them not to register.

By the final day for registration, only a few hundred had complied and thousands had not. The government extended the final date but with little result. Then a series of arrests began and by the end of the year, Gandhi and several hundred other resisters were in prison.[71] General Jan

70. Guilt and self-loathing may or may not exist, depending upon the values of specific groups and nations. Those who have argued for general adoption of nonviolent resistance tend to forget about Nazis and other groups, past and present, whose members neither shy away from nor appear to feel guilty about performing the most sadistic and violent acts against others.

71. Ashe, *Gandhi*, pp. 105–09; Fischer, *Gandhi*, p. 86.

Christian Smuts, the minister charged with enforcing the objectionable registration act, offered Gandhi a compromise, repeal in return for prior voluntary registration. Gandhi agreed, always willing initially to credit the good intentions of others, although some of his followers had urged that repeal precede registration. It happened as the latter had feared; for after voluntary registration, led by Gandhi, Smuts failed to live up to his part of the agreement.

Gandhi then sent an ultimatum to the government of the Transvaal demanding repeal of the act by a given date. He warned that if this were not done by then, the certificates of Indians who had registered would be burned. On August 16, 1908, on the grounds of a mosque in Johannesburg, there was a ceremonial burning of thousands of registration certificates in a huge caldron. This gained attention beyond South Africa, as illustrated by a London newspaper's comparing it to the Boston Tea Party.[72]

This second phase of the campaign included another target, a bill restricting Indian immigration into Transvaal. To test and protest this, Indian volunteers in the adjoining state of Natal entered Transvaal and were then imprisoned. Others already there courted arrest by making clear their lack of registration certificates. At the end of the year Gandhi was also imprisoned. During one period of this campaign, about 2,500 of the 13,000 Transvaal Indians were in prison; many were assigned hard labor and Gandhi himself was also occasionally in solitary confinement.[73]

The act was finally repealed in 1912, partly as the result of a visit by Gopal Krishna Gokhale, a leader of the Indian nationalist movement, who negotiated with Generals Smuts and Louis Botha, who headed what had then become the Union of South Africa. Moreover, Gokhale also received assurances of the repeal of the ban on Asiatic immigration and of an annual tax levied on Indians who had been indentured laborers.

These assurances were not honored, partly because of pressure from the Europeans of Natal. Moreover, the Supreme Court in Cape Colony ruled on March 14, 1913, that only Christian marriages were valid. This

---

72. Fischer, *Gandhi*, p. 90.
73. Details of this part of the campaign can be found in Ashe, *Gandhi*, pp. 114–17, and Fischer, *Gandhi*, pp. 87–93.

made Hindu, Moslem, and Parsi wives legally concubines, subject to deportation, and rendered their children illegitimate. Thus, the final phase of the campaign began not only against three discriminatory acts but with an additional group of volunteers—outraged Indian women.

Gandhi demanded of Smuts immediate implementation of the promise concerning the tax, indicating that otherwise he would urge nonpayment and advise indentured workers to strike. There was no answer and a group of women from the Transvaal went to the coal fields of Natal and successfully urged the workers there to go out on strike. Meanwhile, other women from Natal entered the Transvaal. Both groups of women were arrested and the strike spread.

After the mining company cut off the light and water in the miners' homes, Gandhi organized a march of the miners into Transvaal. More than 2,000 participated. Gandhi was arrested and released on bail several times and then imprisoned. Others were arrested and sentenced to hard labor. The striking miners were sent back to the mines, which were enclosed with wire and surrounded by military police. In spite of whips and other forms of coercion, they refused to return to work. Moreover, thousands of other miners stopped work in sympathy and thousands more indentured laborers joined them.

Concern in India and England was reflected in considerable pressure on the government of South Africa. Gandhi was freed in December 1913 and a commission was appointed to investigate Indian grievances. In January, Gandhi, unhappy with the composition of the commission, announced plans for another march. However, white railroad workers went out on strike and Gandhi canceled the march, stating that it was not part of *satyagraha* to take advantage of an opponent's sudden weakness from another quarter.

This announcement drew praise from abroad and in South Africa. It may also have been one of the factors inducing General Smuts to enter into serious negotiations with Gandhi. Although the negotiations in June 1914 did not remove all the disabilities of Indians in South Africa, they resulted in a victory for Gandhi on all the issues that had given rise to the campaigns.[74]

This feat was widely publicized in India, and Gandhi's reputation

74. Ashe, *Gandhi*, pp. 121–25; Fischer, *Gandhi*, pp. 116–24.

preceded his return. His early campaigns to rectify wrongs in his home-
land, such as the campaign in Champeran in 1917 and that in Ahmedabad the following year, were conducted largely by himself with at most a
few followers. Beginning in 1919 he planned and undertook large-scale
satyagraha campaigns. However, he suspended one after it had begun
and canceled another because of incidents of violence by Indians.

By 1920 Gandhi gained fairly widespread charismatic recognition in
India. Judith Brown's study of Gandhi's rise to power notes 1921–22 as
the years when records from widely dispersed locations revealed popular
perceptions of him as in some way divine.[75] It was also in the 1920s that
Gandhi became paramount leader of the Indian nationalist movement
and that he first was imprisoned in India.

By the end of that decade, the objective of the Indian National Congress was independence or, at minimum, clear transition to dominion
status. A Labor government in England and the viceroy in India, Lord
Irwin, had indicated some possibility of the latter but had then withdrawn it under Conservative and Liberal opposition. In December 1929,
Congress voted for *purna swaraj*, complete independence, and for a
campaign of civil disobedience whose form and timing would be decided by Gandhi.[76]

Gandhi devoted considerable thought to the shape of the campaign
and on March 2 sent a long letter to Viceroy Irwin, outlining the ineq-
uities of British rule for Indians and proposing a "real conference between equals."[77] If Irwin would not begin to deal with these evils, he
promised, he would break the salt laws with a group of fellow workers
from his ashram.

While Gandhi's biographer who called the selection of salt "the weird-
est and most brilliant political challenge of modern times"[78] may have
been overstating the case, there is no doubt that salt was a most felicitous
symbol with which to dramatize colonial exploitation. For salt is a
necessity. In many areas of India it had been a gift of nature, provided by

75. Judith M. Brown, *Gandhi's Rise to Power: Indian Politics, 1915–1922* (London: Cambridge University Press, 1972), p. 346.

76. Ashe, *Gandhi*, pp. 279–82; Fischer, *Gandhi*, pp. 261–67.

77. Mohandas K. Gandhi, *Collected Works of Mahatma Gandhi* (Delhi: Publications Division, Ministry of Information and Broadcasting, Government of India, 1971), 18, p. 7.

78. Ashe, *Gandhi*, p. 284.

the sea and by natural deposits and needing but a little labor for the poor peasant to obtain it. But now the only legal salt in India was government monopoly salt and even though the tax on it was not high, it was onerous enough for the poor.

With the publication of Gandhi's letter to Irwin, excitement and suspense began to grow in India and beyond. Although Gandhi did not write or publicize this letter for suspense—it was part of his practice to notify in advance those against whom a campaign was directed—widespread attention began to focus on his ashram at Sabarmati as reporters and photographers from international as well as national media converged there.

Irwin's—or rather his secretary's—reply arrived to the effect that the viceroy regretted Gandhi's contemplation of action that would violate the law and would be a danger to the public peace. Suspense increased with speculation as to whether Gandhi and his group would be able to begin the projected march. There were persistent rumors of his imminent arrest and thousands of people reportedly converged on the ashram.[79]

Although there had been numerous volunteers for the march, Gandhi chose only those who had been trained in *satyagrahi* discipline at the ashram. Numbering seventy-nine men and women and including some untouchables, Moslems, and a Christian, the group set out on March 12, 1930. Their destination was Dandi, 241 miles south on the coast. They reached it on April 5, twenty-four days later.[80]

Gandhi, at 61, was the oldest person in the group, yet some could not keep up with him on foot and took to bullock carts. During the rest periods, Gandhi kept active, spinning, giving lectures, and working on his correspondence. He addressed villagers in some of the villages they passed, on May 1 urging an audience of 80,000 at Surat to take part in the struggle and break the salt monopoly. Many village headmen resigned their posts as Gandhi passed. He was always followed by crowds as inhabitants of one community escorted him en masse to the next one. Media people recorded the progress.[81]

79. *Indian Social Reformer* 40 (Mar. 15–20, 1930), 458.
80. D. G. Tendulkar, *Mahatma: Life of Mohandas Karamchand Gandhi* (Bombay, 1962), 3, pp. 20–31.
81. Ibid.; Ashe, *Gandhi*, p. 386; Fischer, *Gandhi*, p. 273.

By the time Gandhi reached Dandi, his group was accompanied by thousands of people. On April 6 he waded into the sea and returned with some salt. He then urged Indians everywhere to make their own salt.

They did. Much of India became an illegal salt factory as villagers along the coasts went into the sea with pans and peasants dug in natural deposits and others sold salt in the cities. The wave of illegal salt-making and salt-selling was countered by a wave of arrests, as police arrested fishermen and peasants making salt, Congress volunteers selling it, and leaders of the nationalist movement such as Jawaharlal Nehru and Rajendra Prasad. Local officials who were ordered to stamp out the illegal industry resigned and the salt campaign spread from province to province. Those arrested did not resist, following Gandhi's strictures, but many were roughly handled and beaten nonetheless.

Salt was not the only target of protest. There were boycotts of liquor shops and shops selling foreign cloth, and those picketing these shops were largely women. Civil disobedience was manifested in many ways. When the government tried to censor nationalist publications, for example, they simply stopped publication rather than conform. In some areas, peasants refused to pay the land tax.

A month after Dandi, there were an estimated 60,000 noncooperators in prison. On May 5 Gandhi joined them and his arrest precipitated widespread protest strikes. In Bombay alone, 50,000 textile workers struck, to be joined by the railway workers. In Sholapur the inhabitants took control of the town under the nationalist flag. They established and maintained briefly their own administration until martial law was declared and many of them were shot.

The salt campaign continued, expanded to include raids on government salt depots. A huge one near Bombay involved 15,000 volunteers and spectators. In another large one, 10,000 raiders seized considerable amounts of salt "under the shower of lathis and bullets."[82] The most widely publicized raid was that on the Dharsana salt works on May 21. It was observed and described in detail by Wade Miller, a United Press correspondent, whose dispatch appeared in newspapers throughout the world.

Before his arrest Gandhi had notified the viceroy of his intention to

---

82. Tendulkar, *Mahatma*, 3, p. 41.

lead a group into Dharsana and occupy it. Instead, two of his close followers, one a woman poet, led 2,500 *satyagrahis* to the site, reminding them that Gandhi was with them in spirit and that they must not resist or ward off blows even if they were beaten. They were, many on the head by police with steel-tipped lathis. As one column advanced and fell bleeding under the blows, another took its place. None sought to protect himself. Later some sat down and were kicked in the abdomen or testicles by the police. Miller, who counted more than 300 injured and several dead within the first few hours, wrote that in all his reporting of riots and rebellions in 18 years and 20 countries, he had not seen "such harrowing scenes."[83] The scenes were repeated for several days.

For most of the rest of the year civil disobedience continued and spread. The boycott of foreign cloth, liquor, and all British goods was intensified and immensely effective. There were repeated violations of the salt law, nonpayment of taxes, and boycotts of British banks, insurance companies, and other businesses. There were government countermeasures, police violence, and more and more arrests.[84]

David Low, the British cartoonist, in reaction to a remark of Lord Lothian to the effect that Indians wanted to know where they were, drew a cartoon of a prison with Indians crowded inside.[85] It seemed clear that much of India that was not imprisoned was in active, unarmed revolt. Repressive measures that were taken by the government resulted only in increased defiance. Further repressive measures could not easily be considered, for world opinion was already critical, as was a segment of opinion in England. Lord Irwin finally agreed to the suggestion in Gandhi's initial letter to have a conference between equals.

The campaign was an extraordinary feat in several respects. As was indicated earlier, the aspect that impressed so many was that a small Indian attorney had forced the representative of the mightiest empire on earth to parley with him on equal terms. An aspect, not too often noted, was that Gandhi inspired thousands of middle- and upper-class Indian women, hitherto mainly confined to their homes, to enter the public arena. Not only did they enter the public arena in entirely novel roles, as

83. Ibid.
84. For details, see ibid., pp. 39–49.
85. Ashe, *Gandhi*, p. 293.

pickets, for example, but under his influence they and the men willingly endured provocation and suffering.

Perhaps the greatest tribute to Gandhi's extraordinary influence was the fact that this campaign, in which hundreds of thousands of Indians participated, was so free of violence on their part in the face of countless temptations to return violence with violence. As is observed by a not particularly sympathetic biographer, "throughout most of the country Englishmen went about their ordinary avocations without fear of assault or molestation."[86] This was not only a sign of his charismatic hold on his followers but it undoubtedly was a basis for intensification and further diffusion of his charisma. For among those who held to Gandhi's strictures on nonviolence were members of martial groups such as Sikhs and Pathans. The individual who can induce others to overcome and override a lifetime of training and habit can indeed be seen to possess an awesome power.

86. Moon, *Gandhi*, p. 158.

6
Charismatic Legitimation: The Prodigies of Person

The two preceding chapters deal with two dimensions of the process of charismatic legitimation—association with and assimilation to myth and the performance of seemingly impossible feats. This chapter is concerned with a third dimension—the personal attributes or perceived personal qualities of a leader that cause him to be seen as superhuman, far above the domain of the usual and even beyond the bounds of the rare and exceptional.

As the first chapter of this study specifies, perceptions of a leader as extraordinary or somehow supernatural constitute one of the defining characteristics of the existence of a charismatic relationship. The next chapter mentions some of the qualities traditionally held to be supernatural that have been attributed to some leaders, such as ability to foretell the future, to read minds, to heal or harm by will alone, and to be invulnerable. In this chapter, for several reasons, I focus only on some of the likely sources of such perceptions. The sources are hard to pinpoint, just as it is difficult to pinpoint precisely the acts or statements that form the foundations for rumors. Secondly, I believe, although I cannot provide support for the belief beyond my own observations in the case of Sukarno, that many charismatically oriented followers do not form their beliefs about specific supernatural attributes of their leaders from anything necessarily directly related to those attributes. Rather, they develop a generalized or an undifferentiated notion of the extraordinary power or capability of their leader. In expressing this conviction, they are likely to project it upon or illustrate it by reference to a talent that has traditionally or conventionally been considered supernatural.

This is not to deny that some of the beliefs in "magical" attributes are derived from direct experience or only several degrees removed from it. Sukarno's opponent referred to in chapter 2 who had felt himself to be hypnotized by Sukarno had undergone the experience. He had described it to countless others, I am certain, before I heard it. Each of them had undoubtedly communicated it to still others. By contrast, those who expressed to me their belief in Sukarno's powers of prediction could not tie it to specific sources or incidents; some, when pressed, gave the instance of Sukarno's predictions in his publications at the end of the 1920s of the rise of Japan and a war in the Pacific. It can be argued that although Sukarno showed the acute foresight of a good political analyst, this type of prediction does not evince supernatural powers. It appeared to me that my informants, most of them intellectuals, did believe that Sukarno possessed *sekti* (the Indonesian, Sanskrit-derived term for magical or supernatural power); possessing it in general, he must therefore have had the specific superhuman skills that have traditionally manifested its existence in someone.

I am suggesting that charismatic legitimation through belief in the special personal endowment of a leader may come about through transformation, in the mind of the believer, of one element of belief or object of belief into another. An initial belief in the generalized supernatural capacity of a leader, however derived, may become transformed into a conviction of his possession of a very specific supernatural skill. Conversely, a belief in a specific transcendent quality of a leader, possibly derived from direct exposure to or indirect knowledge of its exercise, may be extended to belief in the leader's general omnipotence. From this belief there may in turn be further derived a specific belief in another transcendent or supernatural qualification.

Thus, these processes of transformation and extension help to explain how political leaders who have become associated with mythical or historic heroes or who have performed outstanding feats or miracles can also be credited with personal powers that they do not possess and that have not been manifested in any way. The modes of charismatic legitimation described in the preceding chapters can have a spillover effect.

Perceptions of the superhuman endowments of political leaders can arise independently of the spillover effect and also independently of actions and achievements in the political domain. A leader may be seen by those around him to exhibit some quality or perhaps several to a degree far beyond that considered "normal" among men. The quality itself may be shared by hundreds or millions of individuals; the exceedingly large measure of it in the person of the leader sets him apart as especially endowed. As will be described below, a number of the charismatic leaders dealt with here, as well as others who were probably charismatic, shared certain characteristics, such as supreme self-confidence and exceedingly high energy. One can argue that self-confidence and high energy are attributes of most successful politicians. However, the prodigious amount of these qualities displayed by these men made them awesome to observers and to those who heard or read the accounts of observers.

A leader may be seen to possess to an unusual degree a capacity or talent or propensity that has been traditionally associated in a culture with supernatural, divine, or demonic power or with its acquisition. This is described below with respect to Sukarno. A combination of qualities, a syndrome of attributes and actions, or a style of life that closely accords with cultural notions of the ideal person can also give rise to beliefs in a leader as being more than human. For the ideal is practically unattainable and he who seems to attain it must be more than human to have done so. This mode of personal legitimation is illustrated below by the case of Gandhi, perhaps its best exemplar in this century.

It may be assumed that beliefs in the outstanding powers of these leaders often begin with their disciples and others close to them and diffuse gradually outward. Even in countries in which newspapers and other media are well developed and most of the people literate, the stuff of which such beliefs are formed tends to be communicated less by formal media than by word of mouth. Especially when the leader is head of state or of a major movement, those who come to the capital to see him or those around him return to their homes in provinces and small towns with the news and stories about him they have picked up in the capital. From provincial towns these stories find their way to smaller towns and villages. Dissemination can also take place through insiders resident in the capital. Some Indonesian villagers I encountered "knew" about Sukarno's magic-laden sword from a market-seller who heard it from a wholesale merchant in the nearest big town who had it from his cousin who was a palace guard.

Sukarno and Sexuality

Sukarno's marital and extramarital sexual activities were seen as scandalous by many Westerners and caused considerable discomfort to Indonesians oriented to Western opinions and values. Few Indonesian men of the upper social stratum during his period availed themselves of the full complement of four wives permitted by Islamic law; Sukarno exceeded it when he took his fifth wife in the early 1960s. However, the number of wives was minuscule compared to the number of liaisons he was reputed to have had. Starting at least in the early 1950s, stories about Sukarno's sexual exploits became a staple of Jakarta gossip.

As I mentioned in chapter 4, these stories about Sukarno's sexual potency did not diminish his political potency but rather enhanced it. This might appear strange to those from Protestant and Puritan cultures of northern and western Europe and the United States, where sex and politics do not publicly mix. The extramarital sexual exploits of some highly placed political figures in Anglo-Saxon countries in recent years have endangered and even destroyed their careers. But the relationship between publicized sexual prowess and public life seems subject to substantial cultural variation. For example, students of Latin American culture have noted the importance of machismo, or the virility syndrome, as a Latin American male ideal and its connection with the dominant type of traditional leader, the *caudillo*.[1]

In Indonesia the perceived linkage between sexuality and *sekti*, or supernatural power, can be traced at least as far back as the East Javanese kingdoms of the thirteenth century. Chronicle histories, court poems, and legends dating from that period and later recount the ways by which rulers and aspirant rulers claimed to partake of the sacred or sought to obtain *sekti* or were seen to have acquired it. One mode by which supernatural power was held to be derived was through union

---

1. John Gillen, "Ethos Components in Modern Latin American Culture," *American Anthropologist* 57 (June 1955), 493.

with the sacred by marriage or sexual encounter. There are references to the nuptials of rulers with the superhuman forces of the cosmos—presumably symbolic rites that were sometimes consummated by actual sexual union with women, temple priestesses, or sacred virgins, standing in for the goddesses.[2] Although such practices were recounted mainly for rulers of the Hindu-Buddhist period of Java's history, they apparently did not entirely disappear with the decline of Hindu-Buddhism. The early kings of the nominally Muslim Mataram Dynasty are recorded in the second half of the sixteenth century as having rites to celebrate their marriage with the Ratu Lara Kidul, goddess of the southern sea.[3]

In Javanese tradition and in the traditions of other areas of Indonesia, the most conventional road to the accumulation of spiritual power is that of fasting, withdrawal, meditation, and abstinence. However, there also existed in Javanese tradition quite an opposite path to the pursuit of *sekti,* presumably less known and less practiced, if one were to judge from the references in the extant Javanese literature. This was the path of a Tantric Buddhist cult popular during part of the Hindu-Buddhist period. Its most noted adept was Kertanagara, the ruler of the East Javanese kingdom of Singhasari in the thirteenth century and Java's first empire builder. The rites of this cult, engaged in by Kertanagara, were presumed to include extremes of sexual indulgence.[4]

The rationale underlying the erotic and other esoteric practices of this form of Tantrism seems to have been a belief that "passion can be exhausted by passion."[5] The subjection of self to extremes of sensuality was held to train one to inner detachment, to an indifference to temptation, and to a maximum of self-control. This was considered to be—and is so still considered by some—a particularly potent means of gaining control over self and command over others.

Sukarno did not claim, and no one asserted on his behalf, that any of his wives or sexual partners was a *yogini,* or bearer of *sekti.* Moreover, Sukarno, a Muslim, did not seek to justify his sexual appetites and ac-

2. Prapantja, *Java,* 4, p. 80.
3. Ibid.
4. Holt, *Art,* p. 68; D. G. E. Hall, *A History of Southeast Asia* (London: Macmillan, 1958).
5. John B. Noss, *Man's Religions* (New York: Macmillan, 1963), p. 242.

tivities by reference to ancient Tantric Buddhist beliefs and practices. I suspect that few of his followers were familiar with the works of the court poets and chroniclers of the precolonial Javanese kingdoms. The accounts of Kertanagara in standard Indonesian histories I have seen fail to mention all the means by which he sought supernatural power.

Nonetheless, my informants who talked on the subject, especially those from rural villages, seemed to believe in a linkage between outstanding sexual potency and *sekti* without knowing the origins of that belief. In the same way, they believed that there was something special about banyan trees and about the number five without knowing their connection to Buddhism and Hinduism. For despite the fact that the Hindu-Buddhistic system of beliefs no longer forms the dominant world view in Java, elements from it remain, if only in attenuated form.[6]

The nature of the linkage was not specifically elaborated by any of my informants. None seemed to see Sukarno as obtaining or increasing magical power through sexual activity. The general notion seemed to be that his scope and degree of activity in this domain constituted one of the signs that he had *sekti*. One of his opponents, a member of the nobility, stated that Sukarno had "debased *sekti*" in consorting with some of the kinds of "low women" with whom he had gone. Finally, it might be mentioned that some of those close to him in later years kept close watch on his casual amours during his trips in the belief that a lessening of his sexual energies would be a sign that his power would leave him and that his political fortunes would decline.

Gandhi and Abstinence

In the later stages of the development of Hinduism a belief arose that the Godhead "descends" or manifests itself from time to time in various forms in order to aid mankind. Such a manifestation is called an *avatara*. In the *Mahabharata*, the great Hindu religious epic, Krishna was presented as an *avatara* of the god Vishnu. In the early 1950s an American anthropologist encountered in Madras several *harikathas* recounting Gandhi's life. *Harikatha* is an art form of recitation of traditional

6. Geertz, *Religion*, pp. 6, 269–78.

stories with musical accompaniment. In the one heard by the anthropologist, Gandhi was treated as an *avatar*, and his life was described in the style generally used to tell about the lives of Hindu saints.[7]

In his lifetime, Gandhi was already seen as an *avatar* by some, a saint by many, and certainly an extraordinary individual by almost all. This was not only because of what he accomplished but also because of the way he lived. His own life exemplified some of the highest ideals of Hinduism, both as he lived and as he strove to live.

One of the ideals professed by many strains of Hinduism has been that of the ascetic life. Asceticism, of which there have been several modes and which has included a variety of practices or disciplines, has long been considered both a means to *moksha*, or salvation from rebirth, and a means to unusual power.[8] The latter aspect can be traced as far back as the Vedic tradition (1200–200 B.C.) and the concept of *tapas*. In this tradition, *tapas*, meaning heat or fervor, denoted both the creative life force and the means to accumulate spiritual power. Techniques such as fasting, meditation, celibacy, and isolation were employed by priests to generate psychic "heat" in preparation for ritual sacrifices. The *rishis*, or poet seers, who composed the early Vedic hymns were thought to have come by the truths they conveyed with the aid of *tapas*.[9]

Asceticism came to play an important role in the later Hindu doctrines and a central role in other Indian religious traditions such as that of Jainism. Of the four stages of life prescribed in the classic Hindu texts for the individual, the final one is that of the ascetic who renounces the world in the search for spiritual self-realization. Of the other three stages, only the second, that of the householder, does not include some ascetic elements. Some texts prescribed the adoption of lifelong asceticism immediately after the first stage of studentship. In India there have been lifelong ascetics, living apart from society either in monastic orders

7. Milton Singer, "The Great Tradition in a Metropolitan Center: Madras," in *Traditional India: Structure and Change*, ed. Milton Singer (Philadelphia: American Folklore Society, 1959), p. 158.

8. George Benjamin Walker, *The Hindu World: An Encyclopedic Survey of Hinduism* (New York: Praeger, 1968), pp. 78–80; Wendy Doniger O'Flaherty, *Asceticism and Eroticism in the Mythology of Siva* (London: Oxford University Press, 1973); Thomas J. Hopkins, *The Hindu Religious Tradition* (Encino, Cal.: Dickenson, 1971).

9. Hopkins, *Tradition*, pp. 25–26, 49–50; G. S. Ghurye, *Indian Sadhus* (Bombay, 1953), pp. 17–19; Walker, *Hindu World*, p. 79.

or as wandering *sadhus*, holy men, since several centuries before Christ.[10]

In Hindu ethos and practice, asceticism appears to have both a passive and an active mode. The passive mode is characterized by renunciation and withdrawal, such as renouncing the use of violence, abstaining from speech, and relinquishing property and possessions. The active mode, with which the old concept of *tapas* came to be associated, involves "an active employment of disagreeable, difficult, unnatural, painful means for the accumulation of merit and the acquisition of spiritual power."[11] Gandhi's asceticism was not restricted to either one of these modes but included elements from both.

One of the ascetic practices that Gandhi most strongly adhered to and proselytized for in his talks and writings was *brahmacharya*, narrowly defined as sexual celibacy. Celibacy was a major component of Indian asceticism from its beginning.[12] The term *brahmachari* literally means "going to Brahman" (i.e., "the holy word") and originally referred to a disciple of Brahman or a student of Veda. Later it referred to the student in the first stage of the four prescribed stages of life and *brahmacharya* became the term for that stage and for the sexual continence that characterized it.[13]

In 1906, when he was no more than thirty-seven years old, Gandhi took the vow of celibacy and remained sexually continent until he died at the age of seventy-eight. It was far from easy for him, for his sexual capacity was well developed and retained until his death. What was moreover impressive to Indians to whom ascetics and celibates were no novelty were the circumstances under which Gandhi remained a *brahmachari*, for according to Hindu prescriptions, this state was to be entered into late in life. Those who took lifelong vows of celibacy early generally lived removed from society and not subject to the temptations of women. Gandhi, on the other hand, lived with, although he did not sleep with, his wife, worked with women, and in later years was con-

10. Hopkins, *Tradition*, pp. 82–83; Ghurye, *Sadhus*, pp. 5–6.

11. Walker, *Hindu World*, p. 79.

12. O'Flaherty, *Asceticism*, pp. 40–42, contains a useful discussion of the relationship between chastity and *tapas* in early Vedic writings.

13. R. N. Dandekar, "Brahmanism," in *Sources of Indian Tradition*, ed. Wm. Theodore de Bary (New York: Columbia University Press, 1958), p. 18.

stantly surrounded by female disciples. For him *brahmacharya* meant more than merely abstaining; it meant self-control and self-mastery.

Apart from the belief in celibacy as a means to master and overcome desire, there is in Hindu tradition a related belief in chastity as a means of conserving and augmenting power. The seed is the life force, and the loss of semen therefore is the loss of power. The theme of erotic desire or virile power transformed by continence into mental power, symbolized by the erect phallus of the god Shiva, has long been a basic theme of Hindu mythology and art.[14] Underlying this theme is a "theory of sexual hydrostatics reminiscent of Freudian sublimation theory."[15]

Gandhi interpreted *brahmacharya* broadly as extending beyond sexual celibacy to restraint and control of all the senses, including diet, emotions, speech, and actions.[16] Thus, he maintained and constantly experimented with a minimal vegetarian diet and fasted, apart from his political fasts. He also observed days of silent withdrawal, reminiscent of the austerity of *mauna*, or silence, practiced by the early ascetics. There was precedent for such a linkage in the Hindu tradition; one of the Upanishads identifies *brahmacharya* with silence and fasting.[17]

Another traditional ascetic virtue associated with Gandhi was disinterest in worldly possessions. According to the Hindu ideal, the *sannyasin*, or individual who decided to enter the ascetic or fourth stage of existence, took vows renouncing ownership of property among other renunciations.[18] Gandhi may not have taken a vow of poverty as he did with respect to celibacy, but beginning with his days in South Africa he simplified his life and that of his family to ownership of the barest essentials. At the time he began this process of simple living, he was earning what was then an extraordinarily high income for an attorney. In South Africa he organized and he and his family lived successively on two communal and relatively self-sufficient farms. After his return to India he lived mostly in an ashram with his family, disciples, and coworkers. An ashram, or a retreat, was a characteristic communal unit

---

14. O'Flaherty, *Asceticism*; Ghurye, *Sadhus*, p. 14; Hopkins, *Tradition*, pp. 97–98.

15. Lloyd I. Rudolph and Susanne Hoeber Rudolph, *The Modernity of Tradition* (Chicago: University of Chicago Press, 1967), pp. 196, 248.

16. Fischer, *Gandhi*, pp. 79–80.

17. Ghurye, *Sadhus*, p. 19.

18. V. Raghavan and R. N. Dandekar, "Hinduism," in de Bary, *Sources*, p. 234.

for ascetics, a kind of hermitage or monastery. The way of life of Gandhi and the other residents of his ashram at Sabarmati included poverty and menial labor; as with the traditional religious ashrams, its income came solely from gifts.[19]

Gandhi and his disciples, however, differed from the traditional ascetics in the emphasis they placed on action in the world as a means of salvation. It was far more common for ascetics to seek deliverance through knowledge and contemplation, shunning the world. But Gandhi had been greatly influenced by the great Hindu religious epic, the *Mahabharata*, and especially its most famous part, the *Bhagavad Gita*. In the *Gita*, the god Krishna propounds the doctrine of *karma-yoga*, the discipline of action. He reconciles it with the earlier emphasis on detachment from the world by emphasizing that actions should be selfless and performed without regard for their outcome, since it is not the actions themselves but the individual's attachment to the fruits of his actions that keeps him chained to the cycle of death and rebirth.[20] The instances in which Gandhi acted with selflessness, with sweetness and absence of rancor under the severest provocation are too numerous to recount but can be found in any of the standard biographies.

Two other doctrinal practices of traditional Indian asceticism were important in Gandhi's life and work, fasting and *ahimsa*, or nonviolence. Not only did Gandhi preach their virtues by word and pen, but he also practiced them in his own life. Moreover, as has been described in the previous chapter, he developed them into techniques of social and political action.

From ancient times in India, fasting was one of the exertions connected with *tapas* and the accumulation of creative energy and then became an aid to the attainment of spiritual purification. It also occasionally played another role, as a form of *dharma*, or seeming self-punishment in protest against an injury done to one, as when a creditor proposed to fast to death at the doorstep of a debtor unwilling to pay him.[21] Gandhi originally turned to fasting to facilitate *brahmacharya*.[22]

19. Fischer, *Gandhi*, pp. 369–80; Ashe, *Gandhi*.
20. Hopkins, *Tradition*, pp. 90–92; Raghavan and Dandekar, "Hinduism," pp. 279–91.
21. Philip Spratt, *Hindu Culture and Personality: A Psychoanalytic Study* (Bombay, 1966), pp. 74–76.
22. Fischer, *Gandhi*, pp. 78–79.

However, after he impulsively decided to fast in 1918 to keep striking millworkers at Ahmedabad firm to their pledge and millowners, as a result, agreed to compromise, Gandhi decided to use fasting as a political as well as a spiritual tool.[23]

Ahimsa, the doctrine of nonviolence, has been important in Buddhism as well as Hinduism and has been one of the major tenets of Jainism, a religion with many adherents in Gujarat, Gandhi's original province, and one to which Gandhi was exposed in his youth. Gandhi modified the more passive element of traditional *ahimsa*, that of withdrawal from the possibility of doing harm, into the more active *satyagraha*, described in the preceding chapter.

Like the saints and sages of the past, Gandhi could thus be seen as exemplifying the great tradition and enlarging it with his interpretation. Insofar as the fast and *satyagraha* worked, Gandhi was a living demonstration of the doctrine that spiritual force could be transformed into other kinds of force. Again like the saints and seers of medieval Hinduism who restored and popularized traditional beliefs, Gandhi restored a traditionally sanctioned but by his time somewhat tarnished Indian cultural ideal. The ideal of the ascetic who cultivated spiritual and moral force rather than physical prowess paled under the impact of British colonialism and British attitudes that favored the Indian martial tradition as they did the similar British tradition of martial valor. What had once been seen as virtue and strength came to be regarded by many Indians also as weakness and impotence.[24] By adhering to asceticism and turning it into a modern weapon that worked in the modern world against those who commanded modern technology, Gandhi indeed seemed superhuman.

It is true that some of the tenets Gandhi adhered to are not solely Hindu and that Gandhi originally came to them not solely through Hinduism. Tolstoy, Ruskin, Thoreau, and British Christian socialists were formative influences in the development of Gandhi's philosophy. But this is less relevant from the perspective of the Hindu believer than

23. Ashe, *Gandhi*, pp. 168–70; Fischer, *Gandhi*, pp. 161–62.
24. Susanne Hoeber Rudolph, "The New Courage: An Essay on Gandhi's Psychology," *World Politics* 16 (Oct. 1963), 103.

that he propounded it in terms of the *Gita* and other Hindu scriptures. Moreover, to the unlettered of India, Gandhi's very appearance was that of the traditional ascetic holy man, the *sadhu*. Gandhi wore a loincloth and little else, which was the dress of many *sadhus*. Gandhi walked with a staff; the staff as an identifying characteristic of an ascetic was said to be older than the code of Manu.[25]

Gandhi himself played no small part in the development of perceptions of himself as a saintly ascetic, for he did not seek the truth, wrestle with temptations, and struggle for self-mastery in the dark. In the pages of *Young India* and *Harijan*, the journals of his movement, and especially in his autobiography, *Experiments in Truth*, he wrote about himself in an unusually frank way, giving his readers a window on the trials and successes of one seeking self-improvement and virtue.

For those Indians and others throughout the world for whom holy asceticism and sainthood were irrelevant, Gandhi nonetheless was seen as of superhuman stature, if only because of the effect he had on the behavior of others. It can, of course, be argued that the most dramatic effects, such as those of the later fasts, came about because Gandhi was already charismatic. People changed their behavior because they could not accept the onus of contributory responsibility for the death of a saint. However, instances of Gandhi's effecting marked modifications in the actions of others, modifications contrary to their usual norms, can be found before his semideification. When he started his ashram in India, he insisted on including an Untouchable family and, admittedly with some difficulty, persuaded his wife and disciples to accept this, a violation of a basic tabu. Moreover, the members of the ashram followed his example in doing work that normally was done by Untouchables, such as cleaning latrines, which was extremely repellent as well as "contaminating" to caste Hindus.[26] Rajendra Prasad has described how he and other lawyers who assisted Gandhi at Champeran in 1917, Gandhi's first *satyagraha* in India, cleaned floors and did all the housework except for cooking. These were men with comfortable households and servants, not to mention positions to uphold in the eyes of the

25. Ghurye, *Sadhus*, p. 79.
26. Fischer, *Gandhi*, pp. 148–50.

community. But Gandhi's example and influence prevailed. What was even more significant, however, was that Gandhi induced them to drop their caste prohibitions in eating together.[27]

There were those who gave up positions and wealth to follow and work with Gandhi and many who gave up comforts. In a world in which these are generally prized above the ideals of truth, morality, and service to others, the person who sacrifices them for these ideals is considered extraordinary. And the person who can cause others to make major sacrifices seems to be endowed with exceptional powers.

Some Attributes in Awesome Measure

It is not only the possession of qualities that are themselves judged supernatural or close to it that lends some individuals the aura of the superhuman. Perceptions of an individual as transcending the normal and even the unusual among humankind can arise if that individual has or is held to have an extraordinary amount of an attribute that many people share. This is especially true if it is an attribute that is somehow associated with power or latent power. An extraordinary amount of determination, characteristic incidentally of all the leaders dealt with here, seems somehow closer to power and to the superhuman than does an extraordinary amount of charm, which incidentally most of these leaders also have had.

One attribute closely allied to perceptions of power is energy or vitality. Admittedly, available data provide few precise or easily comparable indicators of actual levels of energy of political figures. However, actual levels of energy or vitality are less significant for purposes of charismatic validation than the kinds of activities and/or the modes of publicizing them that convey impressions of inexhaustible energy or unflagging vitality.

During the first months of his regime, Castro was reputedly going practically without sleep and working from eighteen to twenty hours per day.[28] Herbert Matthews, the journalist who was largely responsible for

27. Rajendra Prasad, "Gandhi in Bihar," in *The Gandhi Reader*, ed. Homer A. Jack (Bloomington: Indiana University Press, 1956), pp. 148–52.

28. Robert J. Alexander, *Prophets of the Revolution* (New York: Macmillan, 1962), pp. 278–79.

the portrait of Castro that was disseminated in the late 1950s and early 1960s, described him as "working at demoniac speed . . . sleeping little . . . burning the candle at both ends with a fierce flame."[29] And Castro's marathon television speeches, lasting up to four hours or more, also projected the aura of superhuman energy.

Gandhi is said to have exhibited extraordinary energy from early childhood on.[30] The wide range of activities, projects, and visitors he was able to cope with after only a few hours of sleep nightly, the long walks and marches he undertook on his campaigns or in his travels, and the fasts, one of which lasted over twenty days, conveyed the impression of prodigious energy and stamina.

Perceptions of extraordinary energy or vitality can be formed as the result of varied kinds of activity. Ability to work for considerably longer hours than can most men without visible signs of exhaustion can be taken as one indicator, as in the case of Castro. Capacity to exist on very little sleep or food while maintaining a very heavy schedule of activities is another. However, there are also individuals who are capable of dramatic bursts of energetic or frenetic activity followed by periods of lassitude and, if they are public figures, the former phases tend to be publicized by those around them and the latter ones hidden. Observers can sometimes be misled into mistaking magnetism or volubility or vigorous and forceful gestures for vitality.

For example, there is some question as to how energetic Sukarno and Mussolini really were. Yet each of them during the early and middle stages of his career was widely viewed as having great and unflagging vitality. Stories about Sukarno stressed his ability to stay up all night watching *wayang* after a heavy day's work and his tendency on trips to wear out aides and assistants, who became exhausted in his wake. When Mussolini became prime minister in 1922, the *London Times* stated that the "most notable feature of the new prime minister is the energy which reveals itself in every movement."[31] Herman Finer, a political scientist, wrote about his "Herculean" labors and intense concentration.[32] There are numerous accounts of journalists, diplomats, and others who were

29. Herbert Matthews, *The Cuban Story* (New York: Braziller, 1961), p. 160.
30. Rudolph, "New Courage," p. 107.
31. *London Times*, Nov. 2, 1922.
32. Finer, *Mussolini's Italy*, pp. 298–99.

impressed by the vitality they sensed in the presence of Mussolini. The Italian people could form similar impressions of unusual and untiring energy by what they saw in the press. In addition to the usual pictures of a man busy with public affairs, there were pictures of him, almost daily, "making bricks, hammering with fierce concentration in smithies, cutting corn with his great chest . . . naked and glistening in the sun."[33]

Composure or presence of mind carried to the extreme is another characteristic capable of creating awe in observers. Self-control is frequently seen as a manifestation of latent power, and self-control or composure under conditions of stress, challenge, or danger, where most men would be expected to be thrown off balance, can seem somewhat inhuman.

Shortly before his first inauguration Roosevelt narrowly escaped assassination. According to his close associates, he did not twitch a muscle or show any sign of shock, and the descriptions of his courage and calm in the face of danger called forth great acclaim from the press and public.[34] In public, Roosevelt generally projected an aura of smiling imperturbability and easy mastery of himself and his surroundings. His composure under stress has been termed "remarkable" by James Mac-Gregor Burns, his biographer.[35]

Gandhi was also seen as one whose composure and control were extraordinary. Descriptions of his behavior on numerous occasions indicate or suggest that this was one of the facets of his personality that most impressed those who observed him. For example, Gandhi was described as never becoming the least rattled or at a loss in the course of a three-hour discussion with and examination by a group of prominent Oxford scholars, one of whom stated: "The conviction came to me, that not since Socrates has the world seen his equal for absolute self-control and composure; and, once or twice, putting myself in the place of men who had to confront that invincible calm and imperturbability, I thought I understood why the Athenians made the 'martyr-sophist' drink the hemlock."[36]

33. Christopher Hibbert, *Benito Mussolini* (London: Longmans, 1962), p. 40.
34. Burns, *Roosevelt*, p. 147; Edgar Eugene Robinson, *The Roosevelt Leadership* (Philadelphia and New York: J. B. Lippincott, 1955), p. 94.
35. Burns, *Roosevelt*, p. 152.
36. Fischer, *Gandhi*, p. 288.

Hitler is commonly thought of more in terms of lack of control than of its possession, especially since his seemingly hysterical outbursts were widely publicized. Speer, who was close to him, contends that many of the hysterical scenes and other histrionics were deliberately staged in order to obtain agreement quickly. He argues that "self-control was one of Hitler's most striking characteristics"[37] and especially emphasizes Hitler's composure at times of crisis, such as the Allied invasion in June 1944.[38]

Neither Sukarno nor Mussolini seems to have had a high degree of composure or self-control on a day-to-day basis. They were considered by those who knew them, as well as their political opponents, to be cowards.[39] Nonetheless, at least several times in the course of a crisis or when in danger, they were able to rise to the occasion and exhibit impressive self-possession. In at least one instance in the career of each, the circumstances were sufficiently dramatic for their demeanor to have been widely publicized. In October 1952 Sukarno was confronted by a group of army officers with an ultimatum, by a large mob instigated by them and their allies surrounding the palace, and by artillery trained on the palace. He calmly walked out to address the mob and dispersed them, then returned to the palace to talk with the officers whose ultimatum he refused to accept. By the time he had finished with them, some were reportedly close to tears and begging his forgiveness. When he was shot in the nose in an attempted assassination in 1926, Mussolini reacted coolly and proceeded to use the episode for a bravura gesture. In another attempt to assassinate him the same year in Bologna, he was pictured as remaining calm and smiling.[40]

In passing, one might note that escapes from assassination and other narrow escapes from death can give rise or contribute to a belief in the invulnerability or divine protection of the leader. They certainly did so in the case of Sukarno, who survived five assassination attempts, several of

37. Speer, *Third Reich*, p. 97.
38. Ibid., p. 357.
39. Kirkpatrick, *Mussolini*, p. 186. The data on Sukarno were obtained through personal interviews with Indonesians who had been close to him.
40. Kirkpatrick, *Mussolini*, p. 86; Laura Fermi, *Mussolini* (Chicago: University of Chicago Press, 1961), p. 249.

them quite close to succeeding.[41] They well may have in the case of other leaders, but such data are generally not easy to come by except by word of mouth. Thus, none of the sources I have used on Mussolini mentions popular reactions to the four unsuccessful attempts to assassinate him. But one former Abruzzi peasant I knew did recall believing that Mussolini led a charmed life and gave as "proof" the fact that he had survived so many attempts to kill him. It is quite possible that such beliefs are more prevalent among the peasantry, whom journalists and scholars seldom interview. It is also likely that such beliefs arise only after several narrow escapes on the part of the leader.

A third attribute, which in substantial measure conveys an aura of transcendental power, is intellect or learning. Each of the leaders dealt with here had the capacity to project the image of unusually impressive mental attainments. Gandhi, as judged by those close to him and from his own writing, was a genuine intellectual. Most of the others, however, primarily men of action and not of a scholarly bent, have been able to seize upon information and ideas from hasty reading or from other sources and, often by dint of an excellent memory, give the impression of possessing a powerful mind and an unbelievably wide range of knowledge.

Roosevelt possessed an almost inexhaustible curiosity and was in the habit of exploiting his personal contacts almost unmercifully in his search for information. In this respect Burns describes him as "voracious and prehensile in his quest for information . . . [with] a startling capacity to soak up notions and facts like a sponge, and to keep this material ready for constant use. He could overwhelm miners with a vast array of facts about the dismal coal situation; he could impress businessmen with a detailed description of the intricacies of their enterprises."[42] Members of Roosevelt's own family, it seems, were frequently "floored" by his memory.[43]

During his years as a journalist, Mussolini read widely, if indiscriminately and unsystematically.[44] He, too, had a prodigious memory that enabled him to utilize bits and pieces of his accumulated knowledge

41. John D. Legge, *Sukarno* (New York: Praeger, 1972), pp. 292–93.

42. Burns, *Roosevelt*, p. 155.

43. Joseph P. Lash, *Eleanor Roosevelt: A Friend's Memoir* (Garden City, N.Y.: Doubleday, 1964), p. 149.

44. Fermi, *Mussolini*, p. 210.

to amaze and impress. One of his biographers gives the example of the day Mussolini received a historian of parliamentary history who presented him a book. Mussolini leafed hastily through it, stopping abruptly to read a page or two that caught his eye. That afternoon, he used the material in one of these pages in a speech he delivered to the Senate, which led to admiring remarks in the Senate lobby concerning Mussolini's amazing knowledge of a particular parliament.[45] Therefore, it is not surprising that Finer should have picked up the notion in Rome and written that Mussolini had an "exceptionally wide knowledge of science and philosophy" and "reads assiduously, with a wider range than a professor, and certainly with more concentration." Finer, however, would not accept the assurances he received that Mussolini was a great statistician and a great economist.[46] If some of the educated in the capital saw Mussolini as an outstanding social scientist, some of the less lettered saw him as a universal savant, as exemplified by the story of the visitor to the Etruscan tombs of Orvieto. Told that the inscriptions had not yet been deciphered, for the language was unknown, she remarked that this was because Mussolini was not there and he would figure it out when he arrived.[47]

Castro's memorable "History Will Absolve Me" speech gives evidence of the breadth of his reading as of the time it was delivered. Those who have encountered him and spent time with him have been impressed with his skill in logical argument and have found his memory to be "prodigious."[48]

Hitler also read widely and had an excellent memory. He impressed associates and visitors with what appeared to be an uncanny ability to "reel off complicated orders of battle, technical specifications, and long lists of names and dates without a moment's hesitation,"[49] although sometimes with questionable accuracy.

Sukarno, in his youth and especially during the periods when he was imprisoned by the Dutch, read considerably in political philosophy and religion. Like Mussolini, he acquired a reservoir of miscellaneous knowledge, items of which were strategically and seemingly spontaneously

45. Kirkpatrick, *Mussolini*, pp. 161–62.
46. Finer, *Mussolini's Italy*, pp. 292–93.
47. Hibbert, *Mussolini*, pp. 40, 42n.
48. Lee Lockwood, *Castro's Cuba, Cuba's Fidel* (New York: Random House, 1968), p. 78.
49. Bullock, *Hitler*, p. 328.

retrieved in order to impress. To the common people and even to others, Sukarno sounded like a very learned man. His speeches were sprinkled with allusions and quotations, not only from the various ethnic traditions of Indonesia but also from foreign and Western sources, often in the language of these sources. In one frequently reprinted speech, for example, he quoted Ernest Renan, Otto Bauer, Sun Yat-sen, Gandhi, and Jean Jaurès, and in a national day address he developed an extended metaphor from Dante's *Divine Comedy*.[50] Those who were close to him or in frequent contact with him still recall his fabulous memory with awe. He had a particularly impressive ploy of addressing by name someone he had met only once many years earlier and making a specific reference to that meeting.

Another quality that can be awe-inspiring when manifested in extreme degree is self-confidence or self-assurance. Unlike the qualities mentioned above, however, the utility of this one for purposes of charismatic legitimation may be dependent upon cultural context and other contingent factors. It can be argued, for example, that an extreme degree of self-assurance in a political leader is acceptable and admirable in an American context, provided that self-assurance is communicated in a relaxed and occasionally self-deprecatory or self-teasing style. In the same context, Hitler's mode of communicating self-confidence is likely to be seen and rejected as brutal arrogance, even though it might provoke some awe.

The contingent factors referred to above would exclude, for example, the easy self-confidence, no matter how great, of someone bred and schooled to it from an elite background and thus expected by popular assumption to possess it. I refer rather to extreme confidence linked to determination or will in the face of seemingly impossible obstacles or the self-confidence linked to the conviction that one is destiny's child chosen to accomplish what others perceive as an impossible mission. Those possessing and expressing this sort of assurance often seem to many of these others to be close to madness or genius; indeed, a number of charismatic political leaders were initially considered mad by those who later acclaimed them as geniuses.

50. Sukarno, "The Birth of Pantjasila (1945)," and "The Rediscovery of Our Revolution (1949)," in Sukarno, *Toward Freedom and the Dignity of Man* (Djakarta, 1961), pp. 1–21 and 37–76, respectively.

Roosevelt possessed an extraordinary degree of self-confidence and apparently believed that there was no problem that he could not ultimately solve.[51] This assurance might not have seemed so impressive in someone of Roosevelt's background had it not been for two factors. The first was his paralysis, which, although not shown in films or photographs, was well-known. In the face of this condition and the conventional beliefs about the helplessness, dependency, and frequent depression of paralytics, Roosevelt's serene assurance did seem extraordinary. Moreover, he entered office at a time when most Americans, including many of his background, were despondent, if not despairing. His supreme confidence at such a time was not only amazing but contagious and, as the previous chapter indicates, was one of the factors responsible for his charismatic appeal.

Roosevelt did not publicly proclaim himself divinely selected or seized with a mission, but several serious students of his life and works have stated that he did harbor such a belief.[52] As the following chapter shows, he framed his program, as illustrated in several major addresses, in terms of a crusade and implicitly referred to himself as a messiah.

Castro's extremely strong self-confidence and sense of mission were manifest when he was still in his twenties. Whether or not the "History Will Absolve Me" speech was delivered in the closed courtroom during the 1953 trial for the Moncada attack precisely as it was later transcribed, it exudes confidence in every paragraph, a remarkable accomplishment for someone imprisoned and at fortune's low ebb.[53] In a letter also written from prison, Castro compared himself to Christ.[54] Herbert Matthews was much struck with Castro's confidence during the early days of the Sierra Maestre struggle, when Castro's cause still seemed hopeless.[55]

It cannot be said that Gandhi, Hitler, Mussolini, or Sukarno com-

51. Eleanor Roosevelt, *The Autobiography of Eleanor Roosevelt* (New York: Harper, 1961), p. 159; Richard Hofstadter, *The American Political Tradition* (New York: Knopf, 1951), p. 311.

52. Tugwell, *Roosevelt*, pp. 11, 253; Harold F. Gosnell, *Champion Campaigner: Franklin D. Roosevelt* (New York: Macmillan, 1952), p. 4.

53. Fidel Castro, *History Will Absolve Me* (n.p., n.d.).

54. Ward M. Morton, *Castro as A Charismatic Hero* (Lawrence: University of Kansas Center of Latin American Studies, 1965), p. 9.

55. Herbert Matthews, *Castro: A Political Biography* (London: Penguin, 1969), pp. 85, 89–90, and *Cuban Story*, p. 152.

menced his public career with great self-confidence. Yet each one gained it in the course of time and of successes or, if he did not gain genuine inner certainty, developed the capacity to project to all but his closest associates the image of unusual confidence. Gandhi, a shy and nervous barrister when he first arrived in South Africa, became transformed into a man whose iron will and tranquil certainty impressed and sometimes irritated those who dealt with him. What seems to have struck many as extraordinary was his combination of confidence, humility, and humor.

The recent flood of studies of Hitler, especially those from a psychiatric and psychoanalytical perspective, are likely to result in revisions of some estimates of his character and personality. Hitler seems to have been highly labile, confident to the point of megalomania upon some occasions and nearly drowned in doubt and depression on others.[56] He could shout to Otto Strasser, "I never make a mistake. Every one of my words is historic," and vacillate over major decisions.[57] But in public, after about 1925, he managed to convey superb confidence in his powers. In 1930 he told a group of party journalists that his political infallibility was as great as the Pope's spiritual infallibility.[58] And facing a crowd stimulated and transformed him so that he projected to mass audiences an absolute conviction, hysterical at times but nonetheless a conviction, of the correctness of his mission and his capacity to fulfill it.[59] After he came to power, his propaganda machine emphasized his infallibility.

Mussolini has also been portrayed as vacillating between feelings of omnipotence and of inferiority but nonetheless able to communicate to the outer world a strong will and a rugged confidence.[60] During the period when the regime that succeeded Sukarno's in Indonesia was bent on destroying the mystique surrounding the deposed leader, several of his former associates recalled that beneath Sukarno's superb self-assurance there had been manifestations of inner doubt and hesitation.

---

56. Bullock, *Hitler*, p. 60, and passim; Fest, *Hitler*; James H. McRandle, *The Track of the Wolf* (Evanston, Ill.: Northwestern University Press, 1965), passim.

57. Fest, *Hitler*, pp. 285, 448.

58. Ibid., pp. 283–84.

59. For descriptions of Hitler with his audiences, see especially Fest, *Hitler*, pp. 326–28 and passim.

60. Kirkpatrick, *Mussolini*, pp. 159–60; Fermi, *Mussolini*, pp. 292–96.

Because these same informants had seemed convinced, a decade earlier, that Sukarno's self-confidence was both extraordinary and a major factor in his success, one can only conclude that whatever doubts about himself Sukarno had harbored during his heyday had been carefully concealed.

Finally, I should like to note one physical feature that can convey the suggestion of supernatural power in the possessor—eyes of a certain quality. Of all the facial features, none tends to be more perceived than eyes as external indicators of the personal qualities of an individual. Noses, cheeks, foreheads, and ears that are unusual may be commented upon but rarely in conjunction with personality and character. Mouths and chins may be associated with strength or weakness in the possessor. Eyes, however, are in a category of their own.

Only eyes are associated with the capability of exerting force outward. To "hold" someone with one's eyes, to "cut" with a glance, and to "kill" with a look are only a few of the phrases that indicate the power attributed to eyes. The notion of the "evil eye" is common in the Middle East and elsewhere. I have encountered the belief among Indonesian peasants that sorcerers can be distinguished by their eyes. Hypnotic ability is most commonly associated with eyes.

However varied the leaders discussed here may have been in most aspects of their physical appearance—and they were—most of them seem to have shared the attribute of extraordinary eyes. Castro's eyes have been described as "hypnotic in their intensity."[61] One interviewer, Lee Lockwood, who spent a sufficient number of days with Castro not to be overimpressed by brief exposure, refers to his "mantic" (i.e., prophetic) gaze and his use of his eyes "to reduce a listener to surrender."[62]

Hitler was generally undistinguished in appearance, but one feature that stood out and commanded attention was his eyes, which were "persistently said to have had some sort of hypnotic quality."[63] That this was apparently felt by those at some distance to him is suggested by one of the comments in Abel's study of Nazis: "As the Fuehrer addressed us, his eyes became like hands that gripped men never to let go again."[64]

61. Taber, *M-26*, p. 20.
62. Lockwood, *Castro's Cuba*, pp. 78–79.
63. Bullock, *Hitler*, p. 328.
64. Abel, *Hitler*, p. 153.

One of Mussolini's followers observed that upon first meeting Mussolini, he was most struck by his "profound and luminous eyes."[65] This was his most striking feature, according to Kirkpatrick, who offers an explanation for the effect created: "When interested or anxious to emphasize a point, he had a trick of rolling his eyes, as many visitors described it. In reality, he was able to raise the upper eyelid and depress the lower, so as to display two vast white orbs."[66] Roosevelt seems to have had a similar ability to widen his eyes and intensify his gaze so that it had a commanding and compelling quality. Sukarno's eyes were perceived as both luminous and hypnotic.

There may be a physiological basis for this phenomenon. It has been suggested that the effects created are the result of a "relative lack of iridic, ocular tension and a possibly bioelectric brain phenomenon resulting in luminous glitter in the eyes."[67] Whatever its basis, it is well worth considering that the magnetism, irresistible persuasiveness, or emanation of power attributed to charismatic leaders by those who have personally encountered them has been in part due to the effect of their eyes and how they have used them on others.

65. Fermi, *Mussolini*, p. 229.
66. Kirkpatrick, *Mussolini*, p. 156.
67. Personal communication from Dr. John Higgins of East Lansing, Michigan, who has been studying the ocular attributes of leaders, especially those considered "magnetic."

7

The Rhetoric of Charismatic Invocation

Many charismatic political leaders have been characterized as eloquent or spellbinding orators, able to arouse their audiences to heights of enthusiasm and transports of emotion. Their charismatic appeal has sometimes been attributed largely to their oratorical skills. Although there is evidence, as mentioned in chapter 3, that some charismatic conversions have resulted solely from hearing a speech of a leader, rhetoric tends to be one of the several means by which charismatic perceptions are aroused.

Those who have succumbed to the oratorical spells of political leaders or have observed the effects of their speeches on others seem to do little more to explain these spells than describe their own reactions or emotions or those of others. Yet descriptions of effects tell us little about the causes or precipitants of such effects. We are not much wiser concerning what it is the speaker has done to elicit them.

Therefore, in this chapter I will try to explain what accounts for the rhetorical spellbinding that contributes to charisma. The elements I deal with here include only some of those that comprise oratorical eloquence, mainly those that seem to contribute directly to charisma. While it may be argued that all rhetorical eloquence has an uplifting effect that produces at least temporary charismatic or quasi-charismatic responses toward the orator, the linkages between some rhetorical elements and charisma may be obscure.

The rhetorical dimension of political charisma analyzed here deals less with the message and more with the medium through which the message is conveyed. It is true that ideas or messages do play a part in the genesis and maintenance of charisma. But, as has been noted earlier, the major messages of charismatic political leaders have generally been propounded by others before them or others contemporary with them. And it is not uncommon for two speakers to present the same points of view on the same subjects to the same audience and receive different responses to their presentations.

Therefore, rhetorical spellbinding and the charismatic affect it can induce are produced less by logic and ideas than by emotional stimuli, by words as symbols of more than their literal meaning, in short, by the style of verbal communication.

One aspect of style, the use of figurative language, such as simile and metaphor, seems to be strongly conducive to charismatic affect, as will be illustrated below. Related to such linguistic devices is the use of analogy and, for some purposes, of allusion. Since the time of Aristotle, authorities on rhetoric have made claims for the effectiveness of figurative speech in moving audiences. Surprisingly, there seems to have been little contemporary experimental work done in testing the long-held assumption that figurative speech is far more persuasive and effective than literal speech. However, the little that has been done does seem to bear out this contention.[1]

Perhaps even more significant for charisma than the greater persuasiveness inherent in figurative language is its invocation of other meanings and symbols than those that it is immediately intended to denote. By use of such language a speaker can verbally tap selected cultural symbols and elicit the emotions aroused by them.

Two other elements of style are worth noting. One is the level of language used, for example, elevated or literary or colloquial, since different levels may have different associations and emotive power. The second element is comprised of rhetorical devices related to sound, such as rhythm, repetition, alliteration, and balance. Each of these may have

---

1. John Waite Bowers and Michael M. Osborn, "Attitudinal Effects of Metaphors in Persuasive Speeches," *Speech Monographs* 33 (June 1966), 127–55; N. Lamar Reinsch, Jr., "An Investigation of the Effects of the Metaphor and Simile in Persuasive Discourse," *Speech Monographs* 38 (June 1971), 142–54.

particular implications in the oral traditions of particular cultures. Although the emotive content of figurative expression in a language generally can be fully understood only by someone familiar with that culture, there are fewer barriers to cross-cultural understanding of sound devices. One need not even have understood German or Indonesian to have appreciated the force and quasi-hypnotic power of the crescendo effects built up by Hitler's and Sukarno's remorseless repetitions of key phrases in progressively louder tones.

It is highly probable that charismatic rhetorical spellbinders have used both traditional and innovative devices of sound more than their opponents. It is also likely that they have made plentiful use of figurative expression and more so than their political opponents.[2] They have employed rhetoric directly or implicitly to present themselves in a heroic mold, as, for example, prophet, seer, warrior, and protector of the people.

While some examples of the uses of rhetoric in aid of charisma have already been given in chapter 4 in connection with Sukarno, this chapter will deal with charismatic invocation solely through the rhetoric of Franklin D. Roosevelt and his competitors. Of my sample, he was the charismatic leader whose language and culture are probably the most widely known, so he seems the most appropriate to illustrate the process.[3]

Roosevelt and the Great Tradition

In his study of Roosevelt, James MacGregor Burns borrowed his subtitle, *The Lion and the Fox*, from Machiavelli. One can also borrow from Machiavelli to express the dominant image that Roosevelt projected in his major addresses—that of an "armed prophet."[4] Armed with "The Book" and a metaphorical sword aimed at selfish economic interests,

2. This impression is derived from comparing the speeches of Roosevelt and Sukarno with those of their political competitors and a reading (in translation) of speeches of other leaders of the sample.

3. Compared here are speeches of Roosevelt and of his competitors delivered to equivalent audiences on similar occasions. Also, units of speeches that express similar ideas or seem to perform the same function have been selected for comparison.

4. Niccolò Machiavelli, *The Prince and The Discourses* (New York: Modern Library, 1950), p. 22.

Roosevelt rhetorically presented himself as the leader of a crusade of the common people against fear and want.

"The Book" of course was the Bible. If one had to name the single book many or most of whose phrases were deeply etched in the consciousness and unconscious of millions of Americans of Roosevelt's era, it would have been the King James version of the Bible. Not only had Roosevelt been reared on it but so had a large number of his hearers, old and young, urban and rural, of all classes and all occupational backgrounds.[5]

Roosevelt frequently employed elevated Biblical language and cadences in his major addresses. Many of his metaphors were derived from the Bible, as the following extracts indicate:

> Let us be frank in acknowledgment of the truth that <u>many amongst us have made obeisance to Mammon,</u> that the prophets of speculation, the easy road without toil, have lured us from the old barricades. . . . <u>we must abandon false prophets</u> and seek new leaders of our own choosing.
> (acceptance of Democratic nomination, July 2, 1932; emphasis mine)

> Yet our distress comes from no failure of substance. <u>We are stricken by no plague of locusts.</u> . . . Plenty is at our doorstep but a generous use of it languishes in the very sight of the supply. Primarily this is because the rulers of the exchange of mankind's goods have failed through their own stubbornness and their own incompetence, have admitted their failure and have abdicated. Practices of the unscrupulous <u>money-changers</u> stand indicted in the court of public opinion, rejected by the hearts and minds of men. . . . They know only the rules of a <u>generation of self-seekers.</u> They have no vision and <u>when there is no vision the people perish.</u>
>
> The <u>money-changers</u> have fled from their high seats in the <u>temple</u> of our civilization. We may now restore that temple to its ancient truths.

---

5. This was at a time when recital of prayers and religious instruction in public schools still took place and students from various religious backgrounds were exposed to readings from the King James Bible.

(First Inaugural Address, Washington, March 4, 1933;[6] emphasis mine)

The underlined words in the first extract invoked the Sermon on the Mount, the statement of Jesus that "Ye cannot serve God and mammon" and his warning against false prophets. (Matt. 6:24; 7:15). *Mammon*, originating in the Aramaic language, is one of the oldest synonyms for wealth and still carries the connotation of a debasing influence.[7] But if in his acceptance speech, Roosevelt subtly implied an association between himself and Christ, this association was more clearly suggested in the imagery of his inaugural address. *Money-changers* and *temple* obviously alluded to Jesus casting out those who bought and sold in the temple and overthrowing the tables of the money-changers (Matt. 21:12). Despite the use of *we*, what was implied is that what Jesus did, so will FDR.

In these same addresses, there was martial imagery parallel to the Biblical imagery:

This is more than a political campaign; it is a call to arms. Give me your help, not to win votes alone, but to win in this crusade to restore America to its own people.

(acceptance of nomination, 1932)

The only thing we have to fear is fear itself—nameless, unreasoning, unjustified terror which paralyzes needed efforts to convert retreat into advance. . . .

. . . We must move as a trained and loyal army willing to sacrifice for the good of a common discipline. . . . This I propose to offer, pledging that the larger purposes will bind upon us all as a sacred obligation with a unity of duty evoked only in time of armed strife.

With this pledge taken, I assume unhesitatingly the leadership of this great army of our people dedicated to a disciplined attack upon our common problems.

(First Inaugural Address, 1933)

6. Texts of the speeches from which these extracts are taken can be found in *Vital Speeches* and in *Nothing to Fear: The Selected Addresses of Franklin D. Roosevelt*, ed. B. D. Zevin (Boston: Houghton Mifflin, 1946). In all extracts underlining emphasis is mine.

7. Webster's Dictionary.

Not only did the metaphors and meaning strongly suggest a sacred crusade, but the diction employed also did so. Biblical or archaic forms of words were chosen instead of the contemporary ones, as: "amongst" instead of "among"; "made obeisance to" instead of "obey"; "toil" instead of "work"; "seek" instead of "look for." This strengthened the linkage with the prophets who exhorted the people of Israel to return to the true faith and with the prophet who preached the Sermon on the Mount. Even where the choice was between several contemporary words with the same or similar meaning, the one chosen strengthened the dominant metaphors. For example, the word *pledge*, instead of *promise*, was associated with national patriotism by people who as schoolchildren had been required daily to pledge allegiance to their flag.

Biblical imagery was also pronounced in Roosevelt's Second Inaugural Address in 1937, as in the following:

> We of the Republic pledged ourselves to drive from the temple of our ancient faith those who had profaned it. . . . Our Covenant with ourselves did not stop there.

Again there was the association with the cleansing of the temple by Jesus and an even more specific invocation of the many prophets who reminded the people of Israel of their Covenant with God.

Perhaps the most effective metaphoric linkage in this address appeared in its conclusion:

> I shall do my utmost to speak their purpose and to do their will, seeking Divine guidance to help us each and every one to give light to them that sit in darkness and to guide our feet into the way of peace.

Invoked by these words were the messianic prophecy of Isaiah and the account of its fulfillment in the Gospel of Matthew:

> The people that walked in darkness have seen a great light: they that dwell in the land of the shadow of death, upon them hath the light shined. . . . For unto us a child is born . . . and his name shall be called . . . the Prince of Peace.
>
> (Isa. 9:2, 9:6)

> The people which sat in darkness saw great light. . . . From that time Jesus began to preach.
>
> (Matt. 5:16, 17)

Not only was the sacred authority of the Bible invoked in Roosevelt's Second Inaugural Address, with strong overtones of God speaking through the mouth of the prophet, Franklin. Two other works of the classical heritage were drawn upon to add their aura to the Roosevelt persona and message. One was a literary work with religious overtones, Bunyan's *Pilgrim's Progress*. The other was Lincoln's Gettysburg Address.

The former is probably little known today, but until the 1930s it was still familiar to many as a classic. In this religious allegory, the hero, Christian, seeking the kingdom of heaven, encounters in his pilgrimage the personifications of numerous virtues, vices, and other qualities, for example, the giant Despair, Faithful, the Slough of Despond, Vanity Fair.

This work was invoked in the following passage, with its suggestion that Roosevelt was leading the people on to the promised land:

> Shall we pause now and turn our back upon the road that lies ahead? Shall we call this the promised land? . . .
>
> Many voices are heard as we face a great decision. Comfort says, "Tarry a while." Opportunism says, "This is a good spot." Timidity asks, "How difficult is the road ahead?" . . .
>
> If I know aught of the spirit and purpose of our Nation, we will not listen to Comfort, Opportunity and Timidity.

Probably still the best-known and even revered speech in the United States is Lincoln's Gettysburg Address. In the time of Roosevelt many schools still required every student to memorize it. His speech of acceptance of the nomination in 1932 contained one sentence evoking the Gettysburg Address:

> . . . that we here highly resolve that these dead shall not have died in vain.
>
> (Lincoln)

> Millions of our citizens cherish the hope that their old standards of living and of thought have not gone forever. Those millions cannot and shall not hope in vain.
>
> (Roosevelt)

The Second Inaugural Address, however, strongly invoked the Gettysburg Address, not only in its phrases but also in its structure and themes. Although it was considerably longer, Roosevelt's address re-capitulated the form of Lincoln's in beginning with time past and the ideals of the founders, proceeding to discuss the crisis of the present, and concluding with rededication to the unfinished task:

Four score and seven years ago our fathers brought forth on this continent a new nation, conceived in liberty and dedicated to the proposition that all men are created equal.

(Lincoln)

When four years ago we met to inaugurate a President, the Republic, single-minded in anxiety, stood in spirit here. We dedicated ourselves to the fulfillment of a vision.

(Roosevelt)

Now we are engaged in a great civil war. . . . We are met on a great battlefield of that war.

(Lincoln)

This year marks the one hundred and fiftieth anniversary of the Constitutional Convention which made us a nation. . . . Today we invoke those same powers of government.

(Roosevelt)

It is rather for us to be here dedicated to the great task remaining before us.

(Lincoln)

Today we reconsecrate our country to long-cherished ideals.

(Roosevelt)

The Folk Tradition

While it was Roosevelt's masterly use of the great traditions of religion and literature that contributed most to developing his charisma through rhetoric, some other aspects of his speeches might be mentioned as probably having played a subsidiary role. These include the use of the colloquial or folk tradition, the employment of rhythmic devices, and the style of humor and irony.

It is highly improbable that the use of colloquial language and homely imagery is itself conducive to the development of charismatic affect. However, when someone who commands an elevated position and employs an elevated style almost unexpectedly does use the everyday language of the man in the street, there is a special response. For if the posture of elevation can produce awe, that of equality from the elevated can produce affection and love. A touch of the ordinary from the great makes the latter seem somehow greater.

Roosevelt's "folk" imagery was not drawn from any particular type of source but seemed to emerge spontaneously. In his second fireside chat, baseball was obviously the source of the line "I have no expectation of making a hit every time I come to bat." Perhaps a film titled "Death Takes a Holiday" was partly responsible for the sentence in the Second Inaugural Address, "Our tasks in the last four years did not force democracy to take a holiday." Rather popular during this period were figurine or fabric representations of the three little monkeys, one who heard no evil (ears covered), one who saw no evil (eyes covered), and one who spoke no evil (mouth covered). In his campaign speech in New York City on October 31, 1936, Roosevelt evoked their image in the following: "For twelve years our Nation was afflicted with hear-nothing, see-nothing, do-nothing government."

Rhetorical devices, such as certain rhythms, repetition, and alliteration may not add much to meaning, but they do help to fix ideas in people's minds. Moreover, they convey an emotional tone and play upon the emotions. Thus, rhythmically and structurally balanced clauses in the classic tradition of the English language tend to suggest grandeur and authoritativeness. Roosevelt frequently used such clauses, as in the following examples from his Second Inaugural Address:

Old truths have been relearned; untruths have been unlearned. We have always known that heedless self-interest was bad morals; we now know that it is bad economics.

The test of our progress is not whether we add more to the abundance of those who have much; it is whether we provide enough for those who have too little.

Repetition for emphasis was also used frequently by Roosevelt. Only one example, from a campaign speech in New York City on October 31, 1936, is given here:

Nine mocking years with the golden calf and three long years of the scourge! . . . Nine crazy years at the ticker and three long years in the breadlines! Nine mad years of mirage and three long years of despair!

Alliteration, as an effective rhetorical device, may not easily recover from the overkill of Spiro Agnew. It may well have been from study of Roosevelt's speeches that Agnew's speechwriters gained the notion of the efficacy of alliteration. Roosevelt did use it often and in sentences such as the following the measured sonority it adds, especially with certain letters, can be detected when they are read aloud:

Prosperity already tests the persistence of our progressive purpose.
(Second Inaugural Address, 1937)

Nothing would so surely destroy the substance of what the Bill of Rights protects than its perversion to prevent social progress.
(radio address, September 17, 1937)

Another device that might be noted is the sentence in which only slightly different words or phrases are paired for contrasting concepts. Such sentences tend to have an aphoristic quality suggestive of the wisdom of proverbs, as might be seen from the following:

We know that government by organized money is just as dangerous as government by organized mob.
(campaign speech, New York City, 1936)

Hardheadedness will not easily excuse hardheartedness.
(Second Inaugural Address, 1937)

Humor and irony seem far removed from the sort of images that are associated with charisma. Yet if they are thought of as weapons in a verbal duel, there develops the image of a conflict, with the potential for one combatant to emerge a victor. If that combatant seems initially hit and on the verge of defeat but turns the tables unexpectedly upon his opponent in a brilliant thrust, he can seem to take on a heroic cast. This was not quite the image projected by Roosevelt in thrusting back at his critics with humor and irony, for he did not seem on the verge of defeat. If not the tone of heroism, there seemed to be an aura of effortless mastery in the manner in which Roosevelt countered his critics in the following, the first example directed at his critics from big business:

> Some of these people really forget how sick they were. But I know how sick they were. I have their fever charts. I know how the knees of all our rugged individualists were trembling four years ago and how their hearts fluttered. They came to Washington in great numbers. Washington did not look like a dangerous bureaucracy to them then. Oh, no! It looked like an emergency hospital. All of the distinguished patients wanted two things—a quick hypodermic to end the pain and a course of treatment to cure the disease. They wanted them in a hurry; we gave them both. And now most of the patients seem to be doing very nicely. Some of them are even well enough to throw their crutches at the doctor.
>
> (campaign speech, Chicago, 1936)

This metaphor placed Roosevelt in a role of power and sagacity vis-à-vis his critics—the healing physician whose patients were not even appreciative. The critics were not even overtly attacked; they were merely deflated in such a smooth way that the aura of effortless power was sustained. In the following extract Roosevelt reduced his critics by substituting the target of their attacks and at the same time suggested that he and his family were too large-minded and secure to take these critics seriously or to respond in the same manner:

> The Republican leaders have not been content with attacks on me, or my wife, or my sons. No . . . they now include my little dog, Fala. Well, of course, I don't resent attacks, and my family doesn't resent attacks, but Fala *does* resent them. . . . as soon as he learned that the Republican fiction writers in Congress and out had concocted a story that I had left him behind in the Aleutian Islands and had sent a destroyer to find him—at a cost to the taxpayers of two or three, or eight to twenty million dollars—his Scotch soul was furious. . . . I have a right to resent, to object to, libelous statements about my dog.
>
> (address before the International Brotherhood of Teamsters,
> Washington, D.C., 1944)

Landon and Roosevelt: The Plain Phrase versus the Founding Myth

The vividness and evocative power of Roosevelt's rhetoric stood out even more starkly when compared with the rhetoric of other American political leaders of his period and when compared with that of his competitors for the presidency. An electoral competition is also seen as a battle of champions, the incumbent champion challenged by the champion of the opposing party, and the major speeches of these contenders in the American political system are seen as clues to or reflections of their personae as well as of their programs.

In this and the following sections of this chapter, comparisons are made between speeches of Roosevelt and those of Alf M. Landon, the Republican candidate for president in 1936, and Wendell L. Willkie, the Republican candidate in 1940. For equivalence in comparison, it is desirable to select speeches delivered on like or similar occasions and on like or similar themes in such speeches. I have selected the addresses delivered by each of these men in accepting their respective nominations for presidential office.[8]

The 1936 speeches seemed to convey rather unconventional dominant images of the contenders, for Landon did not launch a hard-hitting attack on Roosevelt and Roosevelt did not defend, as is customary with incumbents, but attacked. Both began their acceptance speeches emphasizing the importance of simplicity of expression. Landon's address was decidedly simple and straightforward, both in its structure and in the language employed. Landon started with an outline of the topics he intended to discuss, namely, recovery and relief, debt and taxes, farm policy, labor problems, international relations, and constitutional government. He then proceeded to take up each of these subjects in turn and for each he offered (1) a general statement on principles, (2) a critique of the policies of the Democratic administration, and (3) a statement of his party's program and his pledges for action.

8. The full texts of these speeches can be found in the following issues of *Vital Speeches:* Roosevelt, June 22, 1936, at Philadelphia, 2, no. 21 (July 15, 1936), pp. 634–36; Landon, July 23, 1936, at Topeka, 2, no. 22 (Aug. 1, 1936), pp. 666–70; Roosevelt, July 19, 1940, at New York City, 6, no. 20 (Aug. 3, 1940), pp. 610–13; Willkie, Aug. 17, 1940, at Elwood, Indiana, 6, no. 22 (Sept. 1, 1940), pp. 674–79.

In accordance with this neat and matter-of-fact organization, Landon's tone and language were also prosaic and commonplace, as can be seen in the following examples of the general statements that prefaced each topic:

No people can make headway where great numbers are supported in idleness. There is no future on the relief rolls.

But it must be kept in mind that the security of all of us depends on the good management of our common affairs. . . . Taxes, both visible and invisible, add to the price of everything.

No sound national policy looking to the national welfare will neglect the farmer.

Roosevelt's acceptance speech, unlike Landon's, dealt with no specific issues and no specific policies. Instead, it was an elaborate and extended metaphor, almost a prose poem, woven around the theme of the struggle of the common man and his ally, the Roosevelt administration, against the economic tyranny of the privileged. In dramatizing this struggle, Roosevelt employed the metaphor of the American Revolution, invoking the sentiments and emotions associated with it.

Roosevelt began by reminding his audience that this was Philadelphia, "fitting ground on which to reaffirm the faith of our fathers [note the alliteration]." Referring to the American Revolution as a fight for freedom from political tyranny, he proceeded to elaborate upon the development of a newer tyranny of economic oligarchs, linking the contemporary situation with the historical one through the following images:

The <u>privileged princes</u> of these new economic <u>dynasties</u>, thirsting for power, reached out for control over government itself. They created a new <u>despotism</u> and wrapped it in the robes of legal sanction. In its service, new <u>mercenaries</u> sought to regiment the people, their labor and their properties. And as a result the average man once more confronts the problem that faced the <u>Minute Man</u>.

Thus, the Republican opposition and their backers were not merely tarred with the brush of special privilege; they were cast as contemporary King George III, Redcoats, Hessian mercenaries, Loyalists, the traditional foes of the founding myth of this country.

Both Landon and Roosevelt briefly depicted the plight of people suffering from the depression and both absolved them of blame for the situation in which they were caught. Landon treated the depression as a
depersonalized phenomenon, something that happened to people, as
follows:

> When the depression began millions of dependable men and wom-
> en had employment. They were the solid citizenry of America; they
> had lived honestly and worked hard. . . . Then they found them-
> selves deprived of employment by economic forces over which they
> had no control. Little by little they spent their life savings while
> vainly seeking new jobs.

Roosevelt, however, provided a willful and evil enemy upon whom
blame could be laid and he described the activities of the "economic
royalists" in vivid vocabulary:

> The savings of the average family, the capital of the small business
> man, the investments set aside for old age—other people's money—
> these were tools which the new economic royalty used to dig itself
> in. Those who tilled the soil no longer reaped the rewards which
> were their right. The small measure of their gains was decreed by
> men in distant cities. . . . Individual initiative was crushed in the
> cogs of a great machine.

Roosevelt's depiction of the hardships of the depression was far more
concrete than that of Landon in the selection of words. The effect was
sharpened even further by the alliteration (letters underlined above, r- r-
r-, d- d-, i- i-, c- c-). And the phrase "decreed by men in distant cities"
continued the theme of the royal tyrant.

Landon criticized the policies of the Roosevelt administration, as is
customary for challengers with respect to the administrations of incumbents. The general tone of Landon's criticisms was restrained, even
somewhat bland. In effect, he invited his hearers to reason along with
him. And he reasoned in extremely homey and prosaic language, as the
following examples show:

> The record shows that these measures did not fit together into any
> definite program of recovery. Judged by the things that make us a

nation of happy families, the New Deal has fallen far short of success.

Worse than this . . . is the fact that the administration . . . has gambled with the needed food and feed supplies of the country.

Taking a dispute after it gets into a tangle and rushing it to the doorstep of the President is a bad way to handle a labor situation or any other situation.

Roosevelt presented his critics as enemies of the average person and repeatedly linked them, through simile and metaphor, with the eighteenth-century British royal tyrant. In addition to the passage quoted above, his speech contained sentences such as the following, the first also evoking the War of 1812:

For out of this modern civilization economic royalists carved new dynasties. New kingdoms were built upon concentration of control . . . the whole structure of modern life was impressed into this royal service.

The royalists of the economic order have conceded that political freedom was the business of the government, but they have maintained that economic slavery was nobody's business.

A more detailed comparison of these speeches would show a number of structurally balanced contrasting clauses in that of Roosevelt and only one in that of Landon, figurative language throughout Roosevelt's and only three somewhat pallid metaphors in Landon's, eighteen examples of alliteration in Roosevelt's and two in Landon's. Landon's address included a stereotyped reference to the Declaration of Independence; Roosevelt alluded to it in such a way as to dramatize even more his point concerning the concentration of power.

The conclusions of these speeches presented the same contrasts as the main parts. Landon's was a conventional affirmation of confidence in the country and in God's help:

It is in these aims and in these works that I envision the manifest destiny of America. Everything we need for their realization we can find, I firmly believe, within the principles under which this nation has grown to greatness. God grant us, one and all, the strength and wisdom to do our part in bringing these things to pass.

Having dramatically juxtaposed the current crisis with that of the American Revolution, Roosevelt concluded with a ringing challenge to battle. And in obliquely identifying himself as the chosen commander, he might have also suggested a direct link between himself and the commander who led the American Revolution:

> To some generations much is given. Of others much is expected. This generation of Americans has a rendezvous with destiny. . . . we are waging a great war. It is not alone a war against want and destitution and economic demoralization. It is a war for the survival of democracy. . . . I accept the commission you have tendered me. I join with you. I am enlisted for the duration of the war.

It might be worth noting the receptions accorded these addresses by audiences on the scene. Landon delivered his in Topeka, capital of the state of Kansas, whose governor he then was. Although the local newspaper estimated the audience as upwards of 100,000, the *New York Times* correspondent, Warren Moscow, gave a more conservative estimate of 60,000.[9] The *Topeka Daily Capital* counted "seventy-one hearty rounds of applause," but Moscow observed that after an initial ovation when Landon first appeared, the crowd "listened quietly, intently, applauding only when he paused to give them the opportunity."[10]

Roosevelt addressed an audience of about 100,000 in the Philadelphia stadium. According to the *New York Times*, at several points in the speech he could barely finish a sentence before "uncontrollable" cheers arose.[11] After the line containing the phrase "rendezvous with destiny," the audience reportedly "nearly went crazy."[12] Many of those present apparently remained after the great ovation and after Roosevelt left the arena "as if in a sort of trance."[13]

9. *New York Times*, July 24, 1936; *Topeka Daily Capital*, July 24, 1936.

10. Although a Landon biographer, Donald McCoy, in *Landon of Kansas* (Lincoln: University of Nebraska Press, 1966), p. 273, repeats almost verbatim the version of the Topeka paper, the account in the *New York Times* seems more reliable if only on the grounds that its correspondent was not likely to have been afflicted with local chauvinism.

11. *New York Times*, June 28, 1936.

12. Lash, *Eleanor Roosevelt*, p. 443.

13. Schlesinger, *Roosevelt*, 3, *The Politics of Upheaval*, p. 585.

Willkie and Roosevelt: The Boardroom versus the Arena of History

Wendell Willkie, the dark horse candidate of the Republican Party in 1940, was a far more formidable opponent for Roosevelt to face than Landon. Willkie had suddenly been catapulted to fame and popularity. And sudden emergence onto a national stage in a leading role has a special glamour and appeal superficially akin to charisma. Willkie's candidacy was a political phenomenon practically unequaled in the history of American presidential campaigns. Unlike Eisenhower, whose name had been a household word before he entered the political arena, Willkie had been known only to the small segment of the American public familiar with the names of prominent business executives.

Willkie, in fact, had been a Democrat until 1938, when he switched to the Republican Party. He was not even considered as a possible candidate until April 1940, when a campaign on his behalf was launched by a group of influential eastern seaboard financiers and businessmen on the one hand and a group of publishers and editors on the other. The campaign rapidly gained momentum as Willkie-for-President Clubs were organized throughout the country. Willkie was strongly opposed by the Old Guard of his party. He secured the nomination largely as the result of a well-organized bombardment of the convention delegates by letters, telegrams, and telephone calls from Willkie supporters and a near stampede of the convention hall and its environs by hordes of people shouting and stamping "We want Willkie!"[14]

It is more difficult to compare Willkie's acceptance address with Roosevelt's than it is to make this comparison between Landon's and Roosevelt's, for there are fewer parallel passages. One theme to which both candidates addressed themselves was that of the challenge to this country of the war in Europe and Hitler's stunning victories in Norway, Denmark, Belgium, the Netherlands, and France. Willkie introduced the subject as follows:

> We must face a brutal, perhaps a terrible fact. Our way of life is in competition with Hitler's way of life. This competition is not merely one of armaments. It is a competition of energy against energy,

14. Donald Bruce Johnson, *The Republican Party and Wendell Willkie* (Urbana: University of Illinois, 1960), p. 83.

production against production, brains against brains, salesman-ship against salesmanship.

The strong adjectives, "brutal" and "terrible," in the first sentence pre-pare the auditor for an appalling or awesome phenomenon. After this, the image of "competition" seems anticlimactic and almost in-congruous. A competition of "production" and "salesmanship" evokes the image of the business conference, the boardroom, and the annual stockholders' report and meeting.

In contrast to Willkie's imagery from the world of business, which almost demeaned and made trivial the nature of the danger and the struggle, Roosevelt's words on the same theme placed the challenge in the perspective of the sweep of history and of the times of momentous decisions that shaped the world to come:

> We face one of the great choices of history. It is not alone a choice of government—government by the people versus dictatorship. It is not alone a choice of freedom versus slavery. It is not alone a choice between moving forward or falling back; it is all of these rolled into one. It is the continuance of civilization as we know it versus the ultimate destruction of all that we have held dear—religion against godlessness, the ideal of justice against the practice of force, moral decency versus the firing squad, courage to speak out and to act versus the false lullaby of appeasement.

Apart from the slightly incongruous note in the metaphoric use of *lul-laby*, the rest of the passage communicates a sense of the direness of the situation.

After specifying the nature of the challenge, both Willkie and Roose-velt indicated an appropriate response. Said Willkie:

> In facing it we should have no fear. History shows that our way of life is the stronger way. From it has come more industry, more happiness, more human enlightenment than from any other way. Free men are the strongest men.
>
> But we cannot take this historical fact for granted. We must make it live. If we are to outdistance the totalitarian powers, we must arise to a new life of adventure and discovery.

Roosevelt's words were:

It has been well said that a selfish and greedy people cannot be free. The American people must decide whether these things are worth making sacrifices of money, of energy and of self.

Neither of these passages seems especially inspiring. But if Willkie's began on a reassuring note, although in prosaic words, it concluded discordantly. The urge to adventure and discovery seems unrelated to and incongruent with the challenge of the totalitarian advance. Roosevelt's words were consistent with the challenge as posed and did contain a climactic buildup in beginning with the sacrifice of money and ending with the sacrifice of self.

Different dominant images were suggested also by Willkie's rhetorical mode of coping with criticism of himself as compared with Roosevelt's. Willkie had been accused of being a conservative and a supporter of big business behind the facade of publicity emphasizing his rural Indiana farmboy origins; "barefoot boy from Wall Street" was one phrase coined by one of the opposition that caught on. Roosevelt had strongly been criticized, especially by the isolationists, for trying to bring the United States into the war. Willkie dealt somewhat weakly with the criticism of himself:

Because I am a businessman, formerly connected with a large company, the doctrinaires of the opposition have attacked me as an opponent of liberalism. But I was a liberal before many of these men had heard the word, and I fought for many of the reforms of the elder LaFollette, Theodore Roosevelt, and Woodrow Wilson before another Roosevelt adopted—and distorted—liberalism.

Willkie started by stating the criticism and the reason for it and then denied it. The denial, however, was weakened by what amounted to a "me too" type of statement that did not sharpen the difference between him and his opponent. However much it may be true, to state that one "was there first" has an aroma of "sour grapes."

Roosevelt's mode of dealing with the criticism against himself was masterly:

I would not undo, if I could, the efforts I made to prevent war from the moment it was threatened and to restrict the area of carnage, down to the last minute. I do not now soften the condemnation expressed by Secretary Hull and myself from time to time for the acts of aggression that have wiped out ancient, liberty-loving, peace-pursuing countries which had scrupulously maintained neutrality. I do not recant the sentiments of sympathy with all free peoples resisting such aggression or begrudge the material aid that we have given to them. I do not regret my consistent efforts to awaken this country of ours to the menace for us and all we hold dear. I have pursued these efforts in the face of appeaser 'fifth columnists' who charge me with hysteria and war-mongering.

There is much in this passage that bears minute analysis. Perhaps most noteworthy is the fact that Roosevelt, unlike Willkie, did not begin by mentioning the criticism of himself but ended the passage with it. However, by virtue of what he said before this, the criticism was made to appear absurd and, even more impressive, was transposed into a criticism of those who were his critics.

From the start of the passage, the tone was not at all defensive but bravely assertive, with a repetitiveness of phrase ("I would not undo. . . . I do not now soften. . . .") that would tend to magnify and give momentum to the assertion. The tone of bravery was accentuated by association with those bravely resisting aggression in Europe. Even before the end of the passage Roosevelt was turning the tables on his critics by the terms he used. In stating that he would not "begrudge," for example, he implied that they did and suggested crass selfishness on the part of those criticizing aid to "free peoples." For the Allies were consistently characterized in terms that evoked sentiments sacred to the American heritage, that is, "liberty-loving," "peace pursuing," "neutrality."

The next to the last sentence seemed to bring the danger from Europe to this country. Roosevelt's critics were not only characterized as obstacles to his high-minded endeavors. When this address was delivered in July 1940, *appeaser* and especially *fifth columnist* were terms for new and horrifying phenomena that still had shock value. By applying these terms to his critics, Roosevelt in effect called them the enemy within and made them appear not only absurd in their attacks on him but dangerous to the country at large.

Obviously rhetoric alone did not determine the outcome of the 1940 election. Insofar as rhetoric contributed, however, boardroom and sports-field imagery could not compete with that of ultimate being and civilization for those who knew or feared that war was in the offing and had to choose a commander. In the last passage quoted, Roosevelt was not merely castigating his critics but also obliquely projecting images of himself as commander, images of the preventer and condemner of evil, the succor of the suffering, and the prophet of, and protector against, the danger to come.

8
Political Strategies
in Aid of Charisma

Each of the preceding chapters has dealt at some length with one of the elements crucial to the creation of charismatically oriented perceptions of political leaders. If not all instances of political charisma have contained all four of the elements specified, all those noted have contained at least three.[1] These may therefore be considered the core elements in the creation of political charisma.

In addition, however, there are some other factors that can and sometimes do contribute to the formation of charismatically oriented responses. I treat these separately in this chapter under the rubric of "political strategies." For they are in the main political strategies that have been employed by many political leaders, including those that have not gained charismatic acclaim, in efforts to strengthen their legitimacy and support. They are treated separately from the core elements and in less detail because they are primarily additive or reinforcing factors in the development of charisma and neither necessary nor sufficient for it. While the potential of each strategy for aiding charisma is discussed, it is also conceivable that the actual contribution of any of them in any

---

1. To avoid needless repetition, I have not given illustrations for each of the leaders on each of the elements. There is plentiful evidence, for example, that with the possible exception of Gandhi all the leaders in the sample were perceived as outstanding orators not only by their own countrypeople but also by foreigners who observed their effects on audiences.

specific case was also attributable to aspects of the context in which or the style with which it was employed.

Invocation of the Glorious Past

Clever political leaders who have initiated a change or contemplate a radical revision of their political systems often strive to maintain a sense of continuity while so doing. They may not wish to preserve "the semblance of the old forms," as Machiavelli advised reformers to do,[2] but they try to legitimize their regimes and themselves by linking them to the memories and symbols of one or more previous regimes, particularly those that resonate with glory and grandeur.

Hitler strove to link his regime with that of the Prussian monarchy and those of the early German kings by celebrating the opening of his Reichstag in 1933 at the Garrison Church in Potsdam on March 21. Potsdam had been the royal seat of the Hohenzollern monarchs. The Garrison Church, built by Frederick William I, contained the grave of Frederick the Great. March 21 commemorated the date on which Bismarck had opened the first Reichstag of the German Empire in 1871. In the galleries were admirals, generals, and marshals of the old empire wearing their prewar imperial uniforms.[3]

The spectacularly orchestrated and choreographed party rallies at Nuremberg also contained traditional symbols as well as all the banners, insignia, and paraphernalia of Nazi Germany. The 1938 rally, for example, was opened with a dedication to the First Reich, symbolized by the orb of empire, the imperial crown, the sword, and the scepter.[4]

Mussolini most deliberately and sustainedly sought to surround himself and his regime with the aura of ancient Rome. The very name, fascism, had its origin in the *fasci* or rods carried by the Roman lictors. The fascist militia was organized on the Roman model. It and most paramilitary organizations, even those of small boys, had Roman names for various units. There were the statues of the Roman wolf, a caged Roman eagle on the Capital, the introduction of the Roman form of

---

2. Machiavelli, *Prince*, pp. 182–83.
3. Bullock, *Hitler*, p. 226.
4. McRandle, *Wolf*, p. 13.

address, and other reminders of imperial Rome. Moreover, Mussolini also embarked on a vast program of restoring ancient Roman ruins and monuments as well as building new edifices.[5]

It has been said that, for some Germans, the forest of massed banners, the smoking torches, the columns of light cast by giant searchlights, the bands playing Wagnerian music, and other elements of the spectacles staged by Hitler at Nuremberg and elsewhere turned these spectacles into visions of Valhalla and Hitler into the incarnation of Siegfried. Although I have not encountered any specific testimony to this effect, it is quite possible that these invocations partly converged in perceptions of the person of Hitler as well as of his regime. The linkage of the leader with the heroic and mythical past may not have been so direct or so intense here as in the instances analyzed in chapter 4. But its existence is suggested by the fact that William Shirer encountered people selling postcards displaying the portraits of Frederick the Great, Bismarck, Hindenburg, and Hitler together.[6]

Similarly, I have not encountered any direct evidence that Mussolini's postures on his balcony, the tilt of his head, or his outthrust jaw caused Italians to see him in the guise of a Caesar, although that may have been so for some. Evidence that Mussolini was assimilated to the image of Augustus or Hitler to that of Siegfried or Frederick Barbarossa would have led me to include them in chapter 4. Although it cannot be asserted that their invocations of glorious past traditions associated them in the minds of their peoples with specific legendary or historic heroes or generalized cultural heroic types, it might be alleged that these invocations aroused mass emotions that were projected on them and so enhanced their charisma. Moreover, such invocations could well have contributed to their being seen as the restorers of past glory and the bearers of the new "golden age."

The Demigod Steps Down

In an age of democracy and egalitarian values, political leaders often feel impelled to demonstrate that they are of the people as well as for them.

---

5. Fermi, *Mussolini*, pp. 216–19. See Howard Wriggins, *The Ruler's Imperative: Strategies for Political Survival in Asia and Africa* (New York: Columbia University Press, 1969), p. 102, for other examples of invocation of cultural tradition through personal behavior.
6. Shirer, *Third Reich*, p. 133.

Such demonstrations are often in the nature of a publicity stunt and may carry little conviction. Or if the demonstrations seem in character with the general personal demeanor of the individual, as when President Ford was publicized as making his own breakfast, he is newsworthy mainly by virtue of some related fact, as in the case of Ford by comparison with his predecessor.

However, it is different in the case of someone who is perceived and treated as a demigod, who seems to stand on a lofty pinnacle, whether one of power, prestige, or genius. He partakes somewhat of the aura traditionally associated with royalty. Not only do people not resent a lordly and remote demeanor from him, but it may even be expected by them if one of his roles is to symbolize the majesty or greatness of the state, nation, or people.

Therefore, a special significance is attached to the occasions when someone who is so regarded with awe and at a distance steps down from his pedestal to sound and act as an ordinary being. This phenomenon was mentioned in the previous chapter in connection with Roosevelt's use of colloquial and folksy phrases. Because the great man is not expected to sound or act in ordinary fashion, the fact that he does so lends him added luster and can also increase perceptions of his strength. By making the effort to show his kinship with everyman, when it is not necessary, he is perceived as beneficent and warmhearted. Moreover, to some, the fact that he can do so without concern that he or his position will be demeaned is indicative of his strength and assurance. Thus, both the love and awe components of charismatic perceptions can be furthered by acts of "being one with the people."

Mussolini performed such acts fairly frequently and generally with wide publicity. Some of these activities were intended to show Mussolini as an example of hard work to his people or to demonstrate the variety of skills he possessed. On other occasions he was merely expressing his exuberance of the moment, as when he saluted peasants in their vernacular or sang songs with soldiers at maneuvers.[7]

Sukarno also had such exuberant impulses, wielding a hoe and joining in singing and dancing on his tours. Castro worked as a "volunteer" on the land for two weeks during a sugar harvest.[8] Gandhi's spinning and

---

7. Finer, *Mussolini*, pp. 289–90.
8. Lockwood, *Castro's Cuba*, p. 279.

wearing of a loincloth were primarily intended to discourage Indians from the use of imported manufactured cloth and to revive cottage industry. Yet these symbols of traditional village life, so unconventional for an Indian political leader of his day, were also viewed as an assertion of identity with rural villagers.

The Éclat of Innovation

Priority in achieving a type of powerful result without power, argues Dankwart Rustow, constitutes a strong claim to charisma.[9] Innovation in means or techniques, apart from results, may not be so directly related to charisma, but a dramatic innovation on the part of a political leader can have a magnetic impact. It not only affords him the center of the stage but can contribute to perceptions of him as being daring enough to take a risk. An innovation, almost by definition, is unconventional and the act of innovating can suggest confidence, creativity, and courage in the innovator.

Roosevelt used standard techniques in ways that seemed novel or unprecedented and developed new ones as a campaigner and a chief executive. His first bravura gesture as national leader was to fly to Chicago in 1932 to accept the presidential nomination in person. His predecessors had waited for formal notification. Soon after he entered office, he began his radio "fireside chats," an innovation he had initiated while governor of New York. He revived the presidential press conference as a regular institution and established it "as the American equivalent of the parliamentary question period."[10] In his first term he held 337 such conferences.[11]

The warm and highly personal tone the fireside chats conveyed to millions of Americans convinced many that Roosevelt personally cared about them and their problems, and they saw him in the light of a father and protector.[12] The flight to Chicago could be seen in retrospect as having symbolically heralded the New Deal, a novel attack on the coun-

---

9. Rustow, *Philosophers*, p. 209.
10. Schlesinger, 2, p. 562.
11. Ibid.
12. Leuchtenburg, *Roosevelt*, pp. 330–31.

try's problems. Apart from the issues that arose at the press conferences, their format and tone produced an impression upon reporters that was more widely communicated. At the first one, Roosevelt did away with prepared questions and indicated his readiness to reply impromptu to whatever questions the reporters would ask. This degree of confidence startled many and gave rise to skepticism concerning whether Roosevelt could long sustain this format. He not only did but continually impressed the press people with his knowledge of detail, his wit, his ability to tease and joke with them and be joked with and teased in turn, and his superb self-confidence.[13]

Shortly before Roosevelt flew to Chicago, Hitler commenced to campaign by plane for the elections in Germany. His flights were highly publicized with the slogan "Hitler over Germany." According to one biographer, they "created an impression of brilliant inspiration, bold modernity, fighting spirit, and a rather sinister omnipresence."[14] Other elements of the still new technology were employed in the 1932 electoral campaigns, such as the distribution of thousands of gramophone records by mail and films of Hitler distributed to film theaters whose managers were pressured to screen them.[15]

Within the last decade it has become almost commonplace for political leaders and other political activists to stage media events or conduct political activities in such a manner as to manipulate the media. Castro planned and pulled off a media coup that resulted in his being viewed in mythlike proportions.

In 1957 Castro was holed up in the forests of the Sierra Maestra with a very small group of survivors from his landing on the south coast of Cuba. It was believed in Havana that he was dead. Hearing that Herbert Matthews, a *New York Times* correspondent, was vacationing in Havana, he sent someone to bring Matthews secretly to his hideout. In about a week, Matthews's dispatches appeared over three days on the front page of the *New York Times*. The sympathetic stories about the idealistic young revolutionary caused a sensation. Moreover, because of a temporary lifting of censorship in Havana, they appeared in Cuban papers also.

13. Burns, *Roosevelt*, p. 205; Leuchtenburg, *Roosevelt*, p. 330.
14. Fest, *Hitler*, p. 320.
15. Ibid., p. 318.

The Cuban minister of national defense labeled them a concocted fantasy in the absence of photographic verification. The *New York Times* then published a photograph. In less than two months, an American television team was in the Sierra Maestra to make a documentary film of Castro and his men.[16]

Many of these political innovations have since become institutionalized. Campaigning is routinely done with private or chartered planes; the American presidential press conference is seen to be so much a part of the presidential role that Nixon was strongly criticized for neglecting it; and a revolutionary banner is barely raised in a remote jungle or desert before television correspondents arrive to present the movement and its leader to distant audiences. It is easy therefore to overlook the impact of these innovations when they first took place and the éclat and even awe with which they surrounded the innovators.

The Suspense Tactic

Political leaders as well as actors have long known the value of building up suspense before an announcement or an appearance. The element of suspense, as has been noted in chapter 5 in connection with the outstanding feat, tends to magnify and heighten the importance of whoever or whatever dissipates the tension built up by the suspense. It is even possible in some instances for any factor that relieves the tension of suspense and apprehension to become valued positively if only because it does so. An example of this in the political realm might be the welcome that Mussolini received in Rome in 1922 from non-Fascists who saw him as delivering the country from a prolonged crisis, despite the part played by him and his movement in creating that crisis.

The creation of suspense as part of spectacle was a major item in Hitler's public appearances. As mentioned above, many of them were minutely planned and orchestrated, in part by Hitler himself. In halls, his appearances were often deliberately and artificially delayed and the audiences subjected to various stimuli until he stepped out in a blaze of light after it seemed that the sense of expectation had mounted to a frenzy.[17] Most of his outdoor meetings and rallies were held at night to

---

16. Matthews, *Cuban Story*, pp. 31–61; Taber, *M-26*, pp. 95–100.
17. Fest, *Hitler*, pp. 324–26.

enable the use of artificial lighting to enhance his appearance. However, on one morning, Goebbels delayed his own introductory speech until the sun, which was striving to come out from behind clouds, could break through as Hitler stepped before the audience.[18]

Roosevelt's buildup of suspense before entering office for his first presidential term has been recounted in chapter 5. He also made use of this strategy on other occasions, most notably in connection with decisions about running for a third term and about his vice-presidential running mates. In these and other instances, suspense was deliberately generated for some very specific immediate political reasons. However, a secondary effect was to dramatize before a nationwide audience Roosevelt's power and indispensability.

Sukarno's indispensability was also dramatized by the use of suspense. One of Sukarno's most dramatic and unconventional political strategies was to go abroad in the course of a domestic crisis, including some that he helped to precipitate, such as the one that arose as a result of his charge to the Constituent Assembly in 1959 to return to the Constitution of 1945.[19] These overseas trips afforded a number of tactical advantages, such as allowing trial balloons to be launched on his behalf that he could later disavow or flushing some opposition into the open, to mention only two. Moreover, as disagreement and dissension increased in the country, as in 1959, so did suspense and anxiety about the outcome. All eyes turned toward the returning Sukarno as the sole possibility of surmounting the crisis. He usually did, to his advantage, as in 1959 he obtained the Guided Democracy he had wanted for a number of years. Another result of the suspense was to heighten his image as the all-powerful pivot around whom the country revolved.

Organizational Overlap and Competition

The ways in which a number of charismatic leaders who have become heads of state have handled state administration seem to bear out Weber's contention that charisma disdains formal organizational rules and procedures. The organization of governmental agencies in the administrations of Roosevelt, Hitler, Mussolini, and Sukarno defied many

---

18. Ibid., p. 444.
19. For details, see Legge, *Sukarno*, pp. 229–310.

of the canons of good public administration. Numbers of new bodies were created with jurisdictional boundaries poorly delimited. Authority frequently overlapped and coordination was frequently lacking.

Roosevelt assigned individuals with different outlooks overlapping tasks, such as Welles and Hull in the State Department. He divided control or authority over some area between two agencies and their heads as, for example, public works was divided between Ickes and Hopkins. He did this, Burns has noted, not out of ignorance of management methods but to stimulate effort and assure his control through the process of divide and rule through competition.[20]

In Germany in 1942 there were fifty-eight Supreme Reich boards as well as numbers of other bureaus fighting one another for authority outside the older ministries. Education, the press, the economy, and other areas were "battlegrounds fought over by three or four competing departments, and this guerrilla warfare over territory . . . permeated even the lowest branches of the bureaucracy."[21] Neurath, the foreign minister, Rosenberg, head of the National Socialist Party's Foreign Affairs Bureau, and Ribbentrop, with his own bureau, had an ongoing tug-of-war over foreign affairs.[22]

Sukarno's Guided Democracy was also characterized by a "continued proliferation of . . . administrative bodies with diffuse and overlapping jurisdictions and no clear-cut division or allocation of power and responsibilities among them."[23] During periods when Indonesia was in a state of military emergency and martial law, the competition within the large civil bureaucracy was intensified by competition between some of its units and the parallel national and regional military authority. While Mussolini's corporate state may not have displayed quite as great a profusion of competitive and overlapping units, it also displayed the same general syndrome described above.

The expansion of these bureaucracies may well have resulted in part from the increased intervention of government in economic and social

20. Burns, *Roosevelt*, pp. 371–74.
21. Fest, *Hitler*, p. 419.
22. Shirer, *Third Reich*, p. 380.
23. Ann Ruth Willner, "The Neotraditional Accommodation to Political Independence: The Case of Indonesia," in *Cases in Comparative Politics: Asia*, ed. Lucian Pye (Boston: Little, Brown, 1970), pp. 248–51.

affairs that took place as these leaders modified their political systems. The lack of coordination, however, and the intrabureaucratic rivalries seem partly to have stemmed from a concern on the part of these leaders to prevent the development of subordinate power centers, to maintain alternate sources of information and policy alternatives, and above all, to ensure ultimate control.

By fostering this rivalry they also fostered a sense of dependency in their subordinates and the necessity for the latter to appeal to them and to court their favor. This promoted the image of the omniscient or omnipotent leader to whom all must go and from whom all decisions must ultimately flow.

9
The Impact and Legacy of Political Charisma

This study has been devoted to explaining the origins and development of political charisma. To conclude by dealing in depth with the legacy of political charisma in the twentieth century would be premature and presumptuous. Even to assess what has been wrought by the charisma of a single leader would be a formidable enterprise and one likely to yield controversial results. As Peter Geyl has shown in the case of Napoleon, charismatic leaders and their works have not only been controversial in their lifetimes but have remained subject to controversy for decades and even generations after their deaths.[1]

Some journalists seem to have little trouble crediting some leaders' accomplishments to their charisma. Serious students might find this a hazardous enterprise, for there can be considerable difficulty in discerning whether or how much a particular success can be attributed to a leader's charisma rather than to other factors. There is admittedly an easy way out of this difficulty in the cases of leaders for whom charisma was salient in gaining power. It can be argued that since their power was derived from their charisma, all that they have done with that power can also be treated as derived from charisma.

Apart from the fact that this approach might be begging the question, it cannot encompass the cases of leaders whose charisma was gained

1. Peter Geyl, *Napoleon: For and Against* (London: J. Cape, 1949).

after they obtained power. For when a charismatic political leader achieves the power and authority of public office or when an incumbent of such office achieves charisma, it becomes difficult to disentangle the results that can be attributed to his charisma from the results that can be attributed to the formal powers of his office. It is even more difficult in a closed society. In the later years of Mussolini's regime, could it be determined which of those who volunteered for various Fascist campaigns and auxiliary organizations did so because of Mussolini's charismatic inspiration and which did so in order to play safe? How much of the success of the campaign to eradicate rural illiteracy in Cuba derived from the charisma of Castro and how much from the pressure of government officials working under the direction of Castro as head of government?

Even when one is able to pinpoint charisma as the prime cause of the success of an act or event, there is still an obstacle. How can one measure the range of its impact at any time or over a period of time? The nonviolent resistance of many Indians seemed to be largely the result of Gandhi's charisma. This resistance seemed to be a factor in the ultimate attainment of Indian independence. But how large a factor was it?

After independence, during the postpartition mutual slaughter of Hindus and Muslims, it appeared that Gandhi's charisma had waned and belief in nonviolence had died. Yet one gathers that this Gandhian principle is not absent in the settlement of caste and village disputes in India today. A dramatic consequence of Gandhi's postmortem charisma at a distance was the adoption of nonviolence by Martin Luther King and his followers. We know about this because it was newsworthy, but other manifestations of Gandhi's charisma may not receive notice. The immediate impact of a leader's charisma is often observable; ultimate impacts may be difficult to detect and measure.

Finally, there is the problem of evaluating the impact of charismatic leadership. Here controversy is likely to be endemic. There might be relative consensus, at either end of a spectrum, concerning what followed from the charisma of Gandhi and Hitler. Agreement about what was wrought by the charisma of others is unlikely. For example, Castro, who is positively perceived by some people as having built an egalitarian society, is negatively seen by others as having wrecked an economy and substituted one tyranny for another.

Different basic value premises and different subjective preferences yield different assessments of the results of charismatically induced happenings and consequences. And time may change perspectives and assessments. In recent years, for example, Kemal Atatürk has been frequently cited positively as a prime example of a nation-building leader. Some of the means he used, means that would hardly pass muster if used today, are given scant attention.

Given these caveats, what can be said about the impact and legacy of charismatic political leadership? Obviously, those who undertake minute historical reconstructions of individual cases of political charisma will emerge with many and varied conclusions. The few observations offered here are all derived from most, if not all, of the cases studied.

Charisma and the Road to Power

During the stage of a leader's ascent to formal power, political charisma can undoubtedly be a major asset. A charismatically oriented following can be ordered to the polls or out onto the streets at will. Its members vociferously demonstrate their leader's popularity, swell audiences, and campaign for him with extraordinary vigor and often at sacrifice to themselves. A leader can use such followers as a means of subtle or overt intimidation, provoking them to demonstrations or boycotts and encouraging violence with the threat of further violence to come. He can restrain them from action or violence if it seems advantageous. He has, in short, a most malleable instrument to use at will.

A charismatic hold on some part of his following permits a leader greater flexibility than leaders without charisma are likely to have. Political leaders on the rise generally seek to broaden their support. They run the risk that attempts to attract a new group may lose them some part of their existing support base because stands that are at odds with earlier stands may alienate older adherents while appealing to new ones. Therefore, they have to calculate the costs and limits of major shifts in strategy.

Charismatic leaders are less constrained. It is true that they may lose some of their supporters if they zigzag sharply or seem to act contrary to their earlier proclaimed principles. But those who are charismatically oriented to them stay with them and can be counted upon to do so.

Hitler's early National Socialism contained a considerable element of those strongly oriented to socialism as well as to nationalism. When in 1930 Hitler moved to woo and obtain contributions from bankers and industrialists in Germany, those with socialist orientations were far from happy. Perhaps unhappiest was one of their leaders and one of Hitler's most effective lieutenants, Otto Strasser. In the Nazi newspapers he controlled, Strasser came out in strong support for a trade union strike in Saxony, much to the embarrassment of Hitler, who had ordered party members not to participate in the strike. Moreover, Fritz Thyssen, a leading industrialist, informed Hitler that Strasser's stands might dry up contributions from German industrialists.

In a confrontation with Hitler, Strasser accused him of sacrificing the social revolution for legality and collaboration with bourgeois rightist parties. Hitler soon ordered Strasser to be expelled from the party. Strasser made a very public departure, inviting others of the left wing to leave with him and form a new group. Only a handful did so. For the rest, including Strasser's own brother, Hitler's appeal seems to have been stronger than principle.[2]

The almost automatic obedience a leader can command from a charismatically oriented following gives him substantial leverage in his maneuvers with other leaders and groups. Should he wish to dissimulate, a sometimes useful strategy in maneuvering for power, he can manipulate followers to increase his credibility. Thus, Hitler wished to dissimulate when he saw an opportunity to achieve power through constitutional means. However, the violence of the Nazi paramilitary forces, such as the S.A., or stormtroopers, caused great apprehension in the circles that he wished to cultivate and reassure as to his moderation.

Hitler therefore, in 1931, ordered the S.A. to stop fighting in the streets. He even dissolved one unit that had obtained arms against orders. By the following year the state police accumulated considerable evidence indicating that the S.A. was planning a coup. A government decree was issued, disbanding the S.A. and allied paramilitary organizations. Ernst Roehm, the head of the S.A., whose 400,000 members out-

---

2. Bullock, *Hitler*, pp. 156–58; Fest, *Hitler*, pp. 278–82; John Toland, *Adolf Hitler* (Garden City, N.Y.: Doubleday, 1976), pp. 239–40.

numbered the regular German army, and his associates seriously considered resisting this decree by force. When they got word from Hitler to obey it, they obeyed it.[3]

Charisma can even more directly contribute to gaining formal power. Under conditions of crisis and uncertainty, it can be the major decisive factor in a leader's obtaining office. This happened in Indonesia under the circumstances of a struggle for independence. Sukarno was not then charismatic for most of the other leaders of the independence movement and was not even highly respected by some of the most prominent of them. However, Sukarno's manifest charisma for the masses made him the logical choice of the political elite for president of the new state.

A charismatic hold on a following can also have psychological effects that can be converted into political gains. The conviction and intensity of charismatic commitment can breed new recruits from among those observers who conclude that a leader who can inspire others to such dedication must be well worth following. Another possible effect is the development of a sense of the inevitability of the success of the leader among nonfollowers and opponents. A visible group of fanatic political activists can seem compelling, intimidating, and even unassailable. When General von Schleicher was urged in 1931 to take strong measures against the Nazis, he answered: "Should we try . . . we would simply be swept away."[4] Thus, a sort of contagion effect of charisma can magnify a leader's following, and a steamroller effect can discourage those who stand in the way of his rise to power.

Charisma and the Consolidation of Power

A leader may come to believe that the powers vested in the office he holds are insufficient to accomplish a goal or goals important to him. He may therefore wish to increase them, either by winning grants of special powers from a legislature or through effecting changes in the system. In such cases a charismatic constituency can be a major asset. It can be ordered to put pressure on a legislature or on other relevant structures of government.

3. Bullock, *Hitler*, pp. 202–04; Fest, *Hitler*, pp. 300, 333–35.
4. Fest, *Hitler*, p. 312.

The larger universe of a leader's followers, as well as those who are neutrally oriented or opposed to him, may not necessarily favor pronounced changes in a political order. A notable instance of this was the number of Americans who, while favoring the New Deal measures that were defeated by the Supreme Court, nonetheless opposed Roosevelt's attempt to change the Court structure. There are followers who will support a leader's attempts at structural change, but only up to a point.

For the charismatic constituency, however, the leader's desires become commands and its members are prepared to go to extreme lengths to forward them. When recognized by others, this can become a decisive weapon in a leader's battle to effect changes through persuasion, intimidation, or a combination of both. When Mussolini first faced the Italian Chamber of Deputies as prime minister, he had gained charismatic acclaim from thousands of his Fascist followers as a result of the so-called March on Rome and the apparent triumph of the movement. He had also attempted to conciliate and pacify other political groups by including in his cabinet men from a number of political parties. His cabinet contained only three other Fascists, much to the disappointment of some of his ambitious lieutenants.

Mussolini asked the Chamber to give him "full powers" to institute administrative and financial reforms. His request included a reminder that he could have seized what he was now asking for "with 300,000 young armed men prepared for anything . . . and ready to execute my commands with religious devotion" and that, if necessary, he could still do so.[5] A similar threat was subsequently made to the Senate. Both houses voted him the full powers he wanted. Hitler pursued a parallel strategy when he sought from the Reichstag the passage of the so-called Enabling Act. This was the act that in effect transformed the constitution of Germany and served as the basis for his subsequent dictatorial powers.[6]

Charismatic constituencies can aid political leaders not only in consolidating power but in maintaining it when it is threatened. Two years after the coup as a result of which he had risen to hold simultaneously the posts of vice-president, minister of war, and minister of labor and to

5. Kirkpatrick, *Mussolini*, pp. 145–46; Lyttelton, *Seizure*, pp. 95–102.
6. Fest, *Hitler*, pp. 403–10; Bullock, *Hitler*, pp. 267–70.

become the decisive figure in Argentina, General Perón was forced to resign in an internal revolt of the armed forces. However, after a massive demonstration by members of powerful labor unions for whom he had become charismatic, Perón was released from detention and restored to power. After Nasser's humiliating military defeat in 1967, subsequent to his failure to raise significantly the standard of living of the Egyptian masses, there were rumors of impending attempts to oust him. His demonstration of a charismatic hold on the volatile Cairo populace may well have been a major factor in discouraging such attempts. Shirer attributes the failure of the German army leaders who were conspiring to remove Hitler in 1939 to a "paralyzing sense of futility" that resulted from recognizing Hitler's complete hold on Germany.[7]

Charisma in Aid of Purpose and Policy

A political leader in power may proclaim and proselytize a measure, policy, or program. To carry one out, however, requires the efforts of others, no matter how much persuasion, patronage, bargaining, threat, or other tactic he may employ to stimulate them to marshal that effort. A leader's charisma can also play a role in the implementation of his goals and policies, but how great a role is empirically difficult to ascertain in most cases. We do not have available alternate historical scenarios to tell us what the New Deal or the Cuban Revolution might have been, had Roosevelt and Castro not been charismatic. We cannot send back in time survey researchers and pollsters to ascertain how much of the efforts of aides, civil servants, and others was due to their charismatic devotion to the leaders and how much to a sense of duty, agreement, opportunism, fear, or other motives.

General studies of the regimes of charismatic leaders do yield some impressions of the contributions of political charisma. The charismatic interplay between leader and followers seems to release considerable energy, at least for a period of time, in support of the major goals of these leaders. All accounts I have read of the early years of the New Deal stress the tremendous zeal, enthusiasm, and capacity for work of those in-

7. Shirer, *Third Reich*, p. 742.

volved in developing and implementing its various programs. Also emphasized is the renewed vitality of many groups, including business groups, that were apathetic, a vitality that was manifested even before any significant signs of economic recovery.

Accounts of the early periods of Castro's rule in Cuba and Hitler's rule in Germany also stress the energies and enthusiasm of those members of these states who were not opponents of the regime or treated as such. Their zeal to forward the new order apparently existed despite the increasing curbs on civil rights and the increasing regimentation.

Such observed enthusiasm and energy, however, may not in all instances be correctly credited to charisma. If a leader has tapped the latent desires of people and their goals and his desires and goals coincide or overlap, his charisma was not the major catalyst for their zeal. The nationalist goals and policies of Castro and Hitler may be seen as examples of such ambiguous cases.

Fairly unambiguous cases of charisma affecting the accomplishment of leadership goals are those in which people implement them at a cost to themselves. When they voluntarily sacrifice something, materially or otherwise, or undergo hardships at the bidding of a leader to further policies that are his rather than theirs, the stimulus would seem to be his charisma.

Mussolini's declaration of war against Abyssinia was popular in Italy and people were accustomed to the notion of wartime sacrifices. But Mussolini called upon the women of Italy for a novel sacrifice in 1935, one that meant more to them symbolically than probably did the surrender of more valuable objects. He asked them for their gold wedding rings and those of their husbands. And at Mussolini's call, there was a voluntary outpouring of wedding rings throughout Italy, from the queen in Rome to peasant women in tiny villages.[8]

One of the most dramatic sacrifices offered for a charismatic leader, and perhaps one of the most painful for those who offered, was the surrender of one of their most sacred convictions by Hindus in 1932 on Gandhi's behalf. The British had decided to have a separate electorate for Untouchables, apart from those for other Hindus and for Muslims.

8. Fermi, *Mussolini*, pp. 320–21.

Gandhi, then in prison, was strongly opposed, fearing that such an arrangement would not only harm Hinduism but would serve to perpetuate the untouchability he was striving to eradicate.

For thousands of years the status of untouchability had been institutionalized in Indian society and in the Hindu religion. Those millions who were born into this status, renamed by Gandhi Harijans, were below all castes, literally outcasts. Their touch was considered polluting by caste Hindus. Their livelihood was limited to the jobs rejected by others and they did the dirty work prohibited to others, such as tanning, cleaning streets, and scavenging. They were not permitted to enter the Hindu temples or to touch what other Hindus must later touch. Gandhi had first dramatically violated the strictures concerning their treatment in 1915, when he had welcomed a Harijan family as residents in his ashram.

Gandhi began one of his famous fasts and announced that, if necessary, he would fast to the death. This fast was directed to his own people, for the British indicated that they would accept a voting arrangement that Hindus and Harijans could mutually agree to. As Gandhi's fast began, Hindu and Untouchable spokesmen proceeded to negotiate with each other and with him.

Then there began events that astounded all who knew of the almost automatic loathing and fear felt by caste Hindus at the very thought of being touched by or in close proximity to an Untouchable. Twelve Hindu temples were opened to Untouchables in Allahabad. The members of seven large temples in Bombay voted 25,000 to 445 in favor of admitting Untouchable members. The doors of the most orthodox temple in Benares, the holy city, were opened to them. And so it went throughout India.

Even more astonishing was the public fraternization of Hindus with Untouchables. In the streets of the cities, high caste Hindus, including Brahmans, were seen eating together with the cobblers, street cleaners, sweepers, and scavengers. Nehru's mother, an orthodox Hindu, publicly proclaimed that she had taken food from the hands of an Untouchable. Women from all over the country emulated her. In Yeravada Prison, where Gandhi lay, copies of resolutions and statements against discrimination, sent to Gandhi from individuals, groups, and whole communities across the country, rose to a pile over five feet high.

Five days after the fast began, an agreement was signed. More significant was the fact that Gandhi's charisma had produced a miracle. The long tradition of acceptance and approval of untouchability was shattered and the basis was laid for its ultimate disappearance.[9]

The implementation of a leader's foreign policy may also be facilitated by his charisma, especially if the policy is one perceived as risky. Those who might oppose the policy within his own country might be hesitant to do so openly, not wanting a confrontation with his charismatically oriented supporters. More important, however, can be the credibility he can gain externally because of his known charismatic constituency. Sukarno was determined to secure Irian, or New Guinea, from the Netherlands and by 1960 indicated that he was prepared to go to war for it. Neither the Dutch leaders nor the American leaders, who had offered their good offices, were certain that he was not bluffing. Furthermore, the preparedness campaigns he mounted in Indonesia conveyed the impression that he could count on enthusiastic domestic support if he were not. Negotiations resulted in Sukarno's gaining his objective.

Finally, there might be mentioned the contribution of charisma to the passage of legislation in a country such as the United States with separation of powers and weak party control over legislators. A president or political executive may have a number of means of securing votes, but what legislators are generally most concerned with is the reaction of their constituents and their reelection. Not only did Roosevelt get considerable mail from his charismatically oriented supporters but so did their representatives and senators, often containing threats of defeat if they did not support one or another of his bills.[10]

The Limits of Political Charisma

Reflections on the contributions of charisma to power and policy can lead to some questions about what charisma has failed to accomplish in these areas. As one biographer of Roosevelt has asked, How come his charisma was not translated into full or nearly full employment?[11] If a

9. Ashe, *Gandhi*, pp. 317–18; Fischer, *Gandhi*, pp. 311–14, 322–23.
10. Sussman, *Dear FDR*, pp. 78–79.
11. James MacGregor Burns in letter of comment on manuscript of this work (Mar. 1978).

charismatic leader can count on almost automatic obedience to his commands from followers, why have some explicit goals of charismatic leaders failed to be realized? Moreover, if some, such as Sukarno, were really so charismatic, how could they have been removed from power?

One of the obvious factors affecting what charisma can do is how far charisma extends. The radius of a public figure's charisma has rarely, if ever, extended to include all or most of those under the official bounds of his authority. As was noted in the first chapter, even systems of authority with a strong charismatic component tend to be mixed. A charismatic leader cannot count on constant compliance from followers who are not part of his charismatic constituency and can count on little from his opponents but opposition.

In an open or even partially open political system, the status and resources of those who oppose the charismatic political executive or his policies can limit the extent of charisma's contribution. The really rich who controlled the American media and possibly part of the American Congress were not among Roosevelt's charismatically oriented supporters but were a determined and an active opposition. Roosevelt's charismatic constituency largely comprised members of the lower strata of society, who could contribute little beyond acclaim and periodic votes to promoting his and their objectives. It might be interesting to speculate what might have resulted from Roosevelt's charisma had he been the political head of an English type of parliamentary system, able to control the votes of his party in the legislature and able to call an election on a bill of major importance to his program.

The uses of political charisma can thus be constrained by the type and rules of the political system within which the charismatic leader operates and by whether and how he chooses to circumvent or change them. Sukarno, some of whose major goals seemed blocked by the efforts of other political leaders, some of whom also had charismatic constituencies of their own, manipulated people and events to change Indonesia's political system.

Political charisma in and of itself has rarely, if ever, been sufficient to accomplish a complete reordering of a system or a revolution. In the words of Machiavelli: "It must be considered that there is nothing more difficult to carry out, nor more doubtful of success, nor more dangerous to handle, than to initiate a new order of things. . . . Thus it comes about that all armed prophets have conquered and unarmed ones failed; for . . . it is easy to persuade people of a thing, but difficult to keep them in that persuasion. And so it is necessary to order things so that when they no longer believe, they can be made to believe by force."[12]

Not all charismatic political leaders have chosen to act upon this Machiavellian dictum, but a number seem to have done so. If one were to rank charismatic leaders of this century solely in terms of the magnitudes of changes they accomplished, Hitler and Castro would rank high. Much of their success, however, resulted from charisma plus force, and some of the charisma may have been sustained only because possibilities of dissipating it did not exist.

Thus, the limits of what charisma can do are not only influenced by the size and status of the charismatic constituency and the system within which a leader works. They are also partly determined by what a given charismatic leader may or may not choose to do and by the means he may employ or reject in exploiting his charisma.

Not all objectives can be achieved simultaneously, even by charismatic leaders. Indonesia's Sukarno and Ghana's Nkrumah were strongly criticized for having neglected rational economic development in favor of nation-building and the pursuit of the political kingdom abroad. But was it unwise to direct charisma primarily to the task of trying to meld together the many peoples of a new and fragile state? A country torn by civil war will find any sort of development difficult. Ghana has suffered no major civil war to date. Indonesia's brief internal insurrection was directed more against Sukarno's policies than in assertion of autonomy. Those who launched it were not willing to starve or fight to death for independence as were the Ibos of Nigeria. Perhaps Nigeria and other African countries might have benefited from charismatic leaders oriented to nation-building.

Apart from the goals a charismatic leader may set himself or his priorities, there is the further limitation of the means or measures that might be employed. That Hitler succeeded in solving Germany's unemployment problem and Roosevelt failed to do away with unemployment

12. Machiavelli, *Prince*, pp. 49–50.

in the United States is not a measure of the relative charisma or charismatic effectiveness of either. For Hitler did it largely through a major rearmament program. American unemployment also disappeared when World War II necessitated rearmament.

Finally, it is likely that charisma is limited by how far and how often it can be personally projected. The heroic feats of charismatic leaders are infrequent. Those charismatic leaders who hold office cannot spend the majority of their days touring their countries or communicating through radio or television. Directives of these leaders that are communicated to people through various layers of officialdom may attenuate charismatic effectiveness. It would be interesting to ascertain whether visits of charismatic leaders to factories and other worksites exhorting the workers have resulted in increased rates of production. From descriptions of the catalytic effects of Roosevelt and Hitler on the productivity of those who worked within their orbit, this may have been likely. But if personal presence does indeed augment the impact of charisma, a future in which charismatic leaders might be able to clone themselves offers awesome possibilities.

Perhaps the ultimate limitation on the effectiveness of political charisma is its inability to prevent a leader from being forcibly ousted from office by military forces if they are both united and determined to do so. It is true, as was observed earlier, that charisma can help to deter or modify attempts to remove a charismatic leader. However, its effectiveness in such instances may depend upon division within the military.

When a charismatic political leader is deposed as head of state, it is frequently assumed that he has lost his charisma. While this may be so, it is not necessarily the case. Although charisma and power can be interlinked and each can serve as one of the bases for the other, they are also autonomous in some respects. A leader may lose much of his charismatically oriented following and still retain power, as was apparently the case with Nkrumah and Mussolini in the later years of their tenure. A leader may lose power and still retain charisma for some of his supporters, as apparently was true of Perón and Sukarno. That Sukarno was stripped of power very gradually was not only due to the disunity of the armed forces in Indonesia but also to his continued charisma. For some, Perón's charisma survived his many years of exile and was one factor that led to his eventual return to Argentina.

The Legacy of Political Charisma

Whether or not a given leader's charisma has lasted through his tenure of office or his lifetime, some of its effects have often endured much beyond either. Although the legacies of charismatic leaders have differed greatly in many respects, there seem to be some elements common to those of all or most of them.

It appears that their charisma stimulated political activism on the part of many people who had been apolitical or politically apathetic. As a result of their influence, political participation seems to have increased considerably in their countries. Gandhi brought into politics many more Indians than the Congress Party had been able to mobilize and few of them seem to have withdrawn from it. Roosevelt's mail and telegrams vastly exceeded those received by a number of his predecessors combined and the quantity of White House communications has not declined to a pre-Roosevelt level. Sukarno and Castro aroused even remote village peasants to political action.

Admittedly, arousal to political awareness and activity through charismatic followership does not necessarily lead to autonomous and educated political judgment. But habits of participation may remain long after their original stimulus is gone and may be rechanneled in various directions. We may not know how many of those who had never written to a politician before they wrote to Roosevelt later wrote to succeeding presidents or to their representatives or senators. But it is safe to assume that some of them have done so and that some have written in a critical as well as an adulatory tone. Indonesians I have known whose political activism was stimulated by Sukarno tended to remain active except for those whose activities were curtailed by house arrest, imprisonment, or intimidation.

Another consequence of charisma, although not inevitably a direct one, has been the lessening of social and status inequalities. With the exception of the United States, the countries led by the charismatic leaders with whom we have been most concerned had been marked by relatively rigid class and status distinctions and a strong bias in favor of aristocratic elites. But these leaders seem to have selected their own aides and lieutenants from a range of social backgrounds. Posts of power and prestige were not restricted to those of the upper classes. In their regimes, more of these positions appear to have been occupied by those of middle class origin than in preceding regimes.

Apart from example in allocation of posts and favors, charismatic leaders employed rhetoric and slogans that emphasized social equality and community and that often gave positive reinforcement to the lower strata of their societies. Roosevelt dignified the common man; Hitler hailed the farmer and his soil as well as the Teutonic knights; Sukarno stressed the needs and virtues of the simple village peasant. Although it would be difficult to trace the influence of such emphases on subsequent attitudes and behavior, there probably were subtle but durable effects, if only on how the "lower orders" learned to view themselves.

Other actions, policies, and programs that flowed in part from the exercise of charismatic appeal, directly or indirectly, helped to modify social structures and social attitudes. In the case of Castro there was the deliberate destruction of the previous system in Cuba. The new orders imposed on Italy and Germany by Mussolini and Hitler did not survive their regimes, but the status quo ante was not restored. The monarchies and the dominance of the old elites, the Italian aristocracy and the Prussian Junkers and the military cliques, had passed into history.

It thus can be argued that by and large increased circulation of elites and increased mobility characterized the rule and legacy of charismatic political leaders. In some instances, certain segments of their societies gained appreciably or social distance among some segments diminished. Such changes continued past the periods of these leaders. As was earlier noted, untouchability has never been the same in India since Gandhi and the disabilities of the Harijans have continued to decrease. Sukarno campaigned against the traditional status distinctions in Indonesia and these have markedly diminished. The distances and suspicions among the different ethnic groups, which he also opposed, have declined and continue to do so. In the United States the rights of the underprivileged to public concern, public remedial action, and respectability have been recognized since Roosevelt. Those charismatic leaders who have not dismantled the old orders appear at minimum to have shaken and modified them.

Particularly in the newer states, political charisma seems to have contributed to the growth of a sense of national identity and to the development of national unity among their peoples. These two processes, which are often referred to interchangeably, have somewhat different referents, although they are related. National identity refers to people's identification with and loyalty to the state above and beyond local and other more parochial identifications with their region, clan, tribe, and similar units. National unity refers to a basic consensus among disparate groups in a state and a sufficient modicum of shared values for the state to survive.

The sense of national identity is frail in new states, especially multiethnic ones that were formerly colonies. Rural villagers and peasants tend to know of or identify with few units or figures of authority beyond those in their immediate vicinity. There may have been considerable consensus concerning the goal of achieving independence. After its achievement in most of these states, however, dissension of many kinds developed, including conflict over such basic issues as a constitution and the form of government.

In the new states of Asia and Africa, interethnic conflict was keen as subnations struggled among themselves for greater shares of the benefits to be derived from independence or against whichever groups were perceived as becoming too dominant. Even where ethnicity was not a strongly divisive factor, the achievement of statehood did not in itself produce nationhood. "Now that we have made Italy," a leading figure of the Italian unification is supposed to have said in 1870, "we must begin to make Italians."

Charismatic leadership seems to have aided the growth of nationhood in several ways. The very presence of charismatic leaders, especially when they traveled, helped to promote it. For those people who had little or no knowledge of the abstract entity of the state, much less loyalty to it, the charismatic leader became the concrete embodiment of an authority higher than those they were accustomed to. For those who saw the state and its national capital as remote, alien, and possibly hostile, the presence of the charismatic leader was an electrifying sign that the "country" cared about them and their welfare.

Charismatic political leaders by and large seem to have been strenuous travelers. One of Mussolini's first acts after becoming prime minister was to travel throughout Italy. He appeared in places, such as Sardinia, that no previous prime minister had visited. Gandhi, despite his age after India became independent, continued to travel widely to promote national unity as well as his other goals. To Indonesians it often appeared that Sukarno spent more time traveling around the country and abroad than he did in the capital.

In the United States, Eleanor Roosevelt may have done more through her constant trips to help to allay the sense of alienation that some may have developed as a result of the depression than did her husband in his major addresses and fireside chats. As the "eyes and ears" of a handicapped president, she was one of his major sources of information about conditions in the country and was well known to be.[13] Moreover, she exuded an air of earnest concern and of compassion. In fact Eleanor Roosevelt may well have helped to sustain Franklin Roosevelt's charisma in addition to using it to reassure people that their problems would be looked into.[14]

Because of the charismatic appeal of such leaders, their messages relating to national identity and unity were likely to have been received and internalized with greater conviction than similar messages from others. Or their messages may have been transmitted and heard more widely than those of others. For example, Indonesian peasants who knew nothing of the region or province beyond their district knew that their country extended from Sabang to Merauke, containing people with different customs who were nonetheless one. This, it appeared, they knew because they had heard it from Sukarno.

Some charismatic leaders have used their charisma to create or help popularize national symbols. Even the use of traditional symbols as an aid to charisma, as described earlier, could have a feedback effect so that charisma in turn reinforced the resonance of these symbols. Details concerning traditional symbols employed by Hitler and Mussolini appear in a previous chapter. Here might be mentioned an example of symbols specifically employed to bridge the distances among different ethnic groups. Although the references to legend in Sukarno's speeches were largely from the Javanese shadow-play, his references to heroes of history included heroes of ethnic groups from outlying areas. In other ways he also helped to raise the status of ethnic heroes to that of pan-

13. Burns, *Roosevelt*, p. 173; Schlesinger, 2, *Coming*, p. 525.
14. As is noted in chapter 2 (p. 37), the Roosevelts came close to approximating a case of dual charismatic political leadership.

Indonesian heroes and of specifically ethnic dances, music, and other arts to that of nationally known ones.

It might even be argued that the charisma of some of these leaders could account in part for their ability to undertake vast and expensive prestige projects while some of their people lived under hardship conditions. Mussolini's restoration of ancient Rome may have literally fed only those working class members who worked on it, but it also fed the national pride of members of elite groups. Some of Sukarno's major critics admitted that although they had publicly deplored the sums spent on national prestige projects, they felt pride in their country for its international airline and for some of these projects. The ways in which charisma can contribute to national identity, pride, and unity are indeed somewhat incalculable.[15] For some of these same critics, despite their opposition to Sukarno, felt proud that their country had produced such a leader who could claim world attention.

Perhaps the most lasting legacy of charismatic political leadership is the postmortem charismatic myth in which it becomes clothed. As has been noted, the charismatic leader gains his charisma in part through tapping the traditional myths and symbols of his society. Subsequently, he and his works take on in turn a mythic quality and become part of the reservoir of myths and symbols for that society and perhaps even for others. He and his deeds are then drawn upon by the leaders and generations that follow. Even those for whom he was not charismatic and those for whom he ceased being so did share in the drama he enacted. And they too transmit its awe and aura to their descendants.

The image of a past and even of a defeated charismatic leader may serve as a standard of measure against which those who succeed him are viewed. Twelve years after Perón was forced from power, sugar workers in the province of Tucumán were reported as saying that Argentina was no longer their country, not since Perón had left. No one cared about their welfare as he had. It was reported in 1970 that Italians, when frustrated, often tended to say: "If *lui* were here, this wouldn't happen."

15. For details on the contributions of charisma to nation-building, see Ann R. Willner and Dorothy Willner, "Charismatic Political Leadership as Conservator and Catalyst," in A. R. Davis, ed., *Traditional Attitudes and Modern Styles in Political Leadership* (London and Sydney: Angus and Robertson, 1973), pp. 17–28.

The "lui" referred to Mussolini and the "this" could have been anything from a delayed train or a traffic jam to a riot.[16]

The evocative power of the myth of the charismatic leader for posterity is suggested by the attempts of successors to reenact one or more of its elements. The New Deal, one of Roosevelt's strongest symbols, was followed by the Fair Deal and later by the New Frontier. The "war against poverty" and "affirmative action" are only two of the phrases that have been borrowed from Roosevelt's speeches, presumably to lend the Roosevelt aura to the programs or speeches of presidents who have followed him. Part of candidate Carter's appeal for older people in the campaign of 1976 seems to have been lodged in his smile, which reminded them of the smile of Roosevelt.[17]

Myths of some charismatic leaders seem able to surmount and survive efforts to destroy them by those who dislodge and succeed these leaders. From available reports few followers of Nkrumah were left in Ghana when a military coup deposed him. A systematic campaign was subsequently launched to disparage completely his person and regime. Sukarno was still charismatic for some Indonesians after he was forced from power and a similar and sustained campaign was undertaken against him and his regime. After a decade had passed, Sukarno and Nkrumah were deceased. Their successors had not been notably successful in improving life for the majority of people in their countries. From informal reports it appears that it is again safe to praise these men and that a process of restoring their images is under way. One can already foresee a time when the myths will stress their roles not only as the heroic fathers of their countries but also as the repositories of many virtues they did not possess as well as of those they did.

It is admittedly difficult to imagine restoration of the Hitler myth in heroic cast. Yet one wonders what may be the ultimate result of the current popularity and ubiquity of books and films about Hitler. This may reflect the fascination felt by many toward the Prince of Darkness and toward those who commit unbelievable horrors. It is, after all, the

16. *New York Times*, Apr. 6, 1970.
17. Survey research on perceptions of presidential candidates carried out by students in my class on political persuasion at the University of Kansas in 1976.

"unbelievable" that helps give rise to charisma, to the awe that sustains it and the myth that succeeds it. The charismatic leader is in a sense the Prometheus of politics who also steals from the gods by stretching political reality beyond the bounds of belief and prediction.

Appendix:
Weber and Charisma as Concept and Theory

As I noted in chapter 1, much of the scholarly controversy concerning the definition of *charisma* has stemmed from insufficient attention to analytical distinctions among the various elements in Max Weber's work on charisma. Weber's discussions of the charismatic phenomenon contain a number of discrete ideas about it above and beyond what constitutes a definition in the technical sense.[1]

Some of the major ideas in his formulations may be summed up as follows:

1. The charismatic leader may be inspired by a calling or mission and summon others to "obey and follow him by virtue of his mission";
2. Recognition by the followers or disciples comes about through a "proof" or "sign," originally "a miracle";
3. Recognition arises out of "enthusiasm" or out of "despair and hope" in times of distress;
4. Charismatic authority is exercised through a personal staff of the

---

1. I refer in the plural to Weber's "discussions" of the charismatic phenomenon because each of the two parts of Weber's *Wirtschaft und Gesellschaft* contains a formulation, each of which differs somewhat from the other in emphases and details, as is noted by Guenther Roth in his introduction to his and Wittich's translation and edition, titled *Economy and Society*.

"charismatically elect" among the disciples rather than an administrative staff chosen and working in accordance with formal regulations and routine procedures;

5. The charismatic community lacks a judicial system of formal rules and precedents and adjudicates according to the revelation, inspiration, or will of the charismatic leader;

6. Charismatic authority rejects rational economic conduct in favor of support through gifts, "booty," and extortion;

7. The charismatic leader and followers live in a communal emotionally close relationship, dissociated from routine occupations and normal family life;

8. For charisma to endure, the leader should continue to "prove" his powers or benefit his followers;

9. Charismatic authority tends to transform and reorient values in new directions and is in this sense revolutionary;

10. Charismatic authority is transitory and unstable, tending to become "routinized" or transformed into one or some combination of the other types of authority.[2]

If one assumes that Weber did not do more than draw up a simple classificatory scheme, one might conclude that all the above characteristics are elements defining the concept of charismatic authority. For the logic of classificatory types requires that each type be defined by means of a particular concept that represents the cluster of characteristics essential for membership in that type or class.[3] Therefore, reasoning backward, one might infer that all the attributes mentioned by Weber in his discussions of each type comprise the conceptual definition of that type.

Weber, however, used types not primarily for classification but for explanation. He developed a particular kind of type, an analytic tool called the *ideal-type*, which is formed "by the one-sided *accentuation* of one or more points of view and by the synthesis of a great many diffuse, discrete, more or less present and occasionally absent *concrete, indi-*

---

2. Weber, *Economy*, 1, pp. 215–16, 241–45; 3, 1111–20.

3. Carl G. Hempel, *Aspects of Scientific Explanation and Other Essays in the Philosophy of Science* (New York: Free Press, 1965), pp. 137–39, 156–57.

vidual phenomena, which are arranged according to those one-sidedly emphasized viewpoints into a unified *analytical* construct."[4]

Much has been written about the contributions and limitations of ideal types to the methodology of the social sciences.[5] The relevant point to be made here is that of Carl Hempel on the logical status of ideal types, namely, that they are not concepts, strictly speaking, but theories. "Ideal constructs," he states, "have the character not of concepts in the narrower sense, but of theoretical systems."[6]

Therefore, many of the attributes mentioned in Weber's treatment of the charismatic phenomenon are not to be taken as among the defining properties of the central concept. They are rather propositions concerning the phenomenon designated by this central concept. Stated more simply, they do not tell what charismatic authority or leadership is; they assert something else about it.

Moreover, ideal-type theory, as developed by Weber, is not static but dynamic. Weber's theories about the three types of authority trace and explain the typical process of development of each type over time. Admittedly, this dynamic aspect of Weber's formulations is not so clear in his treatment of the emerging and existing stages of charismatic authority as it is in his treatments of legal and traditional authority.[7] The process emphasized in his treatment of charismatic authority is the process by which it becomes transformed into one of the alternative types. Weber hardly dwells upon the genesis of charismatic authority, touching upon it only by brief reference to the elements that may enter into the process.

Nonetheless, Weber's analyses do contain a rudimentary, if largely implicit, theory about the typical trajectory of the charismatic phenomenon. This becomes clear if the elements in Weber's presentations

4. Max Weber, *On the Methodology of the Social Sciences*, trans. and ed. E. A. Shils and W. A. Finch (Glencoe, Ill.: Free Press, 1949), p. 90.

5. Peter M. Blau, "Critical Remarks on Weber's Theory of Authority," *American Political Science Review* 52 (June 1963), 305–16; Hempel, *Aspects*, pp. 160–71; J. W. N. Watkins, "Ideal Types and Historical Explanation," in *Readings in the Philosophy of Science* (New York: Appleton-Century-Crofts, 1953), ed. Herbert Feigle and May Broadbeck, pp. 723–43.

6. Hempel, *Aspects*, p. 168.

7. For a comparison of the differing emphases in each of the three theories, see Blau, "Critical Remarks," p. 309.

are arranged roughly in the order in which I have enumerated them above. The first group of elements, namely, (1) a time of distress, (2) the claim of the aspirant leader on the basis of (3) a mission or revelation, (4) a "sign" or "miracle," and (5) the despair and hope or the enthusiasm of potential followers can be seen to specify some *antecedent* or contributory factors in the typical emergence of the charismatic phenomenon. Elements (4)–(7) refer to the modes of exercise of charismatic leadership or authority. What is asserted, in effect, is that if or when it emerges, charismatic authority will be exerted in these ways. The reference to the need for proofs or benefits specifies a probable condition for the maintenance of the charismatic relationship and a possible requirement for its genesis. The propositions about reorientation of values and revolutionary impact refer to the probable consequences or results of the existence of such a relationship between a leader and his followers.

These elements, taken together, constitute a theory, however embryonic, about the charismatic phenomenon. The statements concerning them are propositions asserted in relation to charismatic authority or leadership as (1) antecedent, (2) concomitant, or (3) consequence of the phenomenon. They neither define the core concept nor identify its empirical referents.

I stress these logical distinctions, perhaps unduly, because neglect of them, it appears to me, has been responsible for much of the misunderstanding surrounding the meaning of the concept and for some unwarranted criticism concerning its usefulness. Admittedly, the sometimes elliptical and ambiguous style of Weber's prose and the efforts of translators to expand somewhat on his words can easily give rise to variant interpretations of the core of his meaning.

A case in point arose for me in checking back when a respected scholar queried my omission of the element of the leader's claim or mission from the definition of the concept in my initial version of this study. For him this element was a crucial part of the definition. My reason for continuing to omit it follows.

In the original German the first passage in which Weber defines *charisma* reads as follows:

Charismatischen Charakters: auf der ausseralltäglichen Hingabe an die Heiligkeit oder die Heldenkraft oder die Vorbildlichkeit einer Person und der durch sie offenbarten oder geschaffenen Ordnungen [ruhen] (charismatische Herrschafft).[8]

This passage has been translated, somewhat more than literally, as follows:

"Charismatic grounds—resting on devotion to the exceptional sanctity, heroism or exemplary character of an individual person, and of the normative patterns or order revealed or ordained by him (charismatic authority)."[9]

A literal translation of the original German would read more or less as follows:

Charismatic grounds: out of exceptional surrender to the sanctity or the heroism or the admirable qualities of a person and the order revealed or created through any of these.[10]

Of the several points that need to be made about the standard translations, one has to do with the adjective *normative*, for which there seems to be no equivalent in the original German. These translations render the German word *geschaffenen*, which has the connotation of "created" or "shaped," as "ordained," which, while not incorrect, does not clearly suggest an already created or established order. Had the German been translated somewhat more literally, it would have been unambiguously evident that Weber specified two distinct possibilities: (1) the revealed order, that which the charismatic leader projects, and (2) the created order, that which he has established.

Thus, the logical structure of the passage as written by Weber indicates that the objects of charismatic surrender or devotion on the part of the followers can be:

8. Max Weber, *Wirtschaft und Gesellschaft*, 2 vols. (Tübingen: J. C. B. Mohr [Paul Seibeck], 1956), 1, p. 124.

9. Weber, *Economy*, 1, p. 215, and *The Theory of Social and Economic Organization*, trans. A. M. Henderson and Talcott Parsons and ed. Talcott Parsons (New York: Free Press, 1964), p. 328.

10. Assistance in translating from the German was kindly provided by Herta Galton and Heinrich Stammler.

(a) *any* of the following: plus   (b) one of the following:
    sanctity   the revealed order
    heroism   the established order
    exceptional character

This makes for six possible combinations, any of which is adequate for the definition. Therefore, the leader's claim, vision, or revelation of a new order to come, appearing in half the possible combinations, is not essential to the definition.

In a following passage, the earlier translation of Henderson and Parsons also left some room for ambiguity, but the more recent Roth and Wittich edition of Weber makes it clear that the mission or revelation was intended to constitute one out of three possible bases for follower recognition:

> . . . who is obeyed by virtue of personal trust in his revelation, his heroism or his exemplary qualities.[11]

I find only one passage from which it is reasonable to infer that a leader's claim on the basis of a "mission" is an integral part of the charismatic relationship, and even that passage can be subject to an alternate interpretation. The passage reads:

> Pure charisma is specifically foreign to economic considerations. Wherever it appears it constitutes a "call" in the most emphatic sense of the word, a "mission" or a "spiritual duty."[12]

The German word *beruf,* translated as "call," also denotes "profession" or "calling" in the sense of a vocation. *Inner aufgabe,* translated as "spiritual duty," can also mean "inner task." If we take these connotations of the words Weber employs together with the context in which they appear, that is, the repudiation of normal economic life, we can interpret this passage as meaning that wherever charisma does appear, it constitutes a vocation or way of life as an end in itself.

The failure to recognize that many of Weber's assertions constitute propositions and, moreover, that some of them are framed in the proba-

11. Weber, *Economy*, 1, p. 216.
12. Ibid., p. 244.

bilistic mode has produced some logically untenable criticisms of the utility of the concept. Since this is not intended to be a refutation of Weber's critics, I shall mention here merely one example. A critic has taken issue with Weber's statement concerning the likely disappearance of charisma in the absence of benefits to the followers with the statement that in some cases "faith in a leader's qualifications may continue despite the absence of any ascertainable 'benefits.' "[13] This objection in the first place overlooks the logical import of Weber's statement: Likelihood is not equivalent to inevitability and to say that one outcome is likely does not necessarily deny the possibility of another outcome. Even had Weber stated what the critic supposed, the objection would not invalidate the concept but suggest modification of the hypothesis, should empirical investigation warrant it. If empirical investigation yields a number of cases of retention of charismatic faith in the absence of continued proofs or benefits as well as cases of its disappearance, what would then appear called for is a search for the variables that might explain the circumstances under which charisma does not disappear.

I do not mean to suggest that Weber is beyond criticism, for that is something Weber himself would have denied. "In science," he wrote in "Science as a Vocation," "each of us knows that what he has accomplished will be antiquated in ten, twenty, fifty years. That is the fate to which science is subjected. . . . Every scientific 'fulfilment' raises new 'questions'; it *asks* to be 'surpassed' and outdated. . . . We cannot work without hoping that others will advance further than we have."[14]

What is so admirable about Weber is that so much of his work has *not* been outdated in over half a century and that so much of it is so relevant in a world that has changed in many ways since the world of his time and the prior worlds that formed the empirical basis for his theories. If Weber's work has raised new questions, it is the task of those of us who follow in social science to try to answer them and, in doing so, to raise new questions.

13. Ratnam, "Political Leadership," p. 342.

14. Max Weber, "Science as a Vocation," in *From Max Weber: Essays in Sociology*, trans. and ed. H. H. Gerth and C. Wright Mills (New York: Oxford University Press, 1946), p. 138.

Index

Abel, Theodore, 47, 57
Agnew, Spiro, 160
Apter, David, 15
Ataturk, Kemal, 34, 184
authority; Weber's classification of, 3–4;
    charismatic, 15–17

Balbo, Italo, 60
Batista regime, 51, 59, 73, 94
Benedict, Ruth, 64
Bible, 154, 155, 156
Brown, Judith, 123
Burns, James MacGregor, 153, 180
Burujirdi, Ayatollah, 86

Carter, Jimmy, 200
Castro, Fidel, 1, 2, 33, 58; perception of
    invulnerability, 23; evidence of charis-
    ma, 23, 28; follower commitment to,
    28, 51, 189; mission, 59; savior image
    of, 65; invocation of and identification
    with Martí, 65, 72–74, 94; and risk,
    74; heroic image of, 94; perceived per-
    sonality traits, 140–41, 145, 147, 149;
    "History Will Absolve Me" speech, 145,
    147; egalitarian stance, 175; and the
    media, 177–78; impact and evaluation
    of, 183, 195, 196
charisma, impact of: controversy over,
    11–12; problems of evaluating,
    182–84; and type of system, 192–93;
    on social structure, 195–96; on nation-
    building and national identity, 196–99
charisma, political (charismatic political
    leadership): Weber on, 3–4, 9, 10–11,
    15, 202–08; as distinct from other

leadership, 5–7; definition of, 5–8;
    controversies concerning, 8–17, 43,
    182–83; and revolution, 10–11; role of
    goal or mission, 10, 56–59; and the
    media, 12–14, 130, 177–78; and per-
    sonality, 14–15; as authority and/or
    leadership, 15–17; evidence for, 20–33;
    and cultural variation, 24–25, 32–33,
    41, 63–64; and women, 34–38; and
    power, 34, 46, 184–88; dual, 37;
    postmortem, 39; role of myth, 62–64;
    contributions of oratory to, 151–53;
    limits to, 191–94
—concept of, 3–17 passim: overloading
    of, 9–10, 12
—theory of, 8–13, 42–61 passim; sum-
    mary of elements of, 60–61, 203–08
charismatically oriented following: as in-
    dicator of charisma, 18; evidence of,
    20–23; susceptibility to membership
    in, 53–56; spread of beliefs among,
    128–29; in aid of power, 184–86; ener-
    gy and enthusiasm of, 184, 188–89;
    demonstration by, 187–88; sacrifices
    by, 189–91
charismatic political leaders: revolution-
    ary and restorative, 11; and person-
    ality, 14–15; perceived attributes of,
    19–24, 128–30, 140–49; indicators for
    identification of, 19–29; sample, 34;
    contrasted with rivals, 60–61; contro-
    versy over legacies of, 182–83; and
    personal presence, 194; and
    postmortem myths, 199–201. *See also*
    Castro; Gandhi; Hitler; Mussolini; Roo-
    sevelt, Franklin Delano; Sukarno

209